Management of Owner-Operator Fleets

Management of Owner-Operator Fleets

David H. Maister
Harvard University

LexingtonBooks
D.C. Heath and Company
Lexington, Massachusetts
Toronto

Library of Congress Cataloging in Publication Data

Maister, David H
    Management of owner-operator fleets.

    Bibliography: p.
    Includes index.
    1. Motor vehicle fleets—Management. I. Title.
TL165.M34   388.3'25'068   79-5112
ISBN 0-669-03197-6

Copyright © 1980 by D.C. Heath and Company

Published simultaneously in Canada.

Printed in the United States of America.

International Standard Book Number: 0-669-03197-6

Library of Congress Catalog Card Number: 79-5112

To Karen

Contents

List of Figures
and Tables

Preface

This book is, in large part, a sequel to my earlier book, *The Owner-Operator: Independent Trucker*, coauthored with D. Daryl Wyckoff. In that work, we attempted to understand the owner-operator system in the U.S. trucking industry by examining the owner-operators themselves. In this book, I try to complete the picture by examining the other main component of the system: the group of motor carriers that choose to use owner-operators rather than operate company equipment. This work is thus a companion to, rather than a replacement for, the earlier book.

In this study I have tried to answer the following questions:

1. Why do some motor carriers choose to use owner-operators rather than company equipment? What are the advantages and disadvantages of this choice?
2. When motor carriers have decided to use owner-operators, what key decisions must be made to manage them successfully?
3. What can motor carriers learn from other industries that have similar or analogous methods of operation?

I have set out to write a book about *management*, not about the stormy public-policy debate concerning owner-operators and their role in the trucking industry. Inevitably, however, my findings contain implications for the various legislative, judicial, and regulatory activities that surround the owner-operator system. Where these implications are clear, I have not avoided drawing them. However, they have not been my prime concern.

There appears to be a significant probability of substantial changes occurring in the economic regulation of those sectors of the trucking industry most dependent upon owner-operators. As will be clear to the reader, I do not believe that any such events would change what I have chosen to say: I believe that the principles of good owner-operator management explored here will be as important after any deregulation as before (if not, indeed, more important). In spite of this I was faced with the problem of whether to refer to regulations at all and, if so, in what tense—past or present. I was also tempted to delay publication until events took their course. However, the history of regulatory change shows that its pace is unpredictable. Accordingly, I have chosen to describe regulations as they existed in October 1979, with appropriate references to the possibility of change.

I have had more than one audience in mind in writing this book. Above all, I hoped to write a book that would be useful to practicing managers. I have attempted to serve them not only by describing what some companies have done to solve common problems, but by attempting to present concepts and ways of looking at trucking management problems that I hope will be stimulating. This study has been motivated by the belief that the management problems of the trucking industry are not unique; and by focusing on the analogy with franchising, I have tried to illustrate this point.

This book is also addressed to transportation legislators, regulators, researchers, and students. By presenting a view of the owner-operator system as a *system*, and as a *management* system, I hope that this study may contribute to a better understanding of the workings of the trucking industry. Much research on transportation relies predominantly on the approaches and techniques of the discipline of economics, in which the smallest unit of analysis is the firm. With limited (if notable) exceptions, little research has been conducted that employs the approaches and tools of managerial analysis, in which we look inside the firm. I hope that this work will demonstrate the utility of integrating economic and managerial concepts in coming to a complete understanding of the workings of the trucking industry.

In order to obtain the necessary funds to cover the expenses of this research, I approached many institutions and organizations connected with and involved in U.S. transportation. However, when I began I had only a title and a vague, one-page list of the types of questions I thought might be interesting. I am therefore grateful to the American Trucking Associations, Inc., and the Association of American Railroads for their grants made to cover the travel and other expenses of this research. I am grateful not only for their good faith in providing research funds while asking for and receiving no editorial rights over the direction or content of my research (or of the final manuscript), but also for their patience and trust as I struggled to bring the project to fruition from such meager beginnings.

Many individuals and organizations contributed to this book. Given that it was written during a period that saw congressional hearings on owner-operator problems, a revision of the Interstate Commerce Commission's leasing rules, the threat of substantial deregulation, two owner-operator shutdowns, a Teamster strike and a new National Master Freight Agreement, it is not surprising that many (but not all) of the carriers I have interviewed felt some concern in talking about their dealings with owner-operators. The same was also true of regulators, industry association officers, owner-operators, administration officials, and others, all of whom nevertheless gave freely of their time. Accordingly, I decided not to refer to any individual by name in this work, except where I have drawn on previously published sources. However, I have tried to convey my profound gratitude here to the individuals who helped me anonymously.

An earlier version of chapter 2 was presented at the 1979 annual meeting of the Transportation Research Forum under the title "Motor Carrier Use of Owner Operators: Efficiency or Exploitation?'' I am grateful for permission to include the reworked version here. Some of the ideas contained in this book were presented at a trucking industry seminar held at the Harvard Business School in August 1979, and I would like to thank all of the participants for their stimulating discussions. Some of the participants took the time from their busy daily tasks to review this manuscript. I am particularly grateful for the efforts of Duncan McRae, Jr., Donald Schneider, William D. Biggs, Richard L. Few, John M. Smith, and William E. Christensen. Barry Anderson and Jim Yeager of the General Accounting Office assisted (but bear no responsibility for) the analyses presented in the Appendix. Daryl Wyckoff, as always, has been friend, tutor, and guide. The burden of my inability to meet deadlines was borne primarily by Jean Buxton; her assistance was invaluable.

In spite of all this assistance, acknowledged and unacknowledged, the errors and omissions are all mine.

Management of
Owner-Operator
Fleets

1

The Owner-Operator System

Introduction

This book is about trucking companies (motor carriers) that perform their intercity line-haul function not by using company-owned tractors together with employee drivers, but by subcontracting this task to individuals who own and operate a small number of tractors (most commonly, only one). Many terms may be used to describe this practice (subcontracting, leasing, or even franchising), all of which we shall have occasion to use. However, for the purposes of this chapter, we shall refer to *the owner-operator method of operation*, or, more simply, *the owner-operator system*. The term *owner-operator*, of course, refers to those individuals, or small businesses, who perform the line-haul task. While some owner-operators are used in local pickup and delivery operations, most are used in intercity transportation, the primary focus of this book.

As shall become clear, choosing a precise terminology is a difficult task, but it is necessary in order to distinguish the topic of this book from closely allied subjects. First, it is necessary to distinguish between *motor carriers* and *load arrangers* (or *brokers*.) The latter act primarily as intermediaries between shippers and truck operators and perform few other components of the total transportation service. In most cases the distinction is obvious, as, for example, in the case of a motor carrier that uses owner-operators only as a supplement to its own fleet. However, some industry observers believe that the distinction can become blurred, particularly with respect to "motor carriers" that own none of their own trucks and operate entirely with owner-operators. One can usually distinguish such "carriers" from brokers by examining the extent of their activities in services ancillary to the line-haul movement (such as solicitation of traffic, billing, collecting, dispatching, arranging insurance and licenses, and so on). However, it has been argued[1] that, in some cases, the difference in services performed between motor carriers and brokers is not very great. A more fruitful, and perhaps more legally correct approach, would be to observe that, whereas a broker acts as a facilitator between the shipper and the truck operator, a motor carrier enters into a contractual relationship with the shipper for the transportation of the shipper's goods.

The term owner-operator must also be treated with some care, since it may be applied to a number of clearly different types of individuals or or-

1

ganizations. In the first place, and most commonly, the term may refer to a single individual who owns *and drives* his own truck. Such an individual can perhaps more accurately be termed an *owner-driver*. Individuals who own and drive their own truck may be divided into two groups according to their "normal" method of operation: true independents and subcontractors. The true independent is an owner operator that obtains his or her loads either by direct contact with shippers or through the load arrangers and brokers referred to above. As explained below, such operations are limited by law to a relatively limited group of commodities exempt from regulation by the Interstate Commerce Commission (ICC). For this reason, true independents are often referred to as *exempt owner-operators*. For commodities regulated by the ICC, it is necessary to obtain "operating authority" before such goods may be carried for-hire. If an owner-operator wants to carry such commodities, it is necessary to become a subcontractor to a carrier possessing the requisite authority. (It will be assumed throughout this work that the individual owner-operator does not possess operating authority from the ICC. Any individual or company that does will automatically be referred to as a carrier. While the ICC or Congress may make obtaining authority very easy in the near future, it is likely that *some* form of operating authority will still be required.)

It should be noted that it may be difficult to classify a given individual as a "true independent" or a "subcontractor," since an individual may choose to operate in both ways at different times of the year: hauling exempt agricultural commodities in season and switching to being a subcontractor in the off-season. However, while the majority of owner-operators work in both fashions at some time in their careers, it is usually possible to identify a predominant, "normal" method for most individuals. In any event, the focus of this book will be on the subcontractor sector of the owner-operator population. In particular, we shall be primarily interested in owner-operators and carriers that engage in long-term (so-called "permanent") lease contracts. Under certain circumstances (see below), it is permissible for an owner-operator to lease himself and his vehicle to a carrier for a single trip, a practice known as trip leasing. A small number of carriers conduct operations that are entirely or substantially dependent upon obtaining the services of individual trip lessors, and some owner-operators appear to operate only by individual trip leases (although such a practice is not permitted by ICC law). While we shall deal with the topic of trip leasing, this book is primarily concerned with longer-term relationships between a carrier and its subcontractors.

It has been proposed by some motor carrier organizations that the term owner-operator should be dropped, or at least restricted to those operating completely independently. It is suggested that subcontracting owner-operators be referred to as independent contractors. Unfortunately, this terminology is potentially confusing, since "independent contractor" is a term with a particular legal meaning (see below, especially chapter 8). The simple terms "contractor" or "subcontractor" avoid this problem and are used below. However, they are not in general use and the term owner-operator will also be used here. The reader is cautioned, however, that the distinction between true independents and subcontractors is not an idle one. Each group faces distinctly different environments, opportunities, and problems—differences that have sometimes been confused.

Our terminology must also attempt to distinguish between a single, individual owner-operator and someone who owns one or more trucks, employs drivers, and then leases the vehicles together with drivers to motor carriers. The owner of the trucks may or may not drive one of his vehicles. This type of individual will be referred to herein as a *multi-unit owner-operator*. It is unclear what term ought to be applied to the employee driver who works for a multi-unit owner-operator, although in some instances he has also (confusingly) been described as an owner-operator. The picture is made even more cloudy by the fact that, in some cases, an individual or organization may lease to a motor carrier one or more vehicles *without* drivers, the motor carrier then using its own employee drivers to operate the equipment. This type of operation we shall describe as a *pure truck lease*, and attempt to draw a clear distinction between it and leases involving both vehicle and driver. It should be recognized, however, that in practice it is often difficult to draw this distinction, particularly in cases where the employee status of the driver (in other words, whether he works for the multi-unit owner-operator or the motor carrier) is affected by laws and the decisions of various government bodies, for example, Workers' Compensation Boards, the Internal Revenue Service, the National Labor Relations Board, or the Interstate Commerce Commission. The final element of potential confusion is provided by the fact that an individual owner-driver may lease his vehicle to a carrier, sign on as a bona fide employee of the carrier, and thus continue to drive his own truck. In such a case, the individual is simultaneously an owner-operator (or owner-driver), a truck lessor, and an employee.

It may be clearly seen from this discussion that caution must be exercised when discussing the owner-operator sytem, particularly when attempting to make general statements about the system or the relations of the various parties involved. At least part of the potential confusion of terminology derives from the fact that the owner-operator system exists within a complicated system of laws and regulations which, apart from being sometimes contradictory, also frequently fail to make the distinctions we have made above.

The Structure of the Motor-Carrier Industry

Before we can describe (and attempt to explain) which motor carriers use owner-operators, it is necessary to describe briefly the structure of the U.S.

motor-carrier industry. The categorization scheme used here is that devised in 1937 by the Interstate Commerce Commission, the federal body that regulates most of the industry. This scheme was still in force in 1979, and was the basis for the reporting of industry statistics to the ICC. Indeed, as we shall discover, it is only for the regulated portion of the industry that statistics on owner-operator usage (and most other matters) are readily available.

We begin by considering those sections of the industry that are not regulated by the ICC. First, the ICC has no authority over carriers that operate solely within the boundaries of a single state (*intrastate carriers*). In some states there exist public utility commissions or equivalent bodies which exert some regulatory control over their intrastate carriers, but no discussion of such carriers (or regulatory bodies) will be included in this book. The Motor Carrier Act of 1935, which established the ICC, exempted from regulation those trucking operators that do not offer their service for-hire, but transport only their own goods or those of their parent company. Such operators, known as *private carriers*, are an increasing component of the U.S. trucking industry. The third major exemption from ICC regulation is not a group of carriers, but a group of commodities: primarily unprocessed agricultural commodities. Under the Motor Carrier Act, any individual or company may transport these commodities without the prior permission of the ICC, and at rates that are not controlled by the ICC. For all other commodities, goods may not be transported for-hire without the prior issuance by the ICC of the appropriate "operating authority," and the rates to be charged are subject to the approval or disapproval of the commission. One final major exception exists to these rules. There exist some carriers known as *agricultural cooperatives*, which are nonprofit organizations of farmers and other agricultural producers. Under certain circumstances these cooperatives may transport otherwise regulated commodities on behalf of their members, without obtaining the relevant operating authority.

The ICC uses a number of methods for categorizing motor carriers, of which three are of prime interest. First, a distinction is made between *common carriers* and *contract carriers*. Common carriers hold themselves out for hire to the general public and must transport the goods of any shipper who is willing to pay the appropriate published tariff (assuming, of course, that the carrier has the relevant operating authority to haul the shipment between the points in question). This requirement is known as the *common carrier obligation*. By way of contrast, contract carriers do not serve the general public but are restricted to serving a limited number of customers with whom they enter into continuing contractual relationships. Contract carriers have no common-carrier obligation, and they are not required, as are common carriers, to publish their tariffs. Instead, they are free to enter into contractual negotiations with each shipper they serve to establish the rates to be paid.

The second method of categorizing motor carriers used by the ICC is a classification by type of service. The commission has defined five types of "route arrangements": (1) regular-route scheduled service; (2) regular-route nonscheduled service; (3) irregular-route radial service; (4) irregular-route nonradial service; (5) local cartage service.

The term "regular route" refers to operations between fixed termini (origins and destinations), while irregular-route operators may have either their authorized origin or authorized destinations defined not as fixed locations but as general areas. For example, whereas a regular-route carrier may be authorized to serve the "New York City to Chicago" market (origin and destination both fixed points), an irregular-route carrier may be authorized to serve all traffic moving between "New York City and the state of Illinois" (the latter being not a fixed point but a general area). The latter example is of a *radial* irregular-route carrier, since at least one of the origin or destination is still defined as a fixed base point (or points). However, a nonradial irregular-route carrier may have *no* fixed base points and be authorized to serve traffic moving within a general area and another. It should be noted that the distinctions made here among regular route, irregular route (radial), and irregular route (nonradial) are not precise, and do not necessarily reflect the mode of operation of the motor carrier. For example, some nonradial irregular-route carriers in fact operate over relatively regular routes, particularly when the group of customers they serve remains stable over long periods of time.

As noted in chapter 10, there is a possibility that the classification by type of service may be modified by the ICC for certain sectors of the industry. It has been proposed that all route restrictions be lifted and carriers allowed to compete in any market they elect to serve.

The third classification method used by the ICC is that of placing carriers into one (or more) commodity groups. The commission recognizes seventeen such groups, shown in table 1-1. Apart from general freight carriers (commodity group one), the remaining categories are differentiated according to the area of commodity specialization of the carrier, and carriers in these groups are normally referred to as *specialized carriers*. It should be noted that for an individual carrier, the classification into a commodity group reflects the major area of specialty of that carrier. It is not uncommon, for example, for a general commodity carrier to hold authority to transport refrigerated solid products and, in some cases, to form a "special commodity division" within its organization to handle such products. However, when reporting its statistics to the ICC, the carrier will consolidate results for all its divisions. Some caution must therefore be exercised in interpreting the industry statistics reported below. Kogon[2] has identified at least 64 regular-route motor-carriers that have separate, formally organized special commodity divisions, most of which are run exclusively

Table 1-1
Classification of Motor Carriers by Type of Commodity Transported

Carriers of general freight
Carriers of household goods
Carriers of heavy machinery
Carriers of liquid petroleum products
Carriers of refrigerated liquid products
Carriers of refrigerated solid products
Carriers engaged in dump-trucking
Carriers of agricultural commodities
Carriers of motor vehicles
Carriers engaged in armored-truck service
Carriers of building materials
Carriers of film and associated commodities
Carriers of forest products
Carriers of mine ores not including ores
Carriers engaged in retail-store delivery service
Carriers of explosive or dangerous articles
Carriers of specific commodities not subgrouped

with owner-operators. He notes that these are a relatively recent development in the industry, two-thirds of his sample having been established since 1965. The major reasons given by carrier management for the existence of such divisions are that they allow the carrier to utilize more fully its operating authority, that they are established in response to customer requests, and that they allow the carrier to handle otherwise marginal freight. Of the four publicly-held motor carriers that report their special commodity division revenues separately from other activities, three show growth rates in excess of 50 percent between 1977 and 1978.

The relative importance of these various industry sectors in shown in table 1-2, which gives the number of carriers in each of the seventeen commodity groups, together with the number of carriers which fall into the separate "type of service" categories. It will be seen that general commodity carriers tend to be common carriers operating over regular routes, while most specialized carriers are irregular-route operators.

One final method of classifying motor carriers should be noted: categorization by size of annual revenues. In 1979, a Class I motor carrier was defined as one with annual revenues in excess of $3 million. A Class II carrier had annual revenues between $500,000 and $3 million, and Class III carriers less than $500,000. Most of the statistics reported here will refer to Class I and Class II carriers only. Effective January 1, 1980, a Class I carrier will be one having revenues over $5 million, and a Class III below $1 million.

Table 1-2

Relation between Commodity Hauled and Type of Service, Regulated Motor Carriers, 1976

	Number of Carriers	Percentage of Type of Service[a]				
		RR-S	RR-N	IR-R	IR-N	L
General freight	1002	46	16	10	14	15
Machinery	75	—	1	23	64	12
Petroleum	178	2	2	35	56	5
Refrigerated liquids	5	—	—	40	60	—
Refrigerated solids	117	3	3	21	69	3
Dump truck	63	2	2	25	60	11
Agriculture	85	2	5	25	68	—
Motor vehicles	45	—	—	45	53	2
Armor truck	1	100	—	—	—	—
Building materials	114	—	4	28	65	4
Films	7	43	—	29	29	—
Forest products	3	—	—	33	67	—
Ores	5	—	—	60	40	—
Retail delivery	21	5	5	5	33	52
Hazardous	6	—	17	—	83	—
Other	656	3	3	24	64	6

Source: Derived from data contained in *Motor Carrier Annual Reports*, American Trucking Associations, Inc., 1977.

RR-S: Regular route—scheduled.

RR-N: Regular route—nonscheduled.

IR-R: Irregular route—radial.

IR-N: Irregular route—nonradial.

L: Local.

[a]Totals may not sum to 100 because of rounding.

Regulation of Owner-Operators by the Interstate Commerce Commission

The title of this section is something of a misnomer in that the ICC does not directly exert any regulatory control over owner-operators as such. Rather, it regulates the leasing activities of the motor carriers under its jurisdiction. In this section we shall describe the genesis and content of these regulations.[3]

The original Motor Carrier Act of 1935 made no reference to the owner-operator method of operation, or motor-carrier leasing in general. Not until 1948 did the ICC begin formal proceedings to consider this topic, and the first set of rules was issued in 1951. These rules required that lease contracts involving drivers (in other words, owner-operators) were to be in writing, for a period of no less than thirty days. "Exclusive possession" of the vehicle, without the right to sublease, was to be vested in the carrier, and the driver was required to be an employee of the lessee carrier. The rules prohibited the carrier from compensating the owner-operator on the basis of a division of the revenue from the hauls carried by the owner-operator.

These rules were subsequently challenged in the courts, largely on the basis of the ICC's authority to issue any regulations concerning leasing practices. The ICC's jurisdiction was upheld by the Supreme Court, and this was later made even more certain by a congressional amendment to the Motor Carrier Act. In 1956, the requirements that the driver be an employee of the carrier and the prohibition of compensation by division of revenue were both eliminated by ICC decision.

The requirement that leases be for a minimum of thirty days would seem to prohibit the practice of "trip leasing." However, exceptions from the thirty-day requirement were granted for various cases to allow carriers to engage in this practice. Carriers may trip lease vehicles to each other (either their own equipment or owner-operators under "permanent" lease) if the trip returns the vehicle to a point which the lessor is authorized to serve, or if both carriers possess authority to travel the route and haul the commodities in question. Owner-operators (and carriers) working in the exempt sector may trip lease their vehicles as long as the trip is immediately prior to or subsequent to an exempt haul. Special allowances for trip leasing apply to auto and tank truck carriers because of the one-way haul nature of many of those operations.

The regulations as they exist at the time of writing are as follows. Leases must be in the form of a written contract and be for a minimum duration of thirty days. (Such leases are somewhat confusingly termed "permanent leases"). It should be noted that there is no provision in the regulations for a minimum time period for cancellation of a lease, which therefore may occur the day after the lease is signed.

The lease must specify the compensation to be paid, including the timing and terms of compensation. As noted above, the lessee (except in cases of subleasing and for carriers of household goods) must hold exclusive possession and control of the equipment during the period of the lease. The purpose of this clause is to guarantee that the lessee carrier retains its obligations to the shipper for transportation of the shipments tendered to it. As we shall see, this requirement has had an influence on many other aspects of carrier-owner relations, particularly with regard to the employee status of the owner-operator (see chapter 8).

In 1974, the ICC amended the regulations to provide for automatic increases in compensation to owner-operators for fuel cost increases, and, in 1976, further amended them to guarantee owner-operators the right to inspect the freight bills for the goods they carry when they are paid by a percentage of the revenue. In 1979 additional provisions to guarantee "truth-in-leasing" were imposed by the ICC. These are discussed at length in chapter 5.

The regulations distinguish between vehicles rented with driver and vehicles rented without driver. The major significance of this distinction is that private carriers and shippers are (in general) not allowed to lease a vehicle *with* driver, since for them to do so would constitute for-hire carriage and the lessor (owner-operator) would thus require operating authority from the ICC. However, it is possible for owner-operators to work for private carriers under certain conditions. Stripped to their bare bones, the applicable regulations allow this if the owner-operator leases his vehicle and signs on as a bona-fide employee of the private carrier or shipper. However, other conditions may also be required.[4]

Which Sectors Use Owner-Operators?

All motor carriers regulated by the ICC are required to file annual reports with the commission containing selected financial, operating, and employment statistics. Most of the available information on the use of owner-operators by motor carriers derives from this source. The ICC does not itself publish these statistics, but they are available (in somewhat summarized form) from two sources. A commercial enterprise, TRINC's Transportation Consultants, Inc., has published an annual *Blue Book of the Trucking Industry* since the 1950s, which gives selected items from the annual reports made to the ICC. Starting with data referring to 1976, the American Trucking Associations, Inc., has published a similar publication, entitled *Motor Carrier Annual Reports*, taken from the same source. Most of the statistics shown in this chapter are taken from these two publications.

In their reports to the ICC, motor carriers indicate their relative use of intercity miles traveled in their service by vehicles rented with driver. When taken as a percentage of total intercity miles traveled by the carrier, this provides a first measure of the degree of usage of owner-operators. Second, carriers are required to report the average number of trucks and tractors in the reporting year that were rented with driver. This figure may be expressed as a percentage of total power units to obtain our second measure. Finally, carriers report a variety of payments relating to owner-operators. Included among these are wages paid to owner-operators, vehicle rents with driver, and vehicle rents with driver (vehicle portion). A combination of these figures will allow, in principle, a comparison of total expenditures on owner-operator services with, say, total expenditures.

All of these three measures suffer from disadvantages when it comes to practical use. Common to all three potential measures is the problem that inaccuracies and inconsistencies abound in the reports that some carriers make to the ICC. The more blatant and obvious of these are "corrected" before publication in *Motor Carrier Annual Reports* and (to a lesser extent) TRINC's *Blue Book*, but many still remain. The ICC does not audit carriers' annual reports on a routine basis. Apart from this problem, inaccuracies in all three potential measures of owner-operator usage also derive from the different accounting procedures required by the ICC and/or adopted by carriers in their treatment of owner-operators who are classified as employees. In some cases, carriers record the activities of these individuals as vehicles (or miles) rented without driver, which is a separate set of statistics required in the *ICC Annual Report*. The measure of owner-operator usage based on number of vehicles is particularly suspect, since no set procedure is laid down for averaging the number of owner-operators under contract during the year. Given the high degree of turnover experienced by many carriers that use owner-operators, the number under contract at any given point in the year can fluctuate wildly, and a meaningful annual average is difficult to define. Measuring owner-operator usage by payments is certainly the weakest of the three measures, given the multitude of complex financial arrangements that exist between carriers and their owner-operators (chapter 5), and the lack of precision in the definition of statistics required by the ICC. We may conclude, therefore, that all of the following statistics should be treated with extreme caution, but that the measure of owner-operator usage based on mileage is probably the most reliable.

Table 1-3 uses the mileage method to show the relative dependence of carriers of different types upon the owner-operator method of operation for the years 1965 to 1978, inclusive. As has been reported before, it may clearly be seen that household goods carriers show the greatest dependence on owner-operators (between 80 and 90 percent of all intercity miles) followed by refrigerated products carriers (approximately 60 percent). Carriers of building materials and special commodities not subgrouped also depend a great deal on owner-operators, while general freight carriers seem to use them for 8 to 12 percent of their activities. In the latter case, it should be noted immediately that even this amount probably reflects significant special commodity division activity by the general freight carriers, rather than the use of owner-operators in their main, small-shipment ("Less-than-Truckload," or LTL) business. It is interesting that for no group has the relative dependence on owner-operators declined in the thirteen-year period shown. Overall, owner-operators appear to account for 25 percent of all intercity miles traveled by regulated carriers.

The use of owner-operators as measured by relative number of power units employed is shown in table 1-4, and as measured by payments (expressed as a percentage of total operating expense) in table 1-5. It may be seen that they tend to underestimate the use of owner-operators relative to

Table 1-3
Miles Rented with Driver as Percent of Total Intercity Miles, Various Regulated Carrier Groups, 1965-78

Year	General Freight	Petroleum Products	Refrigerated Products	Agricultural Products	Motor Vehicles	Building Materials	Other Special Commodities	Household Goods	United States Total
1965	8.6	23.7	42.3	25.0	2.8	57.0	32.6	80.6	20.1
1966	7.9	22.6	39.2	28.4	2.4	38.0	34.7	83.1	19.9
1967	7.7	19.0	45.5	25.2	1.7	35.5	34.3	88.1	20.4
1968	8.2	22.7	53.1	24.9	2.1	32.7	35.0	87.5	21.5
1969	8.2	22.9	49.9	23.5	2.4	34.7	33.7	89.0	21.3
1970	8.0	22.9	52.8	24.2	3.9	30.9	33.7	88.9	22.7
1971	8.1	23.5	53.1	30.6	2.2	33.2	35.1	90.1	23.2
1972	7.9	22.2	36.6	28.8	2.6	35.0	38.0	38.2	24.4
1973	8.3	23.4	53.5	28.8	4.9	30.8	38.7	83.0	23.9
1974	9.0	25.5	60.5	29.3	3.8	40.9	39.8	89.7	23.0
1975	9.7	22.8	61.5	30.6	3.0	41.8	40.0	90.0	24.3
1976	10.0	24.6	62.4	32.4	4.4	47.2	43.7	91.0	25.6
1977	11.3	24.9	57.8	31.0	5.6	44.7	43.6	91.9	26.0
1978	12.5	25.5	57.5	34.8	4.4	46.2	43.8	91.9	26.4

Source: TRINC's *Blue Book of the Trucking Industry*, various years.

Table 1-4
Vehicles Rented with Driver as Percent of Total Power Units, Various Regulated Carrier Groups, 1965-78

Year	General Freight	Petroleum Products	Refrigerated Products	Agricultural Products	Motor Vehicles	Building Materials	Other Special Commodities	Household Goods	United States Total
1965	9.8	22.1	32.2	18.1	4.1	25.3	25.4	61.9	19.5
1966	7.7	24.6	29.8	18.9	3.6	22.6	28.8	74.8	20.4
1967	8.1	23.1	n/a	17.4	4.9	30.0	27.2	73.5	18.7
1968	8.3	23.4	44.2	18.6	6.2	29.8	28.8	82.7	20.6
1969	8.4	24.9	49.4	19.6	2.5	27.2	27.6	91.1	22.8
1970	8.4	16.9	44.9	20.8	2.7	27.1	28.4	84.2	22.5
1971	8.6	22.9	36.3	23.0	3.0	27.0	30.1	80.5	23.2
1972	9.0	21.5	36.6	23.8	4.7	27.3	32.6	82.6	24.5
1973	8.8	22.1	33.0	15.5	4.3	27.7	33.0	80.3	23.8
1974	5.2	22.8	52.0	20.5	5.0	34.2	32.2	75.6	14.9
1975	4.5	21.5	54.0	20.8	4.7	35.5	35.5	77.7	15.5
1976	5.7	23.6	55.9	27.1	2.6	40.9	35.5	80.6	16.3
1977	6.5	25.5	58.1	25.6	2.6	38.6	37.7	73.4	17.5
1978	7.5	26.5	60.5	28.3	6.5	41.9	40.7	73.1	19.8

Source: TRINC's *Blue Book of the Trucking Industry*, various years.
N/a: not available.

Table 1-5
Payments for Owner-Operators, as Percent of Total Operating Expense, Various Regulated Carrier Groups, 1974-78

Year	General Freight	Petroleum Carriers	Refrigerated Products	Agricultural Products	Motor Vehicles	Building Materials	Other Special Commodities	Household Goods	United States Total
1974	4.4	19.3	47.1	22.9	5.3	31.2	28.1	n/a	12.1
1975	4.3	17.6	45.7	21.6	4.5	29.3	27.8	n/a	12.1
1976	4.8	18.3	46.9	22.7	5.1	30.9	28.2	n/a	12.5
1977	5.2	19.0	48.6	21.9	5.8	31.7	28.4	n/a	13.0
1978	6.1	19.0	46.6	24.5	6.8	34.2	29.9	n/a	14.2

Source: TRINC's *Blue Book of the Trucking Industry*, various years.
N/a: not available.

the mileage measure, except in the cases of general freight and petroleum carriers. If they are to be treated with equal credulity, these varying estimates may be reconciled as follows. First, we can hypothesize that, in general, owner-operators use their vehicles for a larger number of miles per year than carriers use their own vehicles. In such a case, the use of owner-operators as measured by mileage will appear higher than that indicated by percentage of vehicles. Similarly, we may hypothesize that owner-operators work for less money per mile than company vehicles may be operated for, and hence the payments measure will be lower than the mileage measure.

The discussion above focused attention on the relative use of owner-operators by carriers of different types. A further perspective on the owner-operators' presence in U.S. trucking may be obtained by asking the following question: of all owner-operators, how many of them work for carriers of different types? This question is explored in table 1-6 and figure 1-1, which show the total number of intercity miles operated by carriers through "vehicle rents with driver." It may be seen that, although household goods use owner-operators for 90 percent of their intercity miles, the size of this sector of the trucking industry is such that household goods carriers accounted for only 14 percent of owner-operator mileage in 1978, a dramatic decline from 1969, when they accounted for nearly 23 percent.

In fact, the messages of table 1-6 and figure 1-1 are not the decline of usage or owner-operators by household goods carriers, but the increase in usage by carriers of other types. Refrigerated goods carriers have increased their use of owner-operators from approximately 6 to 9 percent of all owner-operators in 1965-67 to around 14 to 18 percent in 1976-78. There appear to be approximately four times as many owner-operator miles in refrigerated goods in 1978 than were used a decade previously. Other sectors of the trucking industry have also posted significant gains, and the number of owner-operator miles used by all carriers shown doubled in the ten years 1968-78. Since the relative use of owner-operators has stayed relatively constant (table 1-3), this is more a reflection of the general increase in activity by motor carriers. An indication of this is shown in table 1-7, which shows the gross operating revenues, by motor carrier type, in the years 1965 to 1978.

It is interesting to note in passing that with the exception of the "depression" year of 1975, the number of owner-operator miles has shown a consistent increase in every year. This is somewhat contrary to prior expectations. It has been asserted that the number of owner-operators in the United States has diminished drastically since the fuel crisis of 1973-74, although this assertion has been previously challenged.[5] The ICC estimated that there were 73,000 power units under permanent lease to Class I and II carriers as of August 31, 1977, although it was 90 percent sure that the true number was between 59,000 and 87,000.[6] Of these, it suggested that only 61,000

Table 1-6
Percent of Total Vehicle Miles Rented with Driver Accounted for by Various Carrier Groups, 1965-78

Year	General Freight	Petroleum Products	Refrigerated Products	Agricultural Products	Motor Vehicles	Building Materials	Other Special Commodities	Household Goods	United States Total
1965	23	9	8	2	1	5	33	19	100
1966	21	8	7	3	1	4	35	21	100
1967	20	8	9	2	1	4	34	23	100
1968	18	8	10	2	1	4	38	20	100
1969	20	9	10	2	1	4	33	22	100
1970	17	9	13	3	1	4	33	22	100
1971	17	8	14	2	1	4	34	20	100
1972	15	7	14	2	1	5	37	18	100
1973	16	8	13	2	1	4	39	16	100
1974	16	8	15	3	1	6	37	15	100
1975	16	6	18	3	1	5	36	15	100
1976	16	6	17	3	1	6	38	14	100
1977	18	5	14	3	1	6	40	14	100
1978	20	5	14	3	1	7	38	12	100

Source: TRINC's *Blue Book of the Trucking Industry*, various years.

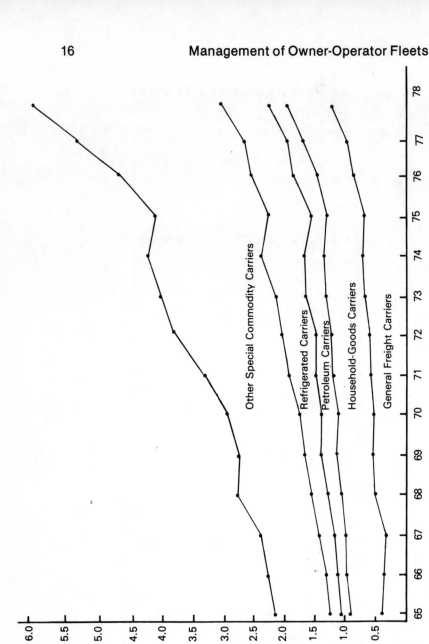

Source: TRINC's Blue Book of the Trucking Industry, various years.

Figure 1-1. Vehicle Miles Rented with Driver, 1965-78

Table 1-7
Operating Revenues, Various Carrier Groups, 1965-78
($ millions)

Year	General Freight	Petroleum Products	Refrigerated Products	Agricultural Products	Motor Vehicles	Building Materials	Other Special Commodities	Household Goods	United States Total
1965	5,753	427	199	82	418	110	1,322	515	8,827
1966	6,348	466	195	98	410	135	1,475	613	9,739
1967	6,523	521	252	95	364	151	1,519	656	10,081
1968	6,571	569	276	101	454	181	1,734	714	11,318
1969	7,471	619	322	110	472	212	1,913	786	12,465
1970	7,749	693	441	115	419	217	2,097	801	12,860
1971	9,125	768	545	151	556	263	2,421	854	15,068
1972	10,215	848	621	158	595	332	2,787	963	16,930
1973	11,584	992	627	180	734	344	3,220	1,047	19,174
1974	12,573	1,071	769	217	681	401	3,582	1,131	19,669
1975	11,986	987	909	258	661	383	3,510	1,110	19,025
1976	14,030	1,109	1,007	283	856	435	4,068	1,291	22,144
1977	16,509	1,092	1,079	373	1,067	598	5,151	1,510	26,272
1978	18,964	1,321	1,351	370	1,242	783	5,995	1,670	30,368

Source: TRINC's *Blue Book of the Trucking Industry*, various years.

were "true" owner-operators in the sense that they owned or drove fleets of less than three vehicles (that is, the ICC did not believe that multiple-unit owner-operators with more than three trucks should be counted as "true owner-operators"), and only 55,000 were owner-operators that owned and drove a single truck.[7] These figures suggest that approximately 25 percent of all "vehicles rented with driver" are rented from multiple-unit owner-operators.

The statistics given above refer only to owner-operator activities by regulated motor carriers. As noted previously, statistics on owner-operator usage by unregulated carriers are very difficult to obtain, since no requirement exists for such carriers to report statistics to a government body. Similarly, there are no statistics accumulated on those owner-operators working as true independents. Wyckoff and Maister[8] discussed the problems of estimating the total owner-operator population and concluded that, as of the mid-1970s, there were probably around 100,000 such individuals. The Department of Health, Education and Welfare, in a letter to the House Subcommittee on Special Small Business Problems, reported that the "number of truckers who consider themselves self-employed, reported more than $400 in net earnings and have not reached the taxable maximum for social security purposes" was 129,200 in 1974.[9]

In the previous section we explored the relative use of owner-operators by motor carriers of different types. In this section we shall attempt to look *within* different sectors and attempt to identify which carriers use owner-operators. As we have seen, owner-operators account for approximately 25 percent of all regulated carrier mileage in the United States. However, as table 1-8 shows, the usage varies significantly by carrier. Over 50 percent of all regulated carriers make negligible use of owner-operators (less than 5 percent of all intercity miles), while for 12 percent this is the predominant method of operation. The ICC has observed that less than 150 carriers account for about 85 percent of all owner-operator miles. Table 1-9 shows the relative use of owner-operators within separate commodity groups.

After household goods carriers, the refrigerated solids groups has the

Table 1-8
Distribution of Motor Carriers by Degree of Owner-Operator Use, 1976

Percent Owner-Operator Use	Number of Carriers	Percent of Carriers
Negligible (0-5)	1,360	58.3
Low (5-30)	309	13.3
Medium (30-60)	216	9.3
High (60-90)	182	7.8
Predominant (90-100)	264	11.3

highest proportion of carriers that are predominantly owner-operator operations, followed by heavy machinery carriers. However, it is clearly shown in table 1-9 that, within each commodity group, all degrees of owner-operator usage may be found.

Which Carriers Use Owner-Operators?

In what terms can we explain which carriers use owner-operators? An attempt to answer this question was made by statistical analysis of ICC annual report data, as contained in *Motor Carrier Annual Reports*. The attempt to fit a linear regression model with "percentage use of owner-operators" as the dependent variable failed entirely to yield satisfactory results, whether applied to the data as a whole or to individual sectors of the industry. The highest R^2 value obtained was only 0.10. Part of the problem in attempting to perform this analysis derives from the fact that many of the financial and operating statistics that potentially could *explain* owner-operator usage may also be the *consequence* of owner-operator usage. This problem could be overcome with a lagged time-series model, but preliminary investigations suggested that this approach was also not likely to yield fruitful results.

In spite of these problems, some insight into which carriers use owner-operators are provided by some simple cross-tabulations of available data. For example, it was not possible to detect any significant difference in owner-operator usage between common carriers and contract carriers of similar commodities. However, a tabulation of owner-operator usage by service type, shown in table 1-10, demonstrates clearly that owner-operators

Table 1-9
Relative Use of Owner-Operators by Carriers within Various Commodity Groups, 1976
(percent)

Type of Carrier	Negligible (0-5)	Low (5-30)	Medium (30-60)	High (60-90)	Predominant (90-100)
General freight	74.1	12.0	4.6	4.2	5.1
Machinery	41.9	10.8	9.5	12.2	25.7
Petroleum	54.5	19.1	14.0	5.1	7.3
Refrigerated solids	28.2	7.7	12.0	17.1	35.0
Dump truck	29.5	19.7	27.9	8.2	14.8
Agricultural	42.4	20.0	15.3	11.8	10.6
Building materials	40.0	13.9	17.4	13.0	15.7
Other specialized	50.0	13.2	11.2	10.4	15.2

Table 1-10
Relationship between Owner-Operator Use and Service Category, 1976
(percent)

	Owner-Operator Use				
Service Type	Negligible (0-5)	Low (5-30)	Medium (30-60)	High (60-90)	Predominant (90-100)
Regular Route— scheduled service	79.1	13.7	3.1	1.8	2.2
Regular Route— nonscheduled service	67.0	11.9	8.2	5.2	7.7
Irregular route— radial	50.7	15.5	10.5	11.6	11.8
Irregular route— nonradial	47.1	13.6	12.7	10.0	16.6
Local service	85.2	5.2	4.3	2.6	2.6

are used predominantly by irregular-route carriers, especially nonradial irregular-route carriers.

There also appear to be significant differences between carriers based upon geographical location of the carriers' home bases, as shown in table 1-11, which uses a classification by geographic location established by the ICC (figure 1-2). Carriers in region 6 (Nebraska, Iowa, Kansas, Missouri) tend to use owner-operators more than in, say, region 1 (New England) or region 9 (the West Coast).

Carrier size also appears to exert an influence, as shown in table 1-12,

Table 1-11
Relationship between Owner-Operator Use and Geographic Region, 1976
(percent)

	Owner-Operator Use				
ICC Region	Negligible (0-5)	Low (5-30)	Medium (30-60)	High (60-90)	Predominant (90-100)
1	77	8	4	7	4
2	53	15	13	8	11
3	64	14	5	7	10
4	55	10	13	6	15
5	59	15	7	5	14
6	44	16	8	14	18
7	62	11	9	7	11
8	46	19	14	7	14
9	64	11	9	11	5

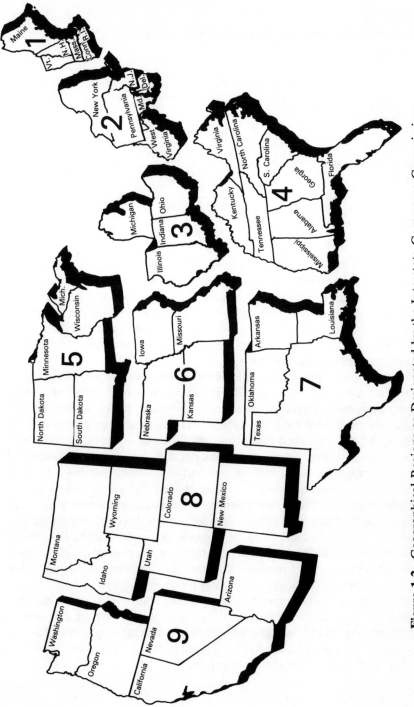

Figure 1-2. Geographical Regions as Designated by the Interstate Commerce Commission

Table 1-12
Relationship between Carrier Size and Owner-Operator Use, 1976
(percent)

	Owner-Operator Use				
	Negligible (0-5)	*Low (5-30)*	*Medium (30-60)*	*High (60-90)*	*Predominant (90-100)*
Heavy Machinery					
Class I	24	8	4	16	48
Class II	51	12	12	10	14
Refrigerated Solids					
Class I	16	7	18	13	46
Class II	39	8	7	21	25

Source: Derived from data contained in *Motor Carrier Annual Reports, 1976*, American Trucking Associations, Inc. 1977.

which shows data for heavy machinery and refrigerated goods carriers. For both of these commodity groups, it is clear that Class I carriers (more than $3 million annual revenues) are greater users of owner-operators than are Class II carriers. This relation between size and owner-operator usage was also suggested by the ICC. Of course, there may be a cause-and-effect problem here, in that large carriers may be large because they use owner-operators, rather than vice versa.

Some final insights into which carriers use owner-operators are provided in table 1-13, which gives operating statistics for carriers of various types, analyzed by degree of owner-operator usage. No completely general rules may be derived from this table, but some trends can be detected. In general, carriers that use a high proportion of owner-operators tend to have lower average revenues per ton-mile and per mile, higher average loads, and longer average hauls. In making comparisons among various figures in table 1-13, it should be noted that many carriers that have a *mix* of owner-operators and company-owned vehicles tend to use these two groups for *distinct* parts of their operation, which may not be directly comparable. For example, refrigerated solids carriers may also have a "flat-bed" division hauling steel in which it uses owner-operators, and a general freight division in which it does not. In consequence, it may be somewhat misleading to talk of that carrier's having, say, 30 percent owner-operators.

For this and other reasons, the published statistics reviewed here are limited in how much they can tell us about which carriers use owner-operators. For further insights, we need to consider the reasons why carriers use owner-operators and why the owner-operator system exists. These topics are the subject of the next chapter.

Table 1-13
Relationship between Owner-Operator Use and Selected Operating Statistics, 1976
(percent)

	Owner-Operator Use				
	Negligible (0-5)	*Low (5-30)*	*Medium (30-60)*	*High (60-90)*	*Predominant (90-100)*
Heavy-Machinery Carriers					
Revenue per ton-mile (¢)	16	86	25	19	7
Revenue per mile (¢)	152	159	132	119	099
Average load (tons)	10.6	7.2	7.8	11.4	9.1
Average haul (miles)	231	289	139	291	427
Refrigerated-Solids Carriers					
Revenue per ton-mile (¢)	25	11	6	6	9
Revenue per mile (¢)	101	74	60	81	101
Average load (tons)	9.1	10.0	11.7	14.5	11.1
Average haul (miles)	453	569	897	658	643
Dump-Truck Carriers					
Revenue per ton-mile (¢)	18	5	5	5	7
Revenue per mile (¢)	104	75	82	75	157
Average load (tons)	7.4	11.1	13.0	12.5	16.5
Average haul (miles)	40	89	79	63	48
Agricultural-Commodities Carriers					
Revenue per ton-mile (¢)	11	7	6	6	5
Revenue per mile (¢)	89	79	74	85	85
Average load (tons)	11.3	11.5	13.5	14.8	13.8
Average haul (miles)	353	264	261	270	600
Building-Materials Carriers					
Revenue per ton-mile (¢)	9	14	9	9	5
Revenue per mile (¢)	89	83	80	93	74
Average load (tons)	11.2	12.6	14.3	10.9	15.7
Average haul (miles)	179	260	233	194	500

Source: Derived from data contained in *Motor Carrier Annual Reports*.

2 Understanding the Owner-Operator System

As we have seen, the owner-operator method of operation is used by a substantial number of motor carriers, accounting for a significant proportion of the industry's intercity mileage. Why is this so? Why do so many motor carriers elect to operate in this way? Why do the owner-operators work for the motor carriers rather than operating in their own right? What role did the economic regulation of the motor-carrier industry that existed through the 1970s play in explaining the existence of this system? These and other related questions are the subject matter of this chapter. We shall begin by exploring the reasons that might lead a motor carrier to using owner-operators.

Why Do Motor Carriers Use Owner-Operators?

The reasons given by motor-carrier executives for their use of owner-operators are many and various. In most cases, I found that no single reason could be given by an individual manager or company owner: the motivations were a complex mix of various distinct objectives. In spite of this, we shall attempt here to distinguish the separate rationales.

One of the most common reasons given is that by signing on owner-operators when traffic levels increase, and terminating the lease contract when they decline, a motor carrier can better match its available equipment capacity to the level of demand, and avoid bearing the cost of idle equipment when traffic levels do not warrant it. I term this the *avoidance of capital risk* rationale, since the motor carrier is passing on the capital risk (that is, the chance that revenue opportunities do not warrant the investment in equipment) to the owner-operator. It should be noted that the source of the capital risk may take two forms: annual seasonality and long-term uncertainty. In the former case, the variation in demand levels is relatively predictable, as in the case of household goods carriers. They know that May through September is their busy period and that relatively few household moves take place in the winter months. By using owner-operators, these carriers are better able to match supply and demand. In the case of unpredictable demand fluctuations in the long term, a carrier may use owner-operators without knowing in advance when, if at all, it will terminate the lease contracts, but it has the security that if demand does decline, the carrier will not have to meet the fixed obligations of making payments on the vehicles (or, it should be noted, paying for an idle work force). The owner-operator is absorbing uncertainty for the carrier.

Apart from these considerations, some motor carriers use owner-operators because they believe that they are more productive than employee drivers driving company equipment. The source of this additional productivity, if true, is said to come from the fact that since owner-operators are paid only for the work that they perform, they have the incentive to work hard, to work efficiently, and to solve problems themselves rather than appealing to supervisory or managerial direction. This rationale may be termed *entrepreneurial incentive* and may take many forms. It has already been observed (in chapter 1) that owner-operators tend to drive more miles per year than company drivers. Because they are responsible for their own maintenance, owner operators will solve minor breakdown problems on the road and proceed, whereas a company driver may wait for a repair service to be sent from the carrier's terminal. If there are problems or delays in getting loaded or unloaded at a customer's dock, the owner-operator has the incentive to solve these problems directly, whereas a company driver, who might be paid to some extent by the hour, would have a lessened incentive to "get rolling" again. Since the vehicle is his or her own, the owner-operator has a greater incentive to take care of the tractor than the company driver, and fewer maintenance problems should arise. Many other specific illustrations can be given of the ways in which the entrepreneurial incentive may lead an owner-operator to be more productive than a company driver.

Some common elements of the two previously given rationales can be combined to yield a third distinct benefit to the motor carrier in using owner-operators. This is that fact that the use of owner-operators gives a carrier the capacity for rapid growth. Since the owner-operator pays for the vehicle, a carrier is not bound by its own borrowing capacity as to the number of vehicles it can add to its fleet in a given year. This advantage may be of particular importance to a small carrier attempting to grow rapidly. However, the increased ability to grow provided by owner-operators derives not only from the relaxed capital constraint, but also from the fact that owner-operators are not only drivers but, for example, are also their own mechanics. In using an owner-operator, a carrier not only avoids buying a new truck but also avoids the expense and managerial problems of hiring (and training) a new driver, and increasing the workload on its maintenance facilities. Because the owner-operator has the entrepreneurial incentive, she or he takes on many of the self-supervisory and self-management tasks that would otherwise have to be provided by the carrier in the form of supervisory and managerial personnel. In principle, this should allow the carrier to avoid the managerial capacity constraint that might otherwise limit growth capability.

The problems of supervision are not trivial. Consider, for example, the differences between a regular-route carrier of general commodities (generally less than truckload) and, say, an irregular-route (nonradial) carrier of (truckload) special commodities. Management control of the driver work force in the former case is relatively simple, since most drivers will be operating between fixed carrier termini: it is easy for the carrier to measure, for example, the time-in-transit that driver takes to complete the assigned run. Standards can be established for these regular runs and monitored on a regular basis. What is more, the intercity driver does not deal with the customer. However, the driver for a truckload, nonradial, irregular-route carrier may *never* report to a carrier terminal. The load is picked up by the driver from the shipper's dock and transported directly to the consignee's dock. The driver must deal with customers at both ends of the trip, and management monitoring and control of the driver can only be accomplished by getting the driver to telephone the carrier at designated stages of the process, a matter that requires the cooperation of the driver. It is a simple matter to see the difficulties of using employees in this situation, and the immense benefits that derive from having the appropriate entrepreneurial incentives placed upon the driver to provide a quality service, that is, to use owner-operators.

A separate set of potential benefits to a motor carrier in using owner-operators rather than company equipment and drivers derives from the assertion that owner-operators are cheaper than employee drivers. It should be noted that this rationale is distinct from the increased productivity argument made above. There we suggested, in effect, that more output could be obtained from an equivalent set of inputs. Here we shall explore the possibility that the inputs (in particular, driver wages) come cheaper by using owner-operators than by using employee drivers. As we shall see, the potential sources of this cheaper labor are numerous.

First, we note that, as identified by Wyckoff and Maister,[1] many owner-operators seem prepared to accept an effectively lower wage than they could obtain by selling off their trucks, investing their capital in Treasury bonds, and going to work as a Teamster employee driver. Wyckoff and I termed this the "price of independence" that owner-operators seem prepared to pay. The fact that they are *prepared* to pay this price does not necessarily account for the fact that in many instances the owner-operators *do* pay this price. For the explanation of this, we must note that since in many companies the owner-operators are classified as "independent contractors" rather than "employees," they are prohibited under antitrust laws from bargaining collectively. The source of the cheaper labor thus derives in part from the lessened ability of the owner-operator to obtain wage levels comparable to those obtained by the bargaining efforts of the Teamsters' Union on behalf of employee company drivers. However, it should be noted that many trucking companies with employee drivers are nonunion: owner-operators are not the only alternative to the Teamsters.

The nonunion status of many owner-operators implies other labor cost savings for the carrier apart from the direct wage labor cost. The carrier using nonunion owner-operators can avoid a variety of "fringe" payments such as union pension contributions, paid vacations, and other indirect labor expenses that are borne by the "employee-driver carrier."

Since the first National Master Freight Agreement (NMFA) negotiated by the Teamsters' Union in 1964, there has been a relatively rapid rise in nondirect fringe costs; this potential source of saving to carriers is nontrivial.

Apart from union-negotiated fringes, a carrier that uses "independent contractor" owner-operators rather than employee drivers also has the opportunity to save on other, government-mandated, fringe labor costs. Among these may be included payroll taxes, social security payments, and, in some states, workers' compensation payments. As in the case of union-negotiated fringes, these expenses have escalated rapidly in recent years and may be perceived as substantial savings to the carrier if they can be avoided. It should be noted that many of these savings may be illusory. While the carrier may not pay workers' compensation or FICA contributions directly, these costs will be borne by the owner-operator and are thus implicitly included in the owner-operator's percentage of revenue. Nevertheless, with total "fringe" labor costs approximately 34 percent of the basic wage bill in the trucking industry, the potential for savings is significant.

Another reason carriers give for using owner-operators is the avoidance not only of union pay scales but of union work rules. For example, in some major cities a union carrier is required to use a *city* driver for pickup and delivery, even on a truckload intercity movement. This necessitates changing drivers, delaying the shipment, and possibly being forced to pay a full-day's wage to the city driver for only a few hours' work. By using owner-operators as a means of avoiding the union (not, as we have noted, the only method of so doing), the carrier can reduce its costs and provide more direct (and speedier) service.

It can be seen that the potential motivations for using owner-operators vary widely. This is not without significance, a significance that is often overlooked by managers and public policymakers alike. For managers, the implication of varying motivations for using owner-operators is that the exact goal to be achieved in using owner-operators can (and, I would argue, *should*) influence the way they manage and deal with their owner-operators. This contention will be explored more fully below, but we can note here that if, for example, a carrier is using owner-operators to capture increased productivity and/or lower input (labor) costs (rather than attempting to grow rapidly or avoid capital risk), then it may need to avoid placing too much of the capital risk on the owner-operator's shoulders in order to preserve the benefits it seeks. To state it more simply: a carrier that is looking for productivity benefits can less afford high turnover and dissatisfaction of owner-operators than one that seeks solely to use them to match supply and demand, and its management practices must reflect this. In the course of my research I have been led to the conclusion that this simple insight is often missed by many motor-carrier executives who have failed to identify their exact motivations for using owner-operators and who have consequently failed to think through how they can best capture the specific benefits they seek.

For public policymakers the varying potential motivations for using owner-operators have significance for the many ways in which they seek to control and influence the owner-operator system. To the extent that cheap labor cost is the prime motivation of carriers in using owner-operators, public policy officials may feel it necessary to enact regulations to prevent the exploitation of owner-operators by carriers, and to view the owner-operator system as an "aberration" that provides no real economies to the motor-carrier system. If, however, increased productivity is the prime rationale, then the owner-operator system offers substantial and real benefits to the industry and should be encouraged (or at least not inhibited) by government action. Implications for public policy also exist in understanding exactly which instruments of public policy are most likely to impact upon the owner-operator system. If the owner-operator system exists for most carriers because of cheap labor input costs, then actions by the ICC in "protecting" the owner-operator may have substantial impact. If avoidance of capital risk is the prime rationale, then slightly increased labor cost due to allowing owner-operators to bargain collectively will not threaten (though it may affect) the owner-operator system. If avoidance of government-mandated fringe costs plays a large role in explaining the existence of the owner-operator system, then the greatest "threat" to the system is not the ICC's action on "truth in leasing" rules,[2] or the National Labor Relations Board's rulings on whether owner-operators may bargain collectively,[3] but whether or not the Internal Revenue Service classifies owner-operators as employees.[4]

At the commencement of my research, I intended to conduct a questionnaire survey of motor carriers in an attempt to discover which of the varying rationales for the owner-operator system really predominated. However, as my interviews progressed it became increasingly clear (as noted above) that many motor-carrier executives have not entirely established in their own minds exactly which of the benefits of the owner-operator system they are attemping to capture.

As a result of my research, I have become increasingly convinced that while all the benefits of using owner-operators are welcomed, most motor-carrier managers, when pressed, will identify one of three basic reasons. For some motor carriers, the capital-related rationales (avoidance of risk, capacity for rapid growth, and so on) and the greater productivity rationale are relatively unimportant (particularly the first). These carriers have sufficient borrowing capacity so that capital constraints do not realistically limit their ability to acquire additional equipment. For many carriers, the level of uncertainty over demand levels (either seasonal or long-term) is not so great that investment in over-the-road equipment becomes a high-risk decision. This is particularly true since the depreciation life of a truck is relatively short (four to five years). For these carriers (and I believe they constitute a high proportion of owner-operator users) the major rationale for using owner operators is reduced labor cost. (As noted above, even this rationale has subcomponents: the lower labor cost may come from lower owner-operator salaries, lower fringe costs, or avoidance of unionization.)

However, in spite of the (hypothesized) predominance of this rationale among many carriers, I have also encountered carriers for whom the other rationales are more keenly sought. Such carriers may have generous health and welfare and pension schemes for their operators, and clearly do not seek to lower "fringe" costs. Some carriers, particularly special commodity divisions of general freight carriers, do not avoid fringe costs or unionization: the parent-company union contract requires all owner-operators to be members and full benefits to be paid. In such cases, capital-related rationales predominate. Finally, I have interviewed carriers who have foregone (or have been prepared to forego) capital-related reasons by financing their contractors' equipment and paying healthy benefits: they just believe that owner-operators are more productive. In spite of this variance, most managers I have talked to will stress one rationale above others.

To a limited extent, one can predict which rationale is favored. Small companies primarily seek growth and the capital that owner-operators bring. Carriers in the South and Southwest are less likely to seek to avoid unionization as their main reason for using owner-operators. Carriers in highly seasonal businesses place great importance on the capacity freedom owner-operators provide. However, these are generalizations and are not valid in all cases. In the final analysis, each manager (or management team) must (and usually does) have his or her own reasons.

The Owner-Operator System in Other Industries

The reader will have noticed that none of the benefits ascribed above to the owner-operator system (avoidance of capital risk, matching supply and demand, absorbing uncertainty, providing entrepreneurial incentive, capacity for rapid growth, cheaper labor cost, nonemployee status) depends crucially for its existence upon factors peculiar to the trucking industry (except perhaps the discussion of the nature of nonradial irregular-route carriers). We may therefore ask whether the owner-operator system exists in other industries. If it does, then our understanding of the system may be increased by consideration of how and why the system works in those industries.

In considering the decision faced by a company as to whether it should use owner-operators or employee drivers there are a number of analogies with firms in other industries that we can draw. First, we can recognize that, in effect, the owner-operator decision is one of "make or buy," that is, shall we make this component of our product (or service) ourselves, or shall we purchase it? There is an interesting literature on this decision as it is faced by firms in manufacturing industries,[5] but it yields few insights into the trucking industry's problems. The same can also be said for the general topic of the "subcontracting out" of work in manufacturing industries such as aerospace, construction, and others. While the decisions on subcontracting in these industries and in trucking appear to be analogous, the existing literature in the field[6] does not, in general, warrant the attention of either trucking managers or public policy officials interested in trucking.

There exists one other analogous experience that we can examine, which, as we shall see, yields a plentiful harvest of valuable insights. This is the experience of the franchising (particularly, fast-food) industry. Consider, for example, the following quotation:

> The following is a more elaborate list of the various advantages for both franchisor and franchisee. . . . Advantages to franchisor: (1) Investment capital . . . , (2) Local, interested management, with cost and sales awareness, (3) Acceptance in the community as a local business, (4) Limited payroll and insurance costs, (5) Better market communications—Local franchise to manufacturer or supplier, (6) Individual ownership giving strong motivation to success, (7) Thorough, fast and selective distribution, (8) Reduced operating expenses.[7]

With only slight vocabulary changes, we can recognize in this list all of the advantages of the owner-operator system that we have described above. To emphasize the analogy also consider this carefully worded attempt to define franchising:

> The problem remains . . . to identify the characteristics of the franchise concept which make that concept unique; and to find a definition which permits a derivation of the boundaries of the franchise form, and which does so in a way which satisfies both the public and the legal conception of franchising. I have adopted a definition . . . which centers on four aspects of the franchise concept which make that concept unique and identifiable. The four aspects are: (1) Although the franchise may be economically

dependent on the franchisor, he is a legally independent member of the franchising system; (2) The franchisee's business is operated with the advantages of name and standardization of the franchisor accruing to the franchisee; (3) The franchisee's business came into being in its present form (although not necessarily physically), with the expressed purpose of marketing the franchisor's products or service; (4) A formal agreement, most commonly called a "franchise agreement" or "franchise contract" is in existence. The agreement calls for a continuing, although not necessarily indeterminate, relationship.[8]

With the possible exception of aspect (3), there is nothing in this definition of franchising that would exclude a motor carrier using owner-operators. It should be stressed that the definition shown above is one of the most restrictive in the literature, being taken from a book devoted to the legal aspects of franchising. Alternative definitions in the more managerially oriented literature on franchising offer even fewer (if any) problems in recognizing the owner-operator system as an example of franchising.

In fact, the analogy between the owner-operator system and franchising has indeed been noted before. In a book designed to assist those considering becoming a franchisee, Metz[9] devotes each of his chapters to the typical franchisee experience in a variety of industries—including that of an individual working for a household goods trucking company! However, the analogy (and the implications it offers) has been scarcely recognized (if at all) in the trucking community, or among those in the public sector who have responsibility for (or have influence over) the trucking industry.

It should be noted that in using the word "franchising" we are not referring to the meaning of the word "franchise" that implies a privilege conferred on an individual by a government. This meaning, which (as does our meaning) derives from the old French word *francher* (to free), has been used extensively to refer to the trucking industry. Interestingly, it was used repeatedly by Representative Millicent Fenwick of New Jersey in the congressional hearings on the regulatory problems of owner-operators[10] to refer to the "franchise" given by the ICC to motor carriers to operate (that is, the certificate of public convenience and necessity). Representative Fenwick was concerned that the motor carriers were abusing their "franchise" by the use of owner-operators. However, it is clear from the transcript of the hearings that she did not interpret the word franchising in the sense that we are using it here.

In spite of this, Reprentative Fenwick's concern does point up the potential importance of recognizing the analogy between the owner-operator system and franchising. The congressional hearings referred to contain many statements, direct and indirect, that seem to suggest that the owner-operator system is a consequence of economic regulation of the trucking industry by the ICC, or at the very least, that many of the problems of the owner-operators in the U.S. trucking industry in the mid-1970s derived from the restrictive entry policies of the ICC. Were it not for the ICC, the argument goes, many (though perhaps not all) owner-operators would not work for motor carriers through lease arrangements, but would haul for shippers directly. In this way, the owner-operator would be able to retain 100 percent of the revenue from the load instead of the (average) 75 percent that he receives frm the motor carrier. It is clear from the transcript that at least one of the major concerns of the congressional subcommittee was that, in retaining 25 percent of the revenue from the load, some motor carriers may indeed be "abusing their franchise" from the ICC by obtaining an "economic rent" for their operating authority. What, it has been asked, does the owner-operator receive from the carrier to warrant the withholding of 25 percent of the revenue?

This question will be addressed more directly in later chapters, but we raise it here to provide the basis for addressing a related set of questions: what is the economic justification for the owner-operator system from the point of view of the owner-operator and society (rather than, as has been explored above, from the point of the motor carrier)? Is the system a consequence of economic regulation of the motor-carrier industry by the ICC? Would the owner-operator sytem exist in the absence of ICC regulation? Are the economic "abuses" of owner-operators by motor carriers reported to the congressional committee due primarily to the lack of alternatives faced by the owner-operators (that is, that they must work for ICC-regulated carriers in order to haul most commodities)?

Our analogy with franchising allows us to shed some light on these questions. First, we consider the potential benefits of the owner-operator system to the owner-operator. Consider the following list of advantages to the potential franchisee (compared to opening up in business for himself) compiled by an authority on franchisng:

1. Risk minimized because of help from franchisor
2. Can open business with less cash
3. Can enter inexperienced, because franchisor provides training
4. Potentially more profitable because of the ability to share in bulk purchasing
5. Benefit from national advertising
6. Obtain merchandising assistance
7. Share in collateral benefits such as insurance
8. Product improvements (R and D) made by parent
9. Continuing managerial assistance
10. Sympathetic personal attention[11]

With some degree of redundancy, we can quote from another list of advantages of franchising found in the *Small Business Reporter*:

1. No previous experience required
2. Less capital required
3. Financial assistance from franchisor
4. Benefits of a consumer-accepted image
5. Maintained quality
6. Buying power
7. Training and continued assistance
8. Location analysis
9. Managerial and records assistance
10. Sales, advertising and marketing assistance
11. National publicity
12. Higher income potential
13. Lower risk of failure[12]

Once more, it is not difficult to interpret these to apply to the situation of an owner-operator who, in a free market, might be considering the choice of whether to sign a lease contract with a motor carrier or operate as a one-person business. Nevertheless, let us emphasize and interpret one or two of these advantages. The "benefits of a consumer-accepted image" to the owner-operator are clear. She or he is likely to have much greater success in obtaining traffic in any market where there is the slightest "service quality" sensitivity by associating herself or himself with a large carrier than by approaching shippers as a one-person operation. The "lower risk of failure" arguent is particularly interesting. Although not unchallenged,[13] there is considerable evidence that franchisees have a markedly lower rate of business failure than the overall small-business failure rate.[14] It would not be difficult to accept this same prediction for the trucking industry if an owner-operator competing in an unregulated market had the choice of working for a large carrier or acting as a one-person business.

The advantage of "location analysis" points out one of the responsibilities of the motor carrier/franchiser to his or her owner-operators/franchisees: the need to provide guidance on what are good markets. In the case of fast-food franchising this will indeed be literally "location analysis." In the case of the motor carrier, this would translate into the need for the carrier to assemble and provide to the owner-operator a profitable set of routes and commodities.

This last point serves to remind the reader that the discussion above is not meant to be interpreted as describing the services and benefits that motor carriers do provide to owner-operators, but rather to illustrate the services and benefits that it could offer to the owner-operator. What we are attempting to establish by the analogy with franchising is that, in the absence of economic regulation of the trucking industry, sufficient incentives would still exist on both sides of the relationship for the owner-operator system to continue.

In the light of the recent investigations of owner-operator "abuses" by motor carriers,[15] it is interesting to evaluate the performance of the franchising industry in this regard. Fortunately for our attempt to establish the analogy between owner-operators and franchisees, the franchising industry has had a history of repeated accusations of franchisee abuse by franchisors. What is more, the forms of these abuses are remarkably similar to those raised in connection with owner-operators in the motor-carrier industry. In 1970 one author noted that "recently a number of class actions have been brought by franchisees against their franchisors. . . . Most actions to date have revolved around the franchisor's 'excessive' methods of control, 'oppressive' contracts, and 'restrictive' buying covenants."[16] Another author (who had previously published a book entitled *Franchising: Trap for the Trusting*[17]) identified in 1973 over sixty prominent franchisors who were then or recently had been involved in franchise litigation.[18] A dramatic description of the franchisee experience has been drawn by Bucklin:

> To devotees of the sport of gambling, Russian roulette is the supreme game in which one places a single cartridge in a revolver, spins the bullet chamber, places the gun to his head, and squeezes the trigger. Franchising may be just this kind of game, except that five of the bullet chambers are loaded instead of just one. Fortunately, the cartridges are packed only with such niceties as seventy-hour work weeks and a minimum wage-busting pay scale, rather than gunpowder. The empty chamber consists of that long-awaited pile of riches at the end of the rainbow.[19]

Like the owner-operator system, concern has been expressed in studies of franchising that the balance of bargaining power is weighed unequally in favor of the franchisor; that deception is used is selling franchises (particularly the use of hidden charges[20]); that misrepresentations of earning potentials are made;[21] that franchisees are exploited in their purchases of equipment and supplies;[22] and virtually all of the other "abuses" that are said to exist in the owner-operator system of trucking. Readers who wish to prove this for themselves have only to read and compare the testimony presented in the Senate hearings on franchise agreements[23] with the congressional hearings on the owner-operator system (referenced above).

Once again it must be stressed that in drawing this analogy it is in no way intended to downplay or exonerate those motor-carrier abuses of owner-operators that do exist. The purpose here is merely to establish that the owner-operator system in the U.S. trucking industry is not unique, and that its existence, its benefits, and its problems do not necessarily derive from the economic regulation of the motor-carrier industry by the ICC. To emphasize this point, we shall briefly examine the experience of other countries with the owner-operator system.

The Owner-Operator in Other Countries

The fact that the owner-operator system is not a consequence of the particular regulatory structure of the United States is amply demonstrated by the reported existence of a flourishing owner-operator sector working by leasing themselves to larger motor carriers in Sweden, Great Britain, Australia, and Canada—all countries with experience of unregulated trucking.

Moore[24] reports that in Sweden the two firms that dominate long-distance (particularly LTL) hauling (together accounting for 90 percent of the traffic) own almost no trucks themselves, but hire independent truckers who work for them under one-year contracts, receiving, on average, 85 percent of the revenue.

The recent Price Commission report on the trucking industry in (unregulated) Britain[25] revealed that 20 percent of the revenues of one-person-one-truck operators was derived from hauls made for other haulage firms and over 9 percent of the traffic carried by large firms was subcontracted to other hauliers. It reports that "sub-contracting is particularly significant between firms operating in the general haulage sector but nevertheless also takes place in other sectors including bulk liquids, tipping and household removals."[26]

In Australia, Rimmer[27] reports a situation remarkably like that of Sweden. A handful of "freight forwarders" dominate the intercity road transport market who employ subcontractors, either on a permanent or itinerant basis to perform the necessary line haul by road. Rimmer notes: "The owner drivers who dominated the industry between 1950-60 operating on their own account received reasonable profits from their operations. Since they have switched to subcontracting, following the decision of several of the larger companies to sell their fleets to individual drivers, their profit margins have been cut severely. . . . This sharing of the returns of individual subcontractors is achieved by requiring more than the agreed number of drops, charging a service fee for loading, an insurance premium on a load and stipulating that the truck must be filled with the firm's petrol."[28] It is notable how close these "abuses" in unregulated Australia interstate transport are to those currently of concern in the United States.

In September 1973, in response to a strike of owner-drivers and subcontractors, the Western Australian government appointed a Commission of Inquiry into the Road Transport Industry of that state, which is de facto (though not de jure) a freely competitive industry. The commission's report described a pictue familiar to anyone who has studied owner-operator behavior anywhere in the world: "The submissions which some of them filled in were woefully inadequate in portraying with clarity operating costs. Many of them kept no proper records at all of expenses. Few of them appreciated that in order for them to obtain a fair appreciation of how the business was operating, it was necessary to make an allowance for their own labour at least at the same rate as being paid to driver members of the Transport Workers Union."[29] As Rimmer has also reported for Australia's (unregulated) interstate markets, the commission observed that "the prime contractors (i.e. the carriers) in effect inform the subcontractors what they will pay them."[30]

In Canada, where each of the ten provinces has a different regulatory environment,[31] the relative use of owner-operators by motor carriers varies widely among the provinces. In unregulated Alberta, over 20 percent of all motor-carrier expenses are incurred by "vehicles rented with driver," that is, owner-operators.[32] The corresponding figure for the regulated sector of the United States is 12 percent. (It should be noted that expressing payments to owner-operators as a percentage of total operating expense leads to an understatement of the degree of owner-operator participation in Canadian trucking, since payments to owner-operators are mainly in lieu of line-haul activities. As a percent of intercity mileage, the relative role of owner-operators would be significantly higher.)

High relative owner-operator usage (measured by vehicle rents with driver as a percentage of total expenses) is also reported in the provinces of Saskatchewan (19 percent) and Manitoba (16 percent), both of which not only regulate entry into the motor-carrier industry but also prescribe the rates that motor carriers may charge. Relatively low owner-operator usage is reported for Quebec (6 percent), British Columbia (10 percent), and Ontario (10 percent), all of whom regulate entry into their respective trucking industries. It should be noted that this variation among provinces cannot be accounted for by differences in the types of traffic that predominate in the different provinces: correcting for the relative proportions of truckload traffic in each province leaves the same pattern of relative owner-operator usage.[33]

An interesting paradox emerges when one attempts to relate relative owner-operator usage in each province to the regulatory structures of the provinces. The three "high owner-operator usage" provinces include an unregulated province and two that control entry and prescribe rates.

A possible resolution of this slight paradox may be provided by the following explanation. It is of more than passing interest to note that the three high owner-operator provinces all are reputed for their low average rates, even after correcting for commodity differences, length of haul, shipment size, and so on. Similarly, the low owner-operator provinces (Quebec, Ontario, and British Columbia) are the three provinces with the highest average rates in Canada. The U.S. trucking industry also demonstrates this relationship between average rate level and degree of owner-operator usage, as chapter 1 showed.

We may push this explanation a little further and offer a more qualitative interpretation. It is perhaps not surprising that the most unregulated province, Alberta, has the highest use of owner-operators. Since competition is more active in that province, with no regulatory barriers to entry, carriers may be less willing to invest in equipment and more eager to pass some of the capital risk on to owner-operators. On the other hand, carriers in Manitoba and Saskatchewan, while they may be protected from "excessive" competition, are faced with low average rates and hence wish to use owner-operators because such individuals provide a cheaper method of operating than employee drivers, who tend to be less productive and have higher wages. While this explanation cannot be "proven" in any sense of the word, it is, nevertheless, a suggestive one.

The problems of owner-operator "abuse" in Canada also show no relation to regulation. In the most closely regulated province (Quebec), an owner-operator "shutdown" in 1974 (against a single carrier), caused by perceptions of poor treatment by the carrier, rapidly turned violent and contributed to a general tightening of that province's regulatory laws with respect to owner-operators.[34] This series of events closely parallels that experienced in the United States. On the other hand, unregulated Alberta was also led, by complaints of ill treatment similar to those in the United States, to conduct a review of the owner-operator system in that province.[35]

Before completing our review of the role of owner-operators in foreign jurisdictions, we should note that the lot of the owner-operator in the U.S. exempt sector is not always a happy one. Johnson, president of the Owner Operator Association of America, had this to say about owner-operators working through brokers in the unregulated agricultural sector: "When you consider that the shipper is inaccessible to the trucker, it doesn't take much imagination to see how this arrangement can be abused. Add to this the fact that the trucker must go wherever the produce is in season and often deals with brokers that he does not know, and you can see that even the exempt trucker is at the mercy of a middleman who can dream up a thousand reasons why he can't pay you yet or why the shipping rate has suddenly changed."[36]

In summary, we can conclude that the owner-operator system (whereby one-person-one-truck operators work by leasing themselves to larger carriers) exists in a wide diveristy of regulated and unregulated environments, and that the problems faced by owner-operators in their treatment by carriers also exhibit remarkable commonality across the world. This conclusion suggests that we should not look to regulation to account for the existence (and problems) of the owner-operator system.

Summary: The Economic Basis of the Owner-Operator System

In this chapter we have explored the reasons for the existence of the owner-operator system in U.S. trucking. We have seen that a variety of possible rationales exist for motor carriers to use owner-operators and that, even leaving to one side the constraints imposed by ICC regulation of the industry, there exist rationales for an owner-operator to want to associate himself or herself with a large motor carrier rather than operate as a one-person trucking business. It was demonstrated that there are close analogies with the owner-operator system in other industries, particularly fast-food franchising, and that many of the problems and potentials of the owner-operator system and the franchising industry are similar. Finally, we have seen that the owner-operator system exists in many foreign jurisdictions, with varying regulatory structures, and that the circumstances of the owner-operator reported in these jurisdictions are remarkably similar.

As noted in the preface, this book is not primarily intended to address public policy questions: I believe that the major importance of my analogy of owner-operators with the franchising industry will be found in the succeeding chapters, where I attempt to use it to provide advice on good management for those carriers that use owner-operators. Nevertheless, no proper advice on management of owner-operator fleets can proceed without a firm understanding of the economic basis upon which the owner-operator system rests. I shall therefore summarize this chapter with an attempt to isolate exactly how the owner-operator system contributes to the efficiency of the trucking industry, and hence to the economy and society at large. As before, this task is greatly simplified by drawing the analogy with the franchising industry.

Judge Dawson, in ruling on a case involving claims of franchisor "abuse" of franchisees, pointed to one of the advantages of the owner-operator/franchise system to the economy. He stated: "The franchise method of operation has the advantage, from the standpoint of our American system of competitive economy, of enabling numerous groups of individuals with small capital to become entrepreneurs."[37] E. Patrick McGuire, in a report on franchising for the Conference Board, phrased the same thought this way: "Franchising, which has been described by certain of its most avid supporters as the 'last best hope of the small businessman,' is generally considered a vital force sustaining entrepreneurship."[38]

In less idealistic terms, Bucklin identified the true ecnomic basis of the franchising system when he noted that it "is derived from an opportunity, through a moderate degree of organization, to tap the economies of standardization that exist within activities at the wholesale level. Through independent ownership, however, the system also has the capacity to adjust to local market conditions."[39] Hunt expressed a similar thought when he observed: "Simply put, the franchise ethic says that franchised units combine the best of both worlds, the sophisticated business procedures of the large company and the drive and initiative of the independent owner-manager."[40] Rephrasing these thoughts, we can easily apply them to explain the prevalence of the owner-operator system in the trucking industry. In essence, the economic basis of the system is that the motor carrier performs those tasks (marketing, selling, dispatching, billing, collecting, and so on) for which "economies of scale" exist, that is, those that can most efficiently be done by a larger company. Those tasks for which few, if any, such economies of scale exist, such as the line-haul transportation, are left in the hands of those individuals best able to perform the service: the entrepreneurial owner-operator. While institutional factors, laws, regulations, and specific industry conditions may cause deviations from this ideal, and the imbalance of power between owner-operator and carrier may create legal and regulatory problems, the owner-operator system will continue as long as this underlying economic rationale exists.

3

An Overview of Owner-Operator Management

In this chapter we shall begin our review of the management tasks involved in running an owner-operator fleet. While succeeding chapters will examine specific functional tasks such as recruiting, dispatching, and control, we shall here take a broad look at the problems and challenges of managing independent contractors. In a preceding chapter we discussed at some length the advantages and benefits of using independent contractors rather than employees. Here we shall consider the *dis*advantages and problems that arise from this choice and attempt to use the analogy of franchising (as well as other, more general, management thought) to shed some light on how these difficulties may be addressed.

The Problems of Using Owner-Operators

Given the very nature of the term *independent* contractor, it comes as no surprise to learn that, as in franchising, the greatest disadvantage in using owner-operators is that of control. While employees may, within the bounds of union restrictions, be told how to operate and what to do at any given time, it is inherent in the carrier-contractor relationship that owner-operators may exercise a greater degree of freedom in their activities. The most commonly cited example of this is in the area of dispatching. Owner-operators normally retain the right to refuse a given dispatch: they may not wish, for whatever reason, to go to a particular destination or to carry a certain commodity. While some carriers do employ a system of forced dispatch, whereby their contractors do not have the right to refuse a load, such a paractice is not only unpopular with owner-operators but also threatening to their legal status (in the eyes of the National Labor Relations Board) as independent contractors rather than employees.

The problems of lack of control show up in other ways. Some carriers complain of owner-operators who do not even report for dispatches, having decided to take a brief vacation without notifying the carrier. For a period of time, the carrier does not know what capacity it might have to haul its customers' traffic. Alternatively, lack of control might reveal itself in the owner-operator's refusal to adhere to company policies such as "calling in" every day to report location, condition of the load, and so on. Other policies, such as those governing the handling of paperwork, may be compromised by owner-operators who fail to complete and turn in completed forms, thus delaying billing transactions and, indeed, the owner-operator's own payments.

A final aspect of lack of control is revealed in the freedom of the owner-operator to terminate her or his contract and go to work for some other carrier. More generally, this is described as the problem of turnover. Most carriers that attempt to use owner-operators report very high rates of turnover. While this term cannot be unambiguously defined, figures of 50 percent and 100 percent are not unknown in the industry.

The Problem of Turnover

The topic of owner-operator turnover is of sufficient importance to warrant particular attention. In the eyes of most managers of owner-operator fleets, high turnover is the number-one problem that they must deal with. The reasons for this concern are clear. A high rate of turnover among the owner-operators in the fleet places extreme burdens on the carrier. It substantially raises the total recruiting budget since a constant influx of new recruits is required. As we shall discuss in the next chapter, recruiting costs are far from trivial. Second, high turnover can have a marked effect upon the carrier's ability to offer quality service, since it implies that the average number of years of experience in the fleet will be low. This is particularly a problem in these sectors of the industry where loading, unloading, and care of the load are important components of the driver's task. Finally, high turnover can hurt the carrier in creating temporary loss of capacity. This "cost" can be particularly severe if the rate of turnover is unpredictable (as, indeed, it normally is).

It should be noted that, for some carriers, there can be some offsetting advantages to a (relatively) high turnover rate. For example, in a highly seasonal sector of the trucking industry (such as household goods) a high rate of turnover will assist the carrier in reducing the capacity of its fleet at the end of the season, simply by cutting back on its replacement recruiting. "That way" one van-line executive said, "we can achieve our required capacity reduction without being seen as the bad guys chopping off contractors because we no longer need them without considering their welfare."

Given the importance of controlling turnover in the overall management task of running an owner-operator fleet, it is worthwhile to consider the problems of defining and measuring this term adequately. Turnover rates are normally considered on an annualized basis and attempt to relate the average size of the carrier's fleet to the total number of independent contractors that the carrier leased during the year. Thus, if the carrier has an average fleet size of 100 tractors during the year, and has had leases with

150 owner-operators during that year, the turnover may be said to be 50 percent. However, this gross calculation may mask two very disparate kinds of problems. On the one hand, each owner-operator may only stay with the carrier for around eight months, meaning that the whole fleet is turning over in two years. Alternatively, ninety of the owner-operators may have remained with the carriers for the whole year, while sixty others were cycled through the remaining ten slots. The latter condition is much less symptomatic of serious problems than the first, or at least of a different kind of problem. If the whole fleet is turning over, there is evidence of poor carrier-contractor relationships. If turnover is restricted to a limited few, this may be evidence either that the carrier cannot generate sufficient traffic to support the last ten slots, or, alternatively, that the quality of traffic, measured by revenue potential, is poor. In general, the extent of an individual carrier's turnover problem should be examined using a variety of measures, including such variables as the percentage of contractors that have been with the carrier for x months or years.

It should be noted (and stressed) that while many carriers may (and do) describe it as their number-one problem in managing owner-operators, high turnover should not be considered as a problem in itself, but rather as a symptom of problems elsewhere. Owner-operators may quit (or be terminated) for many reasons. Some may have been trying out a new sector of the trucking industry for the first time and may have discovered that they do not like the working conditions in that sector. This problem might have been addressed at the recruiting stage by screening out potential candidates unlikely to flourish in the carrier's particular sector. Other contractors might not be prepared to accept the forms and level of control that the carrier exercises. Here recruiting criteria, better training, and a reexamination of the carrier's controls might contribute to a solution.

Of greatest concern are those owner-operators who quit for financial reasons. In a very real sense this can be viewed as the greatest failure of an owner-operator management system. If, as I have argued in chapter 2, the owner-operator system may be viewed as a franchise system, then the responsibility of the franchisor to the franchisee is, above all, to help the latter solve business problems. This responsibility was well summarized in 1967 by H.J. Sonneborn, the president of McDonald's.

> The foundation of our success has not been a good fifteen-cent hamburger, or a sack of crisp French fries or a thick chocolate shake, although these are the elements upon which our system is built. Instead, it has been a system of operations, training and marketing backed up by fundamental rules of business. . . . For us, the key to doing this has been control: a tight control on the operator which forces him into following

good operating and management procedures and which limit his freedom
to make mistakes.[1]

Later in the same speech, he underlined the point by saying, "How can we
make our franchisee successful (even, if necessary, in spite of himself)? This
is our problem."[2] Thus, to the extent that the owner-operators quit for
financial reasons ("unable to make it"), the problem of turnover may be interpreted as a symptom of problems in the carrier's management system for
dealing with owner-operators.

There are many obstacles to the successful implementation of a program for the control of turnover. First, we should note that many carriers
have great difficulty in identifying the true reasons for their turnover, particularly in distinguishing the contractors that quit for financial reasons
from those that quit for other reasons. While many carriers have attempted
to adopt the practice of "exit" interviews in order to determine contractors' reasons for quitting, few report great success in this area. It is
often difficult to get contractors to come in to give such interviews, or even
to talk on the phone. It is also difficult to obtain accurate answers to why
the contractor is quitting. As one carrier observed, "They all say it's
money, whether it is or not. They may not like your dispatcher, but they'll
rarely tell you that. Or they may just want to get home more often and are
afraid that that won't sound 'macho' enough. So they always say they can't
make enough money." Compounding the difficulties of discovering the real
reasons for turnover is the generally accepted perception that many contractors quit purely because of wanderlust, the desire to try something new, go
somewhere different. While this may indeed be an important factor, there is
danger for any carrier in accepting this "answer" too readily, since it may
hide other causes about which the carrier can *do* something.

A final perspective on the difficulty of determining the true reasons for
turnover is provided by the fact that while many contractors may cite "a
better deal from another carrier" as their reason for leaving, it is generally
difficult to compare directly the financial attractiveness of compensation
packages offered by different carriers, since so many variables (percentage
of the revenue, type of operation, deductions and holdbacks, and so on)
must be taken into account. (The complexity of this topic will be further addressed in chapter 5.)

The Conflict of Control

The ideal approach for an effective owner-operator management system as
expressed previously ("How do we make our franchisee successful in spite
of himself?") is a difficult goal to reach. For the owner-operator system in
particular (as opposed to franchise systems in general) there is an important

source of conflict in determining the appropriate degree of control and business guidance to be exercised by the carrier. This is the owner-operator's legal status as an employee or independent contractor. As we shall discuss in greater detail in chapter 8, this legal status (which may be determined by either the Internal Revenue Service or the National Labor Relations Board) primarily turns upon two key criteria: the degree of control exercised by the carrier, and the degree of business risk borne by the contractor. If the carrier exercises complete control over the contractor's operations, or if it acts to reduce substantially the business risk faced by its contractors, then there is likely to be a determination that the owner operator as employees and *not* independent contractors. This will have the consequence of introducing fringe labor cost (in the case of an IRS decision) or the opportunity for collective bargaining (in the case of an NLRB decision). Such consequences would remove the "lower labor cost" benefit of the owner-operator system to the carrier. To the extent that this particular benefit played a large role in the carrier's decision to use the owner-operator method of operation, the control/independence tradeoff would be a difficult one to make.

In addition to this particular problem, there is a more general difficulty to establishing the appropriate degree and forms of control. As with the franchise systems there is a paradox at the heart of the carrier-contractor relationship: on the one hand the need for (and benefits of) contractor independence, and on the other the need for the benefits of system coordination. As Stephenson and House note, "franchise relationships are based on the potential for greater gains through group membership rather than independent action. Thus the very nature of the relationship raises the question of how much latitude for independent action should exist and, alternatively, to what extent decision authority should be constrained by centrally developed programs."[3] They offer their own conclusion: "From the point of view of strict operational efficiency, there is probably little or no value in a high degree of franchise autonomy."[4]

Unfortunately, the goal of "strict efficiency" is not the only criterion by which an owner-operator management system is to be judged. Efficiency may dictate that, for example, the carrier advise the owner-operator on (for example) cash management and a preventive-maintenance schedule in order to help avoid business failure due to poor self-management. However, many owner-operators might resist the infringement on their independence and resent the direction provided by the carrier. This suggests that the key to the success of an owner-operator management system is winning the confidence and cooperation of the contractors. As Emmons phrases it, "there is little doubt that the key element in achieving long-term objectives in a franchised business is the maintenance of a close quasi-partnership working arrangement between the franchisor and the franchisee."[5]

Capacity Management

There can be no doubt that winning the confidence and cooperation of independent contractors is a challenging task. In large part this difficulty derives from the fact that the carrier is in the greater position of power in the relationship and has the ability to influence not only its own profitability, but also that of its contractors. This breeds a (natural) suspicion on the part of the contractors that any actions, decisions, or changes made by the carrier are being done for the carrier's best interest and hence are a threat to the owner-operator.

A good (and central) example of the inherent conflict in a carrier-owner-operator relationship is provided by the *capacity* decision that every carrier must make in deciding how many owner-operators to sign up. It is clearly in the best (short-term) interests of the carrier to have a slight excess in capacity over (forecast) traffic volumes, so that the level of service it can provide, in the form of availability of equipment, will be high. On the other hand, the best interests of an individual owner-operator might be that the carrier should have a slight shortfall in capacity, so that there would be plenty of traffic for that individual.

Capacity planning by irregular-route motor carriers is, at best, a difficult task. The volumes to be hauled cannot be forecast with any reasonable degree of accuracy, and the uncertain, widespread geographical nature of operations are such that short-term capacity in the form of an empty truck may be available but unusable since the demand for that capacity may be hundreds or thousands of miles away. It is, therefore, difficult for an irregular-route carrier to determine in advance its capacity needs for anything but the immediate short term. Indeed, competition in the irregular-route industry is often competition by available capacity. Although there is less uniformity of rates in this sector than in general commodity trucking (due in part to less reliance on tariff bureaus), the most important distinguishing characteristic between carriers is often whether or not the carrier has the equipment available to haul the tendered loads when the customer desires. It is, therefore, not surprising to discover that most carriers have the attitude, to a greater or less degree, that they will sign up as many owner-operators as they can. Of course, *too* substantial a growth in capacity will create problems in generating demand to fill the trucks, so expansion goals must be controlled. Nevertheless, many irregular-route carriers do have aggressive expansion plans.

As an aside, we may note that the "available capacity" nature of competition in many parts of the irregular-route industry may help explain one of the paradoxes of the owner-operator sector. During the course of my research one particular carrier, with a significant size of operations, was repeatedly held up as an example of a carrier that did not treat its owner-operators well and was allegedly involved in many of the dubious practices then receiving much attention from the congressional subcommittee investigating the industry. Why, I asked, was this carrier able to "get away" with treating its contractors so poorly when other carriers appeared to offer such better working conditions? The answer I received, from many sources, was that "he [the carrier] has got the traffic, so he gets the owner-operators. Since he's got the owner-operators, he gets the traffic. It's as simple as that."

The importance of capacity management in carrier-owner-operator relationships is further illustrated by considering the problems faced by a carrier when it has a downturn in traffic volumes. At such times the carrier is faced with the problem of whether to allocate the available traffic equally among all its owner operators, thus reducing by a relatively small amount the earning potential of all its contractors, or to cut the size of its fleet by directing the traffic to its "best" operators and "starving" the poorest ones. The former tactic has the advantage of equity and the preservation of capacity; the latter has the advantage of maintaining the income level of the "core" group and reducing the possibility of turnover among them. I have observed both strategies in practice, and the advantages and disadvantages of both are clear. In general, carriers tend to favor "share the burden equally" strategy because of the importance that owner-operators tend to place on equitable dealings in their judgment of how well they are treated by the carrier. This is particularly true in the less seasonal sectors of the industry where downturns in available traffic tend to be temporary and shortlived. In the more highly seasonal sectors, the protection and support of the core group tends to take on higher priority. It should be noted that the issues of capacity levels and demand allocation are intimately related. The greater the excess capacity possessed by a carrier, the greater the allocation problem it will face.

Carriers' attitudes to the question of capacity management have important implications for the rest of their owner-operator management system. We can best illustrate this by considering two extremes, Carrier A, which follows an aggressive "chase demand" strategy by adding and firing owner-operators as demand fluctuates, and Carrier B, which follows a "level capacity" strategy of signing on new contractors only where long-term demand conditions dictate. Carrier A, on average, will have a lower "quality" of driver than the stable group at Carrier B. By definition, turnover of owner-operators should be less at Carrier B, and more attention may be given to long-term training and the development of carrier-owner-operator relationships. However, overall training costs may be higher at Carrier A, since there will be a higher proportion of new owner-operators. Carrier A will probably require more detailed and complex supervision of its owner-operators than Carrier B, and will require more sophisticated management information systems to enable it to match supply and demand as the market varies. Working conditions for the owner-operators are likely to be more pleasant at Carrier B, since there will be less concern over who is likely to "let go" in the next downturn. Hiring and firing costs will be greater at Carrier A. On the other hand, Carrier B will, to a greater extent than Carrier A, have to turn down business because of the lack of available capacity, and, correspondingly, occasionally have to support its owner-operators in some way during weak market periods.

Mixed Fleets

Another major carrier decision that may act as a conflict source is the question of whether to retain any company (employee) drivers as well as using owner-operators. As in so many areas of owner-operator management, I discovered sharply differing viewpoints on this topic.

Carriers that do "mix" employee drivers and owner-operators argue that the mix allows them to avoid "putting all their eggs in one basket." In the words of one carrier, "the threat of increased owner-operator usage keeps the employees in line, and vice versa." Other carriers point out that the existence of carrier-owned and -operated equipment allows them to keep a close watch on the costs of operating the vehicles, information that is often difficult to obtain directly from the owner-operators. "If you don't know their costs very well," one carrier noted, "you're going to be in trouble very quickly. You'll end up with rates out of line, too high or too low. The only way to really understand what these guys need is to bear the costs yourself by operating at least a few company trucks." Another reason given for mixing owner-operators and employees is that there are some loads that owner-operators will not take (see chapter 6). One carrier I interviewed maintained a small fleet of company vehicles to handle such loads (primarily short-haul and low revenue).

In spite of these advantages, most carriers avoid mixing of employees and owner-operators. There are two major reasons for this. First, many carriers use owner-operators to avoid the threat of unionization by the Teamsters, and the existence of even a few employee drivers is seen as providng an opportunity for the union to organize the firm. Second, and perhaps more importantly, the use of a mixed fleet reduces the level of trust between the owner-operators and the carrier. "When we operated our company trucks in the Reefer Division with the owner operators," one carrier told me, "each group of men thought dispatch operations favored the other group. This led to many problems. Therefore, we have attempted to keep the contact between the groups to as small a degree as possible."

The Management of Conflict

The problems of capacity management and the decision on mixed fleets are but two examples of the areas for potential conflict between the interests of the carrier and the owner-operator. Other more obvious potential areas of conflict are in the fair division of the revenues from the traffic and the sale of trucks by the carrier to its contractors. Little useful advice can be given about the resolution of these conflicts beyond the simple (but nevertheless valid) observation that if the carrier attempts to resolve all inherent and unavoidable conflicts in its own favor in the search for short-run profits, then it is unlikely that a stable and contented owner-operator fleet will result. Or, as one motor-carrier executive summarized our discussion of the problems of owner-operator management, "if they think you're trying to screw them, nothing you can do is going to work. And if you *are* trying to screw them, nothing you can do is going to hide that fact."

Unfortunately, even in the absence of malicious intent, any motor carrier is likely to face the problems of owner-operator suspicion, that is, to be faced with the task of winning the willing cooperation of its contractors. In part this is due to the current existence of certain motor carriers that have "given the industry a bad name." However, it is important to recognize that, even without such a history, there will inevitably be some degree of natural suspicion felt by a small businessperson dependent for his or her livelihood upon the actions of a large company.

From this perspective it is useful to consider some of the insights gained from research into the channels of distribution (or marketing channels) used by manufacturing concerns. In many such industries the same scenario of an "imbalanced mutual dependency" exists. For example, a network of dealers or distributors may be very much dominated by a large manufacturer that has the power to influence their economic well being. The manufacturer in such a situation faces the same problems as the motor carrier in needing to win the willing cooperation of its smaller business associates, to get them to accept direction and change that is in the best interests of the channel as a whole. As in the owner-operator system, it is the combination of manufacturer and distributor that is the unit of competition competing against some other manufacturer-distributor combination: they must act together for success in the marketplace.

The study of marketing channels is a well-developed field of academic endeavor, with a wide literature.[6] Much of it tends to deal with abstract and difficult terminology. Nevertheless, it is worthwhile to consider some of the concepts that have been developed by researchers in this field.

Mallen provides a convenient point of departure when he observes, "If . . . channel members view one another as part of a total distribution system . . . then this interacting, interdependent channel situation is more realistically viewed as a political-social system—'social' because it consists of interacting group activities and 'political' because it is a social system which can, and often does, make use of power to pressure some members to behave in the way the leader would like."[7]

The key word here is *power*: where it comes from and how it is used. While sociologists and political scientists have written many treatises on the nature of power, we shall here, with Mallen, distinguish between two types of power: economic and sociological. Economic power derives from the ability to reward or punish channel members. With their control over rates and the generation of traffic, there can be no doubt that carriers have economic power over their contractors. However, there are limits to this power. It is a useful insight to consider that power is more usually *given* than it is taken. The owner-operator always has the option of quitting the carrier and going to work for another. The owner-operator thus may be seen as giving power to and accepting control from the carrier in exchange for the profit opportunities the carrier provides. Naturally, the greater the profit opportunity the more control the owner-operator is prepared to accept. This insight, powerful in its simplicity, has a chicken-and-egg quality. If the owner-operator will accept more control and give the carrier more power, then the carrier can, and hopefully will, provide greater profit opportunity. Unfortunately, the owner-operator will not accept more control until greater profit opportunity is provided. In spite of this difficulty, it is a common observation in the motor-carrier industry that the owner-operators most satisfied with their carrier are those who work for carriers exercising the greatest degree of control.

In spite of the ability to control that economic power confers, it has been argued (by Bucklin,[8] in particular) that there is an upper limit to this. This limit has been called the "tolerance function," or burden that the channel member feels from sacrificing his or her freedom of action. As Mallen phrases it, "one can consider power to be not only a process but also an inventory, the overuse of which can deplete its effectiveness."[9] To restore and replenish its inventory of power, the channel leader should look to the alternate, sociological bases of power as well as the economic. Stripped of its jargon, channel theory tells us that weaker members will yield (sociological) power and control to the dominant firm to the extent that (1) it is perceived as acting in the best interests of the channel as a whole and not only in its own best interests; (2) it is perceived as being competent ("expert") in performing this role (that is, in selecting markets, setting prices, advising on operating procedures and the like).

Among the most valuable insights yielded from the study of channels of distribution is an analysis of why conflict (that is, lack of cooperation) arises in the interorganizational relationships between firms in the same channel. With some degree of oversimplification these causes can be divided into three categories: roles, goals, and communication. "Role theory" (a sociological concept) suggests that a channel member is expected by other members to perform certain functions in a certain way. When anyone deviates from the role expected by others, then conflict arises. Fortunately, the owner-operator system has a built-in mechanism for the resolution of role-conflict: the contract. Together with recruiting literature, training periods, and "operating procedures" manuals there should be little room for conflict in an owner-operator system as to who is responsible for what duties, and how each is to be performed. However, it is important to note that agreement on roles must be worked for and not assumed. In addition, the perception of role includes performance characteristics. Failure to perform such functions adequately means that the channel member is failing in his or her role. This perspective may be related to our previous discussion of the franchisor's role and responsibilities in the franchise "channel."

Conflict may also arise through a disparity of goals. A good example of this is provided by the work of Dixon,[10] who demonstrated that gasoline producers and retailers had differing goals not only because of different "philosophies" (desires for growth versus stability, income versus a "good life," long-term views versus short-term views), but also because of differing cost curves. Where the producer has high fixed costs, he may aggressively try to maximize sales. However, the service station, with higher variable costs, will have less incentive to do so. We shall give detailed attention to the nature of owner-operator goals in the next section of this chapter.

Finally, conflict between channel members can arise from poor communication. Communications concerning the behavior of costs, trends in the marketplace, and other important factors in the environment need to be shared among the members of an interorganizational system: any barrier to the free flow of such information can create different perceptions of reality and cause conflict. A number of causes of communication distortion or ommission have been identified by Mallen:[11]

1. The required information is not provided or collected in the first place.
2. The required information is provided or collected but somehow disappears in the process.
3. The required information is delayed in transmittal, making it partially or completely useless.
4. Information is provided or collected and passed on to decision makers, but is, in fact, irrelevant for decision-making purposes.
5. The correct information is provided or collected, but during the collection or transmittal to the proper decision makers it becomes distorted.

6. The correct information is provided or collected but is done so in an er-
ratic manner in order to "put out fires," i.e., for tactical purposes, but
is not provided on a regular basis so that it may be used for strategic
purposes.

The importance of communications, and the role of information collection, processing, and sharing in the design of an owner-operator management system will be discussed in detail in chapter 7.

A good summary of the lessons for owner-operator management that
can be provided by the study of distribution channels is contained in Donald
L. Price's "Key Elements in a Sound Distributor System."[12] He summarizes
the process of managing the interorganizational relationships in the following way:

1. Establish well-defined distribution policies and objectives.
2. Develop and publish a distributor sales agreement.
3. Help the distributor determine what it costs to sell your product.
4. Provide training for distributor salespeople.
5. Establish performance evaluation procedures.
6. Educate your own sales force on the value of the distributor to your
    marketing effort.
7. Cooperate with your distributors in developing overall market poten-
    tials and sales quotas.
8. Provide the distributor with an adequate profit.
9. Develop efficient channels of communication with distributors.

It does not take much translation to relate this to the owner-operator
management experience. For example, step 6 could be read as, "Educate
your own supervisors and other contractor contact personnel on the value
of the contractor to your operational effort" and would remain as sound
advice.

What Do Owner-Operators Want?

We have seen, in our discussion above, that one of the central tasks of
owner-operator management is winning the cooperation of the contractor
fleet; further, that an important component of this task is identifying and
recognizing the owner-operator's needs and goals. As one carrier said, "it
sometimes seems as if getting the owner-operators is no problem: keeping
them is another matter altogether! What do these guys *want*?"

In simple terms, it is easy to identify some of the specifics that owner-
operators want. They want to be kept busy. They want to be treated

equitably, in the sense that there is no "playing of favorites" by dispatchers. They don't want too much paperwork. They want quick payment. Many of these specifics will be brought out in subsequent chapters.

However, I believe that one can go deeper in an analysis of what owner-operators really want: from the carriers, from their profession, and from life. It must first be stated that not all owner-operators want the same thing. Indeed, it is this very diversity that makes managing an owner-operator fleet so challenging.

One of the most important insights to come out of the study of franchise system management is the recognition that there is a "life-cycle," or evolution, in the relationship between a franchisor and its franchisees. As noted by Thompson,[13] "initially, most franchisees are fairly anxious to cooperate with the franchisor, particularly when they recognize the value of his services and the franchise package. As the franchisee grows and matures, this may change, particularly if the services provided by the franchisor are intangible." In many, if not most, franchise systems, the benefits to the franchisee are heavily weighted at the beginning of the relationship, that is, when the franchisee is new to the business. It is at such times that the franchisor's expertise, guidance, and training are most required. This may be verified by examining the list of "benefits to the franchisee" provided in chapter 2. It may be seen that such benefits as location assistance, training, and the like are most likely to be of importance to the new franchisee. The same may equally be said of an owner-operator whose need for carrier training and guidance changes over time.

Oxenfeldt and Kelly summarized the franchisee's evolution well:

Initially the franchisee may be primarily interested in obtaining an outlet for his energy and initiative in a situation which provides some security while giving him stimulation through at least partial autonomy. As he prospers, however, his monetary (security) needs ordinarily become less pressing while his desire for identity is likely to grow. When he has become established and prosperous he may seek more independence—a plot of ground that is truly his own. The need for stimulation may make change attractive just for its own sake. . . .

Even as the franchisee's goals change, so do his capabilities. At first his major strengths may be his ambition, willingness to work hard, local knowledge and finances. Because of his lack of certain important skills (for instance, planning) he may initially welcome the close attention and training provided by the franchisor. Through time, and especially as he grows, he acquires managerial skills of his own. His self-esteem grows and he comes to resent the constraints placed upon his actions by the franchisor.[14]

This evolution will be readily recognized by managers of owner-operator systems in the motor-carrier industry. It has a number of important implications for owner-operator management. First, it reveals the importance of recognizing that there exist *categories* or groups of owner-operators, each of which has its own goals, opportunities, needs, and strengths. Accordingly, any system of owner-operator management must be sufficiently flexible to respond to the individual needs of particular owner-operators. This is a challenging task, which in turn has another important implication. Given the need for individual (or, at least, flexible) dealings with owner-operators, we may wonder what kind of carrier will be best suited to provide this flexibility.

On the one hand, we may expect that the small, owner-managed carrier could retain the flexibility to deal with its owner-operators on an individual basis. At such carriers, the small size allows the relevant management personnel (often, the owner himself) to know each of the owner-operators personally, and to be accessible enough to deal with their individual needs. At such carriers there will often be an open-door policy so that any owner-operator can walk in and meet with "the boss" at any time.

At the other extreme, large carriers have the capability to establish driver counseling departments with key personnel dedicated to the sole task of dealing with individual owner-operators about their personal needs. Such departments are common among the larger household goods carriers. As we shall discuss in greater detail in chapter 6, it is important that such counselors are made distinct from the dispatching, record-keeping, and payment (that is, business-related) functions. Their role is to deal with the owner operator's *personal* needs.

The problematical period comes, as does so much in motor-carrier management,[15] when the carrier is too large to retain the intimacy of the small firm, but too small to establish systems and departments that can compensate for this loss. At such carriers there is the danger of being too busy to respond to individual owner-operators and to institute standardized methods of dealing with the contractor fleet that fail to reflect the fact that individual members of the fleet may be at different stages of their life cycle and have different needs. It was at one such mid-size carrier that I heard the comment, "The biggest problem with running an owner-operator fleet is that they take up so much management time. They're always on the phone with some bitch or another, or wanting to come by and chew the fat. Often they don't really have a problem at all—it's just that they're on the road for eight hours not having spoken to anyone, have brooded about some slight dissatisfaction and just want to get it off their chest." It is clear that providing a suitable mechanism for such "steam-letting" is one of the essential tasks of owner-operator management.

This insight leads us to the second implication of Oxenfeldt and Kelly's "life-cycle" analysis. It will have been noted that they refer to a variety of needs: security, identity, independence. This suggests that the task of good owner-operator management is to recognize and deal with these needs. The carrier that views its relationships with owner-operators in purely business or monetary terms is unlikely to have a stable and contented fleet. (One carrier asked me, "Why do I have such high turnover? They're earning good livings from my traffic! What do these guys *want*?")

What human beings want is a subject that has been endlessly debated by psychologists, sociologists, and organizational behavior theorists. Many contending theories have been presented, but there is not the space to present a full review of them here. (An excellent review is presented in Gellerman's *Motivation and Productivity*.[16]) However, it is worthwhile to consider some of the most famous of these theories, beginning with Maslow's "hierarchy of needs."[17]

Abraham H. Maslow suggested that man works to satisfy his needs according to a hierarchy in which there are "lower order" needs and "higher order" needs. The former are the basics of life: physiological comfort, safety, and security. The latter, higher order needs deal with the individual's ego: self-fulfillment or self-actualization. People are thus initially motivated by their basic needs (for example, sufficient earnings to live on). If these are not met, they are motivated to fulfill them. As these become met, the power of money (for example) as a motivator declines (at least in the sense that money is used to satisfy basic needs: it still may be sought as a symbol of status or success). As their basic needs are met, individuals are motivated to fulfill their social needs, which include "belongingness," "status," and personal growth (see figure 3-1).

While these categories are largely self-explanatory, it would be as well to expand upon one or two. The third level of needs, belonging, includes the

Figure 3-1. Maslow's Hierarchy of Needs

individual's desire for friendship, membership of a group, teamwork, helping others, or being helped. Being trusted is also a component of this need. It is relatively easy to see the relevance of this category of needs to the owner-operator. As we have noted elsewhere in this chapter, the owner-operator/franchise status is one of *quasi*-independence. The typical individual suited to this life is not completely entrepreneurial, but has clearly recognized needs for association. In the case of the truck driver, these needs are likely to be more accentuated than the typical franchisee because of the loneliness of the life on the road.

Various tools are available to the motor carrier to help fulfill these needs, apart from the creation of a caring attitude through open-door policies or driver counselors. Not all of these tools are readily applicable in each circumstance, but all have been used with some degree of success. They include painting the truck and/or trailer in the company colors, or providing jackets with the company logo. (One carrier reports a desire on the part of its owner-operators to have a company uniform, a move that the company is considering.) This may be considered extremely unusual, since most carriers would predict substantial resistance to a policy of company uniforms, because of the owner-operator's desire for independence. However, this example perhaps illustrates the potential success of efforts to promote "belongingness" and goes beyond the simple acceptance of the owner-operator's independent status. Other tools might be a contractor newsletter, or at least some form of regular nonbusiness-related communication. Such newsletters (common enough in other employee-based industrial settings) might be used to pass on personal news ("Congratulations to Fred and Mary Bartlett, who have just had their third child"), give driving and business "tips," or explain the latest activities of the carrier ("We've applied to the ICC for rights out of Podunk, and hope to have lots more business for you in the near future"). Unfortunately, given the mobility of owner-operators and the need to keep the fleet operating, it is unlikely that any motor carrier (except perhaps short-haul operators) can make use of one of the most powerful group association methods employed by franchisors: regular conventions of franchisees. However, some franchise systems have developed franchisee advisory councils, composed of franchisees usually elected by their peers, whose role it is to speak for the franchisees in dealings with the franchisors. In suitably modified form, this is a technique that might be adapted to large owner-operator systems.

The fourth level of needs in Maslow's hierarchy, ego needs, includes the needs for self-respect, achievement of status, personal recognition, and the esteem of others. These are needs that may easily be overlooked in the management of owner-operator fleets. The need for self-respect may conflict with the carrier's need for explicit managerial controls and directives. The achievement of status may conflict with the need to treat all owner-operators with equity (in dispatching priority, for example). Personal recognition is easier to fulfill, perhaps through the "newsletter" described above.

The fifth level of human needs, self-actualization, is, according to Maslow, very rarely attained. It is the need to reach one's potential and grow. In an owner-operator contract this need is particularly problematical, since it involves discovering what the individual's ambitions in life are. In many cases, the desire to be an owner-operator may not be the limit of the individual's potential. As Wyckoff and I noted,[18] many owner-operators enter the industry with dreams of one day owning their own fleet of vehicles. If the carrier has a policy of not utilizing multi-unit owner-operators, such a goal might eventually take the owner-operator out of the carrier's fleet. In essence, the carrier would be helping to train and establish its own competition. It should be noted, however, that this is not a conflict peculiar to the owner-operator system. In many professional service organizations, such as consulting firms or advertising agencies, employees' self-actualization goals include the establishment of their own consulting or advertising firms. Whether or not these goals can be dealt with, it is clearly important that the management of such professionals involves the recognition of such needs and the correct identification of those individuals for whom those needs are strong.

The view of owner-operators as professionals raises the whole question of the appropriate attitude of management to their independent contractors. In this context we should review another well-know theory of human motivation, Douglas McGregor's[19] "Theory X and Theory Y." Like Maslow's need hierarchy, McGregor's theories have become close to doctrine among some behavioral scientists and others involved in management thinking about employee motivation.

According to McGregor, a "Theory X manager" is one who believes employees to be essentially lazy and unmotivated and who, if left alone, would perform indifferently on the job. A Theory X manager would tend to rely on external controls and the threat of punishment to encourage employee effort. A "Theory Y manager," on the other hand, is one who believes that individuals have desires to achieve and will work hard toward goals to which they are committed. (The "assumptions" of Theory X and Theory Y managers are summarized in table 3-1).

While McGregor attempted to keep his classification neutral, recognizing that in some situations each style of management is more appropriate, there has been a tendency to characterize Theory X as bad and Theory Y as good. Such has not been my intention in presenting his classifications here. Rather, it serves to remind us that underlying the design of any management system is a set of assumptions about human motivation, and that systems and management style tend to reject those assumptions even where they are not explicit.

Table 3-1
McGregor's Theory X and Theory Y

Theory X Assumptions	Theory Y Assumptions
People by Nature:	*People by Nature:*
1. Lack integrity.	1. Have integrity.
2. Are fundamentally lazy and desire to work as little as possible.	2. Work hard toward objectives to which they are committed.
3. Avoid respnsibility.	3. Assume responsibility within these commitments.
4. Are not interested in achievement.	4. Desire to achieve.
5. Are incapable of directing their own behavior.	5. Are capable of directing their own behavior.
6. Are indifferent to organizational needs.	6. Want their organization to succeed.
7. Prefer to be directed by others.	7. Are not passive and submissive.
8. Avoid making decisions wherever possible.	8. Will make decisions within their commitments.
9. Are not very bright.	9. Are not stupid.

Source: D. McGregor, *The Human Side of Enterprise* (New York: McGraw-Hill, 1960). Reprinted with permission.

One additional (and controversial) contribution to the field of behavioral science should be acknowledged here: Herzberg's "Two-Factor" theory (figure 3-2). Frederick Herzberg[20] concluded, from survey research, that the factors influencing a worker's motivation could be divided into two groups: (1) those that are intrinsic to the job itself and relate to achievement, recognition, the work itself, and opportunities for advancement and recognition (that is, the upper part of the Maslow scale); and (2) job *context* factors, such as company policy and its administration supervision and the social relations between supervisors and subordinates, and work conditions. Herzberg terms the first group "satisfiers." If these were present, people would be satisfied with their job and motivated. The second group he termed the "maintenance" or "hygiene" factor, and suggested that while these considerations could do little to motivate an employee, their absence could be the cause of *dis*satisfaction. In a sense, they are thus negative in their effect: they do not necessarily increase motivation and morale if they are present, but can substantially decrease them if they are absent. The significance of this distinction (which has not been unchallenged) derives from the fact that while, in an owner-operator context, not much might be able to be done about the work itself (the "satisfiers") to improve the work environment (that is, there are few opportunities for job enrichment in the truck driver's life), there might appear to be opportunities to change the factors that lead to dissatisfaction.

Summary

This chapter has attempted to provide a brief (if simplified) review of some of the basic concepts of franchising, channel theory, and behavioral science

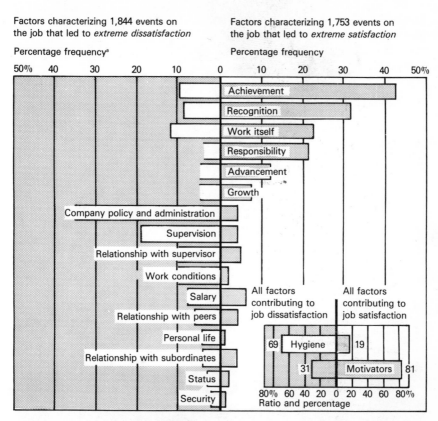

Factors characterizing 1,844 events on the job that led to *extreme dissatisfaction*

Factors characterizing 1,753 events on the job that led to *extreme satisfaction*

Percentage frequency[a]

Percentage frequency

50% 40   30   20   10   0   10   20   30   40   50%

Achievement
Recognition
Work itself
Responsibility
Advancement
Growth
Company policy and administration
Supervision
Relationship with supervisor
Work conditions
Salary
Relationship with peers
Personal life
Relationship with subordinates
Status
Security

All factors contributing to job dissatisfaction

All factors contributing to job satisfaction

69 Hygiene 19

31 Motivators 81

80% 60 40 20 0 20 40 60 80%
Ratio and percentage

[a]The data were derived from twelve studies.

Source: Frederick W. Herzberg, "One More Time: How Do You Motivate Employees?" *Harvard Business Review* 46 (January-February 1968):57. Copyright © 1967 by the President and Fellows of Harvard College; all rights reserved. Reprinted with permission.

Figure 3-2. Herzberg's Data on Dissatisfaction and Satisfaction

that are applicable to the problems of owner-operator motivation and control. In so doing, it is not intended to downplay the importance of financial incentive upon the owner-operator, or the importance of adequate revenues in keeping the owner-operator happy. As one carrier observed to me: "esprit de corps went out the window several years ago, when the costs of operations [for owner-operators] and freight rates reached disparity." This view is in accordance with Maslow's analysis described above: until the minimum pay needs are satisfied, few of the concepts discussed in this chapter can be applied. Nevertheless, it has been the theme of this chapter that too much reliance can be based upon money as a motivating force. The carrier that looks *only* to revenue needs to motivate and retain its owner-operators is likely to experience low morale and high turnover. The other human needs, discussed above, still need to be met, and met by *active* management recognition of, and response to, these needs.

4

Recruiting

According to Lewis and Hancock,[1] the single most pervasive operating problem of running a franchise system is the selection of qualified candidates as franchisees. Oxenfeldt and Thompson also note that "a continuing managerial problem facing franchisors concerns the recruitment of new franchisees. . . . The situation is made worse by the rapid growth in the number of franchisors competing for the available supply of the competent franchisees. Also, ideally, the franchisor must be able to define these activities and attributes that are essential to franchisee success—and surprisingly few franchisors can."[2]

The same situation exists in the owner-operator system. We have already noted (chapter 1) that an ever-increasing number of motor carriers are seeking to run owner-operator fleets, and that there is at least a *perceived* shortage of owner-operators. As with franchisors, many motor carriers have reported their difficulties with recruiting, particularly their lack of ability to identify in advance which of a number of candidates is most likely to turn out to be a successful operator. The problem is made more acute in the motor-carrier industry due to the rapid rate of turnover of owner-operators experienced by most carriers. As noted above, it is not unusual for a motor carrier to lose 50 percent of its owner-operators each year, and some carriers have turnover rates even higher. Recruiting is thus not only competitive and difficult, it is also a continuous task.

In this chapter we shall review all stages of the recruiting process. We begin with consideration of the task of stimulating inquiries from owner-operators, and then consider the initial contact and prescreening of unsuitable candidates. The next section deals with the recruiting interviews: the attitudes, attributes, and characteristics that carriers look for in attempting to select successful operators. We conclude with a discussion of recruiting costs, and the role of the recruiting program in an overall owner-operator management system.

Stimulating Inquiries from Owner-Operators

The first task in the recruiting process is to generate inquiries from owner-operators willing to consider "signing up" with the carrier. The prime technique used by many motor carriers is, not surprisingly, advertising.

Most trucking magazines aimed at owner-operators, such as *Overdrive, Owner Operator, Open Road*, and *Heavy Duty Trucking*, contain advertisements from carriers, describing various attractive features of their business and usually giving a toll-free number to call. We shall discuss the typical content of these advertisements below. However, it is first necessary to consider the media in which carriers choose to advertise.

The range of magazines chosen for advertisement is remarkably large. Apart from magazines specifically aimed at owner-operators, other (generally carrier-oriented) trucking magazines (such as *Fleet Owner, Commercial Car Journal*, or *Transport Topics*, a news weekly published by the American Trucking Associations, Inc.) also contain regular recruiting advertisements. It is not clear whether carriers that advertise in such magazines do so because they believe owner-operators read them, or whether such advertisements are but one method of getting the grapevine working. Except for isolated exceptions, few of the carriers I interviewed attempted formally to measure the effectiveness of advertisements in different magazines, or, indeed, the effectiveness of different advertising copy.

A remarkably large number of carriers use the business opportunities section of the classified advertisements in local newspapers to stimulate inquiries, and many report great success with the medium. At least one major van line has used such magazines as *TV Guide* and *Reader's Digest* with some degree of success. This action largely reflects the fact that, due to their need for a large number of owner-operators, many large van lines are forced to recruit new entrants into the trucking industry rather than attract existing owner-operators from other carriers.

At the other end of the spectrum, another carrier has experimented with a highly *focused* advertising campaign, using radio spots on country-and-western stations, aimed at working owner-operators dissatisfied with their current carrier. It is reported that late-night ads are particularly effective, especially if a twenty-four-hour toll-free number is given.

Carriers have experimented with a wide range of other advertising media: direct mail, billboards, or notices pinned up in truckstops or even attached to the rear of the carriers' trailers so that they will be read by any driver following behind. Various personal reference techniques are also employed: truck dealers and salespeople may be asked to recommend the carrier when an owner-operator purchases a new truck (sometimes obtaining a commission if the owner-operator signs up). Many carriers offer prizes or cash rewards to their existing owner-operators if they bring in a friend (sometimes as much as $1,000 is offered per sign-up: $250 when the friend signs on, and $750 if he or she stays with the company for a given period of time, such as a year).

The most important personal reference technique is, of course, general word-of-mouth or the owner-operator grapevine. Virtually all carriers I interviewed gave this as the most effective recruiting tool. Indeed, it was because of the power of word-of-mouth that one carrier ceased its driver-incentive program of offering cash rewards for bringing in new owner-operators. "There's a fellowship or brotherhood among owner-operators, and if your current drivers like how you treat them, they'll recommend you to their buddies. If they don't, then no amount of cash incentive is going to get them to tell lies on your behalf. Give them a good deal, treat them right, keep them busy and you'll have applicants breaking down your doors."

In spite of a wide consensus about, at least, the underlying sentiment expressed in this quotation (the importance of word-of-mouth), most carriers continue to employ advertising to attract owner-operators. However, their use of advertising remains an inexact art or science. As noted above, relatively few carriers perform formal appraisals of their advertising programs. The reasons for this are not clear, since such appraisals are not complex and there exists a wide body of literature (practical and theoretical) on how to perform such reviews.[3]

The selection of media for any advertising campaign involves a set of tradeoffs between cost and various factors influencing the success rate. These factors will include the total readership of the magazine (or audience for the radio spot), the portion of that audience the advertiser is trying to reach, the number of inquiries generated (that is, inquiries by owner-operators or potential owner-operators that the carrier is prepared to consider), and, finally, the number of inquiries from individuals that are not only qualified but are particularly desirable for some reason. With isolated exceptions, many carriers give too little attention to the *quality* of responses rather than quantity. Local newspapers, for example, may be cheap and generate many inquiries: however, much time and expense may be wasted in telephone conversations screening out obviously unqualified prospects. It is relatively simple to monitor the effectiveness of different advertising media (and appeals) by asking prospects where they heard of the company (or why they called at this time). Accumulated statistics will then reveal which element of the advertising campaign yielded the most successful sign-ups, and at what unit cost. The importance of such appraisal is illustrated by the experience of one major van line which, with a fleet of 2,000 owner-operators and a turnover of 40 percent a year generates 25,000 telephone inquiries per year at a cost of $32 per inquiry for advertising. Since the carrier signs up only one in thirteen of these inquiries, this represents an advertising cost of $400 per successfully acquired owner-operator. Just to maintain its fleet size, the carrier must spend close to half a million dollars per year on advertising. With such statistics, the importance of considering the "demographics" of who is likely to read advertisements in different media is clear.

In their selection of advertising *content*, carriers use everything from specific rates to social conditions in the attempt to distinguish themselves from other carriers. In most advertisements, revenues and rates (in various forms of presentation) take pride of place. The basic rate may vary widely (from 40 to 80 cents when stated as earnings per mile, or from 70 to 90 percent as a percentage of revenue), but these rates are often supplemented by a variety of promises such as full loads, payment for backhauls, tolls and licenses, unloading and layover times, immediate settlements, advances, and so forth. One advertiser offered hourly pay or salaries for owner-operators, while another, paying on a mileage scale, guaranteed minimum miles. Other appeals that may be found are to furnish all fuel, bonuses for longevity with the company, or bonuses for top producing operators.

In accordance with the maxim that "you may keep them with how you treat them, but you get them with money offers," no other working condition is as widely advertised as revenues. After direct revenues, job security is the most commonly advertised appeal. While the usual line is "steady year-round work," one company went so far as to note that most of their owner-operators had been with the company for ten to forty years. The availability of steady work is, of course, another way of looking at the owner-operator's earning potential with the company, although distinct from unit (per mile or percent) payments. Other ways in which carriers conveyed the promise of regular earnings were to stress that they were "an established, first-class company with high growth," although other cariers have relied on their newness to indicate growth. Many carriers indicate "long-haul nationwide operations" with twenty-four-hour central dispatching.

While rates and revenue potential are common interests of all owner-operators, different working conditions do appeal to different types of owner-operators. Evidence that some carriers recognize this and capitalize on the specific nature of their operation is given by selected advertisements which offer short-haul operations "guaranteed home every night," or "home every weekend." Appeals to husband-and-wife driving teams are also common, particularly in the household-goods sector. However, such instances of special interest or special appeals are not common. It is surprising, for example, that few advertisements stress (or even, in many cases, indicate) the commodity to be hauled, in spite of the fact that the type of work and working conditions vary so substantially among sectors. The type of individual who hauls steel is unlikely to be at home in the household-goods industry, where loading and unloading activities are such a large portion of the task. Similarly, refrigerated hauling differs from petroleum hauling in its demands and requirements. Carriers would seem, from their advertisements, to be missing the opportunity to prescreen potential applicants by accentuating the specific work conditions they can offer. This point may be underlined by noting that relatively few advertisements for owner-operators indicate conditions that the owner-operator applicant must meet (type of equipment, financial conditions, and so on). However, given the current perception of a shortage of owner-operators, it may be that carriers wish to generate as large a pool of applicants as they can, in order to meet their hiring requirements. It remains for each individual carrier to determine whether this shotgun approach is justified when the costs of processing and interviewing applicants, and the costs of hiring owner-operators unsuited to their industry sector, are taken into account.

Managing the Initial Contact

In managing the initial contact between an owner-operator and the motor carrier, there are normally two major objectives. The first is to establish whether the applicant is qualified to be considered further, and the second is to convey information about the company in order to interest the owner-operator.

Most owner-operators contact carriers by telephone ("These are not the sort of guys that sit down and write letters"), and many carriers stressed the importance of a well-managed telephone operation. On the one hand, there is the desire to attract as many owner-operators as possible. To this end, carriers try to ensure that (1) there is always someone qualified to accept owner-operator's calls ("They're probably calling, on impulse, from a truckstop: you can't say you'll call them back") and (2) their name and address is obtained as quickly as possible, so that promotional literature can be sent out. On the other hand, th first telephone contact is a major opportunity to avoid wasteful interviewing time by eliminating unsuitable candidates from further consideration.

Most carriers have established standardized forms to be used by their telephone answering clerks in conducting the initial contact. Such forms usually require such information as the make, age, and specifications of the owner-operator's equipment, his or her age, residence, and years of experience, whether or not he or she has worked in this sector of the industry before, and so forth. In some cases, accident history is also sought at this stage. Based on examination of many carriers' procedures, it would appear that only the most extreme candidates are "eliminated" at this stage by most carriers. Most elimination that does take place is often due to self-selection on the part of the owner-operator when he or she learns of the company's rate base, areas of operation, and commodities hauled.

The prime information that most carriers seek to obtain at this stage, and which serves as the major tool for carrier-eliminated prospects, is the owner-operator's monthly payments on his or her equipment. Nearly all carriers have some such rule as "Never hire anyone with more than $1,000 per month payments to make: there's no way they're going to make it." However, it is notable that the cut-off point appears to vary widely, even between carriers in the same sector of the industry with similar operations and rate bases.

As noted above, the second objective of the initial contact is to provide the owner-operator with information about the company. The prime vehicle for this is, apart from the telephone call, an initial mailing of various materials. Those generally fall into two groups: promotional materials and application materials. Promotional materials are usually more detailed explanations of contract terms and work conditions, as well as general information about the company. In the larger companies, special booklets directly aimed at owner-operators are employed, while in smaller concerns use is made of general-purpose promotional materials also sent out to shippers and other company contacts. Revenue promises or claims are often stressed at this stage and more specifics are given. While most carriers continue to rely on rate quotations and general statements such as "we'll keep you busy," others provide more detailed information as to the earning potential actually experienced by owner-operators working for them.

Practices in this regard vary widely and many different schools of thought appear to exist. Some carriers are very reluctant to make specific claims, either because of fears of creating undue expectations or because of the desire to avoid commitment. There has been at least one court case brought by an owner-operator against a carrier for misrepresentation of earning potential. However, some carriers do offer "typical" figures, or, in one case that I observed, a table showing the distribution of gross earnings for all owner-operators working for the company. These were structured so that the applicant could determine her or his expected earnings (and variations in such earnings) in the first year, in the second year, and in the third and subsequent years.

The question of the appropriate level of revenue disclosure is surrounded by controversy, as it is in the franchising field, due to the possibilities for misrepresentation. One motor-carrier executive interviewed by an owner-operator magazine observed, "[A prospective contractor] shouldn't expect to make any more money than a carrier's promotion materials says he can make. Chances are, what the carrier advertises is the best the contractor can do."[4]

Apart from the possibility of misrepresentation, any attempt to provide a "typical" pro-forma for an owner-operator is fraught with difficulties, due to the large number of distinct payment systems in use in this field. Since some carriers pay for licenses, insurance, and other cost items, while others do not, it is difficult for an owner-operator to obtain and compare *net* earnings (rather than gross receipts) from the carrier. Similarly, due to different cost experience by individual owner-operators, it is sometimes difficult for carriers to provide a "typical" pro-forma of net earnings without including many qualifying statements such as "Assumes you keep maintenance below 4 cents per mile" or "Assumes 100,000 operating miles."

We should also note the inherent conflict in providing such pro-formas.

Given that other carriers may be offering optimistic pro-formas, a carrier is faced with the conflicting desire on the one hand to appear as attractive as possible, and on the other to be as accurate as possible in order to avoid future disappointment.

Finally, it must be observed that many carriers do not provide pro-formas of net earnings for the simple reason that they do not know the financial experience of their own owner-operators. They may be able to provide gross earnings data but do not possess additional information on owner-operator expenses. As we shall discuss below, the lack of such information is the source of many problems.

Screening Applicants: The Interview

While some carriers await the return of completed application forms before calling owner-operators in for interviews, others (particularly smaller carriers) proceed directly to the interview stage and have applicants fill in application forms during the interview. While this practice eliminates a potential stage of prescreening, it (probably) does increase the number of applicants that the carrier sees, since so many owner-operators dislike completing forms and will not do so in advance. Indeed, one carrier observed, "A lot of applicants walk out the door when they see the paperwork. We don't mind that, because it's a good guide to their attitudes and practices. If they can't deal with the forms, then they're not going to be good businesspeople and we don't want them."

There exists a great diversity of interviewing practices among carriers. These range from informal personal conversations between the owner-operator and one individual (often the owner and general manager in smaller firms) to highly complex, full-day procedures at the larger carriers. Which individual sees the owner-operator often reflects the carrier's attitudes toward recruiting and recruiting criteria. In a number of small and medium-sized carriers the bulk of the interviewing is conducted by the officer in charge of safety, who also conducts the (mandated) inspection of the equipment. At such carriers, there may be some question as to whether sufficient discrimination is shown in selection.

In part, this may be due to the difficulty of applying hard and fast selection. Many motor carriers would express sympathy with the fast-food franchisor who was reported as saying, "We have been unable to determine what produces the most successful franchisee. We have analyzed our own franchisees and can seem to find no definite pattern which will enable us to draw any definite conclusion."[5] Certainly, no generalities can be obtained from my research, particularly as the most successful owner-operator in one sector of the trucking industry is quite likely to have different characteristics than will a successful operator in some other.

Table 4-1 shows a list of characteristics which carriers reported to me as being important in selecting owner-operators. It may be seen that many (if not most) of these criteria are very intangible, involving extremely judgmental decisions. Some, such as marital status, are clearly surrogates for other such characteristics as "stability" or "willingness to be away from home." (Indeed, marital status appears to be very important to many carriers. Some urge wives to accompany their husbands to inter- views, or at least to training sessions when and if the owner-operator signs on. "The wife is key," observes one carrier. "If there's trouble at home, you'll have nothing but trouble with the guy. Besides, the wife is often the owner-operator's vice-president of finance and controller, looking after all his accounts.")

An officer of an owner-operator association has aptly summed up the characteristics of a good owner-operator. He observes that an owner- operator must simultaneously be (1) a manager, to run his business; (2) a buyer, to get the best deal on his supplies; (3) an engineer, in order to "spec" his truck; (4) a salesman, of himself to the carrier and to shippers; (5) an accountant, to keep his records well; (6) a mechanic, to do his own maintenance and repairs as much as possible; (7) a lawyer, to understand his contract and various ICC and state laws; (8) a personnel manager, to motivate himself; (9) a financer, to purchase his truck; and (10) a trucker.[6]

Table 4-1
Criteria Used for Selecting Owner-Operators

Honesty
Ambition
Willingness to work
Attitude toward money
Domestic tranquility
Responsibility
Intelligence
Willingness to accept direction
Character
Driving record
Desire to learn
Age
Experience
Credit rating
Ability to get along with people
Willingness to be away from home
Marital status
Type and condition of equipment
Appearance
Approach toward business
Willingness to accept responsibility
Stability

While such a litany could probably be created for any small businessman, this list does indicate the range of characteristics that a carrier must attempt to identify in the recruiting process.

In order to identify these intangibles, carriers have few facts to rely on. Past work history is often the most reliable, and it is remarkable that many carriers fail to check out personal and work references. As K. Thomas, in an article entitled "You Hire Your Own Problem," observed, it should be a first rule that one should "read the application: don't just file it."[7] On the other hand, as one carrier observed to me, "no-one wants to be accused of blacklisting, so I rarely get useful answers when I do call up previous employers."

However, it is often the case that the number of previous employers, and length of time with them, offers a good guide to stability. Recruiting can often be simply a means of moving operators from one carrier to another without changing the size of the total power fleet: "Unless we're careful, we end up hiring everyone else's rejects and mistakes."

In the absence of hard information, some carriers have employed various testing procedures to try to identify the desirable characteristics. These have varied from psychological "dirty hands" tests (most often used by carriers recruiting new owner-operators to test whether they are suited to the driving life) to lie-detector tests to determine honesty. However, the use of such tests is not widespread, and most carriers depend on clues to determine the aptitude of a driver. My research indicates that the most important characteristics are likely to be cooperativeness and businesslike attitude, primarily determined through conversation. A carrier with one of the lowest turnover rates in the special-commodities sector (and, it is reported, a waiting list of drivers wishing to sign up), Red Ball, attributes its success to picking "drivers who either follow good business practices already or who are open to the kind of training that they know will garner them maximum financial reward."[8] The determination of whether or not applicants currently follow "good business practices" may be made by asking about their record-keeping system, their allowances for depreciation, and preventive maintenance.

Such a conclusion is supported by the experience of franchisors. The head of Dunkin' Donuts has observed that lack of realism (that is, business expectations and experience) is the chief cause of failure of franchisors, and that the essential qualities required by a franchisee are (1) proper motivation, (2) willingness to accept direction, and (3) tolerance of stress.[9]

The Costs of Recruiting

In the course of my research, I inquired of every carrier that I interviewed how much its recruiting programs cost. While many carriers could provide such statistics (particularly the larger ones), it was noticeable that many others were unable to do so. In part, this was because many of the costs of recruiting are indirect, and not necessarily accounted for as recruiting costs. A prime example of such an expense is the time executives spend interviewing potential candidates.

The costs of recruiting may be substantial. The van line that estimated its advertising cost of $400 per successful recruit further estimated that recruiting costs were $1,000 when other factors were included. Another van line estimated its total recruiting costs at $3,000 per successful recruit! While the van-line recruiting costs may be expected to be higher than other sectors of the trucking industry (because they tend to rely more heavily on attracting new or inexperienced drivers), the figures may remain high for other sectors. As a basis for comparison, it is interesting to note that, in 1966, the *Motor Fleet Safety Manual* (published by the National Safety Council) estimated the cost of hiring and training an employee truck driver at $1,000.[10] It is to be expected that, more than ten years later, this cost has risen dramatically.

In calculating its recruiting cost, a carrier should take into account the following categories of expenses: (1) expenditures for advertising; (2) cost of promotional materials; (3) expenses incurred in maintaining telephone service to handle inquiries; (4) direct payments (if any) to potential recruits to come to office for interview (some carriers offer to pay gas and other expenses for any out-of-route mileage incurred); (5) full allocation of the time of executives and other salaried employees (plus fringes) which is spent interviewing candidates. In addition to these expenses, the carrier has yet to include what may be termed "sign-on" expenses. These fall into two categories: training and other.

Other expenses include all the activities that are necessary to qualify the driver to operate legally under contract. These include obtaining valid licenses and registration; administering the medical, road test, and written exams required by safety laws; performing a safety inspection on the owner-operator's vehicle; examining the driver's log (to ensure that he or she has not exceeded the maximum eight-day driving time allowed by law); obtaining a "driver's abstract" from various states to verify account record; obtaining insurance; and so on. These activities will normally take in excess of two days to accomplish and, since they will often be performed by salaried personnel, may involve costs that are easy to omit from recruiting cost calculations.

Training activities vary substantially among companies, largely depending upon the type of recruits that a company usually attracts. Carriers that frequently hire new or inexperienced drivers, or drivers that are unused to the carrier's sector of the trucking business, will normally have fairly substantial training programs. It is not unusual, for example, for a household-goods carrier to require an orientation program (as much as ten days) for inexperienced drivers who have not previously worked in the household-goods field, although the sectors of the trucking industry will normally require less. (The high time requirements in household goods are due to the extensive paperwork and loading/unloading practices that must be learned.) For inexperienced drivers or new entrants to trucking, a carrier will often require the new recruit to ride with an experienced driver for up to four months in order to learn the business. At some companies the carrier will pay the new recruit a small salary ($100 to $150 per week) during this period, while other carriers do not. (The experienced driver gets the benefit of a two-man operation in exchange for training the new recruit.)

Finally, in estimating the total cost of recruiting, a carrier will need to include any costs that it incurs as part of its compensation package for the owner-operator. For example, many carriers will require the owner-operators' equipment to be painted in the carrier's colors, and some bear the cost of so doing (others pass this cost on to the owner-operator). In addition, the carrier may pay for the owner-operator's base (license) plate in the first year of operation, or for the insurance. Even if the carrier does not pay for these items, it is normal for the carrier to finance such expenditures, recouping the cost in deductions from the owner-operator's revenues during the year. Given the high cost of insurance and licenses, this finance cost (both direct and administrative) should be included as the cost of signing on new recruits.

Financing the New Entrant

The shortage of owner-operators that existed in the late 1970s, together with the rising cost of new equipment, has forced an increasing number of carriers to consider the option of assisting potential owner-operators in the financing of their equipment. This assistance may vary from casual conversations with (and introductions to) a friendly banker, to the carrier's actually selling the equipment to the new entrant, deducting the monthly payments from the owner operator's settlement checks.

Carrier financing, particularly where this takes the form of sale of equipment by the carrier, is often looked upon with distrust by owner-operators, because of the potential conflicts faced when the carrier is not only the sole source of revenue to the owner-operator, but also his main creditor. The suspicion in which carrier financing is held was accurately captured in testimony presented at the 1976 congressional hearings:

> Another practice the subcommittee should take a long look at is the sale of trucking companies to aspiring owner-operators. The buyer is at the mercy of the seller, obviously, otherwise he would go to a truck dealer if he had the necessary downpayment and financial standing.

In actuality, under this setup the trucker has little or no chance of ever owning a truck. Payments are deducted by the company from the trucker's pay. This way the company not only controls the trucker's earnings but is assured of getting its money and the trucker gets what is left. If it is a used truck, the trucker will find that when it breaks down—and it will—the company gets it back, repairs it, and sells it again. If it is a new truck, there will be plenty of work from the company to keep the trucker busy while the purchase is being paid off. After that, the trucker will suddenly find available work has dropped off sharply; either he is not in the right place at the right time to get loads or there are trucks ahead of him. If he manages to survive, he may unexpectedly find a large claim for damaged goods on a load he has hauled, which comes out of his pay. Short of cash for a payment on his truck, the truck is repossessed by the company, the trucker gets little or nothing for his equity, and the truck is sold again.[11]

Naturally, such shady dealings are not inherent in carrier financing: there may be many benefits to such practices. Since the carrier can buy equipment in large numbers, it is often able to obtain substantial discounts in the purchase price from manufacturers. These discounts may represent 15 or 20 percent of the retail value of the vehicle. The carrier may also be able to obtain funds for the financing at lower rates than the individual owner-operator. The savings that these represent may be passed on to the owner-operator, thus promoting her or his chances of financial success. Finally, the carrier may be better able to "spec" the equipment for the particular needs of the traffic it hauls. (It is often remarked that owner-operators "tend to buy equipment that is 'overspec-ed': too much horsepower for requirements, and certainly too much chrome!'") These advantages are perfect examples of the appropriate use of the franchisor power referred to in chapter 2: the carrier is using its size to keep economies of scale of benefit to the whole system (and to shippers in the form of lower costs, if not to equipment manufacturers). In addition, by control over equipment selection, the carrier has the capability of using its experience to help the owner-operator make wise business decisions. (It should be noted, however, that few franchisors *require* equipment purchases from them by their franchisees: the legal problems surrounding such a practice are great!)

In spite of these potential benefits, carrier financing does have some inherent problems. First, it obviously negates or compromises much of the "capital risk" rationale for using owner-operators (chapter 2). Second, the carrier must accept the problems and difficulties involved in the inevitable if rare instances of repossession due to owner-operator bankruptcy. (The ICC estimates that 10 percent of carrier-financed equipment is repossessed.[12])

Greater than these problems is the inevitable fact that any owner-operator financed by the carrier will be "locked in" to that carrier for at least two years. This observation may be easily demonstrated. Most carriers that finance equipment will (quite reasonably) include a provision in the sale contract that, if the owner-operator terminates its lease contract with the carrier and hauls for some other carrier, then the outstanding equipment loan must be paid in full. Because of the relatively low earning potential of new entrants in the trucking business, the carrier is forced to set monthly repayments at not-too-high a level. Since a new tractor (or trailer) depreciates quite rapidly in its final year, repayments in the first year fail to cover the loss in value. Accordingly, owner-operators will have built up no equity: if they attempt to find refinancing for a year-old vehicle, they will find that the resale value (upon which any loan will be made) is less than the outstanding loan. In such a situation, owner-operators have no choice but to continue to work for the same carrier until sufficient equity is built. If monthly repayments have been set at a low level (a temptation for any carrier in order to facilitate the recruiting task), this can take a number of years. In such a circumstance, the potential for resentment by the owner-operator is obvious.

In order to avoid these problems, some carriers prefer to seek ways of obtaining finance for new entrants without themselves being the prime source of capital. One way in which this might be done is to discover investors prepared to finance a vehicle and lease it to a new entrant. In some cases, tax-break opportunities are available to facilitate convincing investors.

Multi-Unit Owner-Operators

While it may be difficult to persuade nontrucking investors to buy and lease tractor-trailers (or just tractors), another form of finance is available in the form of multi-unit owner-operators (or fleet operators). As noted in chapter 1, these individuals own more than one vehicle, hire drivers themselves, and then lease vehicle and driver to the carrier.

In some respects, this is a curious (if not new) practice since at least one of the major motivations for using owner-operators is thus lost: the incentive upon and motivation of the driver. Since the driver is now an employee of the multi-unit operator, he or she does not have the incentive for service, productivity, and maintenance-avoiding driving practices that are often given as a major justification for using owner-operators. However, the other two major advantages to the carrier—nonunionized and cheaper labor and the availability of equipment without capital risk—remain. This practice thus offers some insight into the *major* motivations of some carriers in using owner-operators.

Among these carriers that use multi-unit operators, the advantages are seen as follows. First, it is noted that many owner-operators get into the business with the explicit goals of owning their own business, and one day owning a fleet of vehicles. The opportunity to expand into multi-unit operations is an incentive to good performance, and, to some extent, loyalty to the carrier. The multi-unit operator provides the carrier with a sizable amount of capacity at a significantly reduced recruiting cost, since the carrier does not need to recruit each owner-operator individually. Opponents of the multi-unit contractor system (and there are many carriers who will never consider their use) argue that this very advantage also constitutes a grave disadvantage, in that such a multi-unit operator has too much power over the carrier due to the threat posed by the chance of losing this capacity all at once.

Another advantage of the multi-unit contractor often cited is that such contractors can maintain small maintenance and repair shops and thus achieve lower maintenance costs than can an individual owner-operator. Major repair work for a single vehicle is less likely to be financially catastrophic for the multi-unit contractor in the way that it sometimes is for the individual owner-operator, thus leading to greater stability. It is also noted by some carriers that dispatching is easier with multiple-unit drivers, since the drivers, with no investment in the equipment, are less likely to refuse dispatches. The owner of the equipment, the multi-unit operator, is prepared to take a slightly longer-term view of his or her revenue needs than the typical individual owner-operator, who often seeks to maximize the revenue of every individual load.

In spite of these advantages, many carriers avoid the use of multi-unit contractors. There can be no doubt that the multi-unit contractor system creates additional administrative problems for the carrier. First, it has less control over the drivers, since they are neither its employees nor its contractors. However, most carriers reserve the right to veto any driver that the multi-unit contractor wishes to provide. The driver's salary is determined not by the carrier, but by the multi-unit operator, although the carrier may handle the payroll accounting for the multi-unit operator, issuing separate checks to the driver as salary and to the multi-unit operator for use of the equipment. (It should be noted that such a practice might be viewed by the National Labor Relations Board as evidence of an employer-employee relationship between the carrier and the driver, thus negating another of the benefits of using owner operators.)

It is possible that a conflict may exist for the carrier in trying to satisfy the separate needs of the driver and the multi-unit operator. For example, one carrier noted that its "peddle runs" (that is, short hauls) made its multi-unit contractor rich because of the high revenue and utilization that flowed from this traffic. However, the contractor paid its drivers by mileage, and peddle runs involve a high proportion of loading/unloading activities. Consequently, the drivers were not receiving high wages. The carrier was thus faced with unhappy drivers about whom it could do very little.

The topic of multi-unit contractors, as so much about the owner-operator system, has its analogy in the fast-food franchising business. Some franchisors, particularly in the early stages of their development, seek to grow rapidly by granting "master franchises" covering entire states or regions. The master franchise then may develop multiple units in that area, or even subfranchise. Vaughn[13] reports that "this procedure has not worked too well with many firms," citing the following reasons as typical of the problems encountered: (1) subfranchisees were not properly coached by the master franchisee; (2) controls slipped away from the parent company; (3) the parent company lost its rapport with the subfranchisee.

It is also notable that many of the large franchisors (such as McDonald's and Wendy's) have begun, in recent years, to buy back many of their larger franchisee networks. Few, if any, of the mature franchise systems now grant multiple-unit franchises, which suggests that the use of multiple-unit contractors is largely a phenomenon of small, new, and/or rapidly growing companies. Such a conclusion for the motor-carrier industry is largely borne out by my investigations.

Conclusions

As noted at the beginning of this chapter, recruiting is one of the most pressing, continuous, and difficult tasks in owner-operator management. Its difficulty lies in the fact that most motor carriers have problems in identifying either which applicants are most likely to succeed, or exactly how to attract owner-operators. ("What do owner-operators *want*?" is the question I have been asked most frequently.)

The question of recruiting is a problem not only for individual companies, but for the trucking industry as a whole. As we have seen, the demand for owner-operators is increasing and there is a constant need for new recruits into the industry. However, many companies stress *experience* in their recruiting activities. Only the household-goods sector can be identified as one that specializes in recruiting new entrants. Indeed, a van-line executive compared his company to IBM in that it served the role of recruiting and training new entrants into the industry, only to lose them to other companies and other sectors that offered better pay or better conditions. As the demand for owner-operators increases, it is likely that other sectors will be forced into the task of recruiting owner-operators from outside the trucking industry, with the attendant problems of more difficult selection (in that carriers will need to identify those individuals most suited to trucking), increased training cost, and closer supervision.

There may, however, be some attendant benefits to dealing with new recruits rather than attempting to hire experienced drivers. First, by attracting new recruits the carrier will avoid the problems of having to deal with drivers who have not worked out for other carriers. Indeed, one carrier that performs little or no advertising to experienced drivers noted that a large proportion of its problem drivers were those that were recruited as a result of an aggressive advertising campaign, while its most successful drivers were those that were brought in by owner-operators already working for the company. It is likely that word-of-mouth is the best recruiting tool not only quantitatively, but also qualitatively.

A second potential benefit to recruiting new entrants into the industry is the fact that such entrants may be more cooperative and willing to learn than hardened, experienced drivers. Increased cooperativeness will facilitate the task (which should be performed by all carriers) of teaching owner-operators how to manage business well, handle accounts, and deal with the paperwork. It was commonly reported to me by various carriers that "we'd like to help these guys but they resist our advice in the name of independence. They've got their bad business habits and they're not going to let anyone tell them what to do." An increased reliance on new recruits may allow carriers to overcome this problem.

It is notable that there exist a number of carriers that do little or no active recruiting, and yet have (reportedly) long waiting lists of owner-operators waiting to drive for them. For such carriers, word-of-mouth alone performs the recruiting task. This leads, inevitably, to the conclusion that it is the treatment of existing owner-operators that is the key to the recruiting task. Keeping existing owner-operators happy not only brings in more potential recruits but also lessens the recruiting task by reducing turnover, and hence the need for new recruits. It is possible that a number of carriers could benefit by explicitly considering the tradeoffs between expenditures on recruiting and those on raising the level of satisfaction of their existing owner-operators. The minimization of turnover will also have benefits in the quality of the owner-operator fleet. With 50 percent turnover, the average experience of the carrier's drivers will be less than two years. Such inexperience may affect productivity as well as the degree of customer service. With recruiting costs in excess of $3,000 per owner-operator, it would appear that there might exist some opportunity to divert resources away from the recruiting task.

5 Contracts and Payment Systems

We have seen that the relationship between owner-operator and carrier, while basically one of mutual dependence, is often characterized by potential conflicts of goals, disagreements over methods of operation, share of responsibility, division of revenues, and many other rights and obligations. The lease contract, the foundation of this relationship, can be a powerful tool to help eliminate many of the causes of misunderstanding or friction between the parties. As such, it may be viewed not merely as a legal document but as an important and integral component of the carrier's management system.

In this chapter we shall examine the lease contract: its structural components, the options open to management in its design, and the principles that should guide that design. As before, we shall use the analogy with franchising to assist in our understanding of this aspect of the owner-operator management system.

Problems in Contract Design

To fulfill its role as a management device for the elimination of conflict, a lease contract needs to be comprehensive. It should delineate the rights and obligations of each party in detail, so that rules are established for adequately dealing with all aspects of the business transactions between the carrier and the owner-operator. However, this ideal is difficult to reach.

McGuire has noted of franchise contracts that

> although a contract supposedly represents a "meeting of minds" between two knowledgeable consenting parties, some critics have complained that the "meeting" in the case of the franchiser and franchisee is often imperfect on two counts. First, they argue, the franchisee is sometimes unable to comprehend the complicated clauses common to many contracts. It is not unusual for franchisee contracts to run 15 to 20 pages in length.

> Secondly, they note that it is extremely difficult for an individual franchisee to get the franchise organization to modify its standard agreement in any way. The franchise proposition is thus a "take it or leave it" possibility for most franchisees.[1]

These comments may be equally well applied to the owner-operator system. As Wyckoff and I have already noted,[2] many owner-operator contracts are heavily weighted in favor of the carrier, in that they impose (as we shall see below) many duties and obligations upon the owner-operator and few upon the carrier. As in franchising, the owner-operator has the option to "take it or leave it." It is also true that to many owner-operators, contracts are impenetrably complex. "They hate this twenty-five-page stuff," one carrier told me.

The conflict between comprehensiveness and comprehendability in contract design is a real and important issue. On the one hand, if the contract is too abbreviated it will not only fail to serve the function of removing conflict sources, but may also open the carrier to charges of misrepresentation. The carrier, by conscious or unconscious omission, may fail to establish explicit rules for adequately dealing with various aspects of its business dealings with owner-operators. In some cases, this may be done "in the hope of preserving greater flexibility in interpreting to its own advantage matters not covered in the contract."[3] However, this can lead not only to potential friction, but also to regulatory and judicial questions.

On the other hand, if the contract is too comprehensive and detailed, many owner-operators will be put off and will either not sign up with the carrier or will fail to read and understand the contract. The first of these possible consequences may not constitute too serious a problem: the carrier may benefit from discouraging contractors who are not prepared to take the time to examine the document that will rule their business lives. Too extreme an aversion to complicated forms may be a good indicator of a lack of the appropriate business attitude that is necessary to succeed as an owner-operator. However, the latter consequence, failure to read and understand the contract, can be a serious problem for the carrier. It will mean that the owner-operator has failed to learn and, more importantly, agree to the terms and conditions of the work. While future disputes *may* be resolved by appeals to 'look at your contract," such appeals are more likely to increase conflict ("caught by the fine print again") than to resolve it.

On balance, therefore, the argument for comprehensiveness in lease contracts would seem to dominate, as long as the carrier is sure to make efforts to keep the language of the contract as straightforward as possible (within the confines of legal constraints) and to ensure that the terms and content of the contract are well-understood.

Regulatory Requirements for Lease Contracts

The regulations of the ICC controlling motor carriers' use of owner-operators[4] impose certain requirements upon the lease contract to be used.

In January 1979, in the wake of an investigation of leasing practices, the ICC substantially revised the relevant sections of the regulations, largely to embody a truth-in-leasing principle so that contracts would involve "a full disclosure between the carrier and the owner-operator of the elements, obligations, and benefits of leasing contracts signed by both parties."[5] In this section we shall review the requirements that the regulations impose upon lease contracts, as modified by the January 1979 decision.

The first requirement of the regulations is, naturally, that there shall be a *written* lease, made between the carrier and the owner of the equipment. The duration of the lease is to be specific (that is, to indicate when it begins and ends), and, in any event, is to be of a minimum duration of thirty days. (Any lease of less than thirty days is termed a *trip lease* and is governed by other regulatory requirements. Thirty-day leases are termed *permanent leases*.)

It has long been an ICC requirement that the lease shall include language to the effect that the carrier "shall have exclusive possession, control, and use of the equipment for the duration of the lease. The lease shall further provide that the authorized carrier lessee shall assume complete responsibility for the operation of the equipment for the duration of the lease."[6] This clause has proven to be a source of difficulties for many carriers, since its language conflicts with the desire of most carriers to establish an *independent contractor* status for its owner-operators. As we shall discuss in chapter 8, the phrases "exclusive possession and *control*" and "complete responsibility for the operation of the equipment" have been combined with the common law "control of means" test to establish the owner-operators' status as employees rather than independent contractors. Possibly because of this threat, there do exist some carriers that have failed to include this language in their contracts. This is plainly illegal.

The requirement for exclusive possession, use, and control of the equipment does not mean that the carrier may not sublease the equipment to another carrier (for example, allow the owner-operator to trip lease a load for another carrier in order to have a loaded backhaul). The regulations expressly permit a provision in the lease that characterizes the lessee carrier as the "owner" for the purpose of subleasing to other authorized carriers.[7] A similar exception is provided for household-goods carriers. Since many of these carriers operate on an agency basis, whereby the national van line coordinates the activities of equipment that is leased not only to the van line directly but also the equipment leased to the member agencies, the regulations allow the van line to control the activities of the agency's drivers. This arrangement, which allows the owner-operator to be (variously) under the control of the agent and the national van line, is often termed an "intermittent lease."[8]

One of the major changes effected by the 1979 revision of the leasing regulations was the inclusion of a clause which requires lease contracts to state (*on the face of lease or in an attached addendum*) the amount to be paid by the carrier for the equipment and driver's services. The "amount" may be expressed as a percentage of gross revenue, a flat rate for mile, "or by any other method of compensation mutually agreed upon by the parties to the lease."[9] To back this up, the ICC also ruled that the lease should "clearly specify the responsibility of each party with respect to the cost of fuel, fuel taxes, empty mileage, permits of all types, tolls, ferries, detention and accessional services, base plates and licenses, and any unused portion of such items."[10] Further, "the lease shall clearly specify all items that may be initially paid for by the authorized carrier, but ultimately deducted from the lessor's compensation at the time of payment or settlement."[11] Particular attention was given to the question of insurance. Under commission regulations, a regulated carrier must "maintain insurance coverage for the protection of the public."[12] Such insurance may be broken down into four categories: (1) cargo insurance, which protects against loss or damage to the loads being transported; (2) collision insurance. which covers damage to vehicles or equipment involved in an accident; (3) bodily injury and property damage insurance, which covers injury damage to third parties as a result of an accident; and (4) bobtail insurance, which covers any accident while tractor is operating without a trailer (for example, on its way to pick up a load). It is the responsibility of the carrier to ensure that adequate insurance exists to cover all these contingencies. However, the applicable regulations do not specify who is to pay for such insurance. Accordingly, the ICC's leasing regulations make it a requirement that (1) the lease establishes the carrier's legal obligation to ensure adequate insurance coverage and (2) the lease clearly specifies who is responsible for the payment for such insurance. If the owner-operator purchases insurance coverage from or through the carrier, then the lease must specify that the carrier will provide the owner-operator with a copy of the insurance policy at the request of the owner-operator.

The regulations also deal with the matter of responsibility for the payment of cargo or property damage claims in the wake of an accident (in practice, for the deductible portion of any insurance coverage). It is a regulatory requirement that the lease specify the conditions under which any deductions for such claims may be made from the owner-operator's settlement. While few, if any, carriers hold owner-operators completely responsible for all of the deductible, it is common that owner-operators are held responsible for some portion, in order to ensure care for the cargo and equipment.

This issue of the responsibility of the owner-operator for claims arising from accidents is one in which there has been some legal activity. In 1975, the Supreme Court held that carriers were permitted to include an indemnity clause in their lease contracts which placed the responsibility for claims upon the owner-operator and indemnified the carrier against such claims. The Court was careful, however, to point out that the ICC could, if it chose, prohibit such clauses.[13] Such clauses had previously been determined to be contrary to public policy because they tend to mitigate against the *carrier's* responsibility to the public under the terms of its ICC operating authority. The enforceability of such clauses has not generally been tested in law.

It may be seen that most of the contract provisions mandated by the ICC refer to the allocation (between carrier and owner-operator) of charges for various operating expenses. This emphasis is continued in other provisions not yet discussed. Among the most important of these is the topic of *escrow funds*. It is a common practice among carriers (see below) to require the owner-operator to provide an initial deposit of funds to the carrier. These funds may be used by the carrier to finance "trip advances" paid to the owner-operator in anticipation of revenues from hauling a load; to protect the carrier against the owner-operator's quitting while still in debt to the carrier for such items as insurance claims; or for many other purposes. Because of reports of abuses of this practice (nonpayment of interest on such funds, difficulty in obtaining reimbursement upon termination) the ICC in 1979 made it a requirement that the lease contract specify the amount of any escrow fund or performance bond, indicate the specific items to which these funds can be applied, and provide to the owner-operator (on a monthly basis) a statement of all transactions involving this account. The carrier is required to pay interest on the net balance of these funds (that is, less the average outstanding advance made to the owner-operator) at rates based on ninety-one-day, thirteen-week Treasury bills. The lease must also specify all the conditions the owner-operator must fulfill in order to have escrow funds returned, which return must be completed no later than forty-five days from the date of termination.

Three other regulatory requirements for leases exist. First, the lease must specify that payment to the owner-operator will be made within fifteen days "after submission of the necessary delivery documents and other paperwork concerning a trip." The necessary paperwork must be clearly specified. Second, the lease must specify that the owner-operator is not *required* to purchase or rent any products, equipment, or services from the carrier "as a condition of entering into the lease arrangement." If the carrier is a party to any equipment purchase or rental contract which gives it the right to make deductions from the owner-operator's settlement, then the lease must specify the terms of any such agreement. Finally, the regulations require that the carrier give copies of rated freight bills to any owner-operator paid on a percentage basis for all loads that he or she hauls. (The carrier may delete confidential information such as the names of shipper and consignee.) Prior to the 1979 revision, the regulations required only that such freight bills be available for inspection by the owner-operator. The lease contract must include a statement to the effect that freight bills will be provided. The contract must also specify the right of all owner-operators to inspect the carrier's tariff to verify that the correct basis for payment is being used.

It will have been noted that, while detailed, the ICC's regulations concerning the content of lease contracts leave large areas for management discretion. First, they are primarily concerned with financial interaction between the parties, rather than the rights and responsibilities of the parties. Second, while the truth in leasing principle has led to regulations that required clear statements of responsibility for various charges, the ICC has not imposed any rules concerning who (ultimately) has to pay for any item. (The required payment of interest on escrow funds is a possible exception.) This condition is largely a result of the limited jurisdiction of the ICC. In the course of the investigation which led to the revision of the leasing regulations, trucking associations argued forcibly that the ICC did not have the authority to intervene in contract negotiations. Accordingly, while ICC Chairman Dan O'Neal and two other commissioners would have protected the interests of owner-operators by setting minimum standards on such matters as fuel, permits, tons and the like, these matters remain open to be decided by the carrier in designing its contract.

It is therefore of some interest to examine carrier practices in this regard. We shall begin with a discussion of the bases of payment.

Forms of Payment

According to a series of surveys performed by the ICC in 1977 and 1978,[14] approximately 75 to 80 percent of owner-operators are paid on the basis of a percentage of the carrier's revenue from the loads they haul. The remaining 20 to 25 percent are paid by the mile.

The percentage paid can vary widely. According to one ICC survey[15] in 1977, household-goods carriers generally paid 50 to 65 percent of line-haul revenues if the owner-operator provided only the tractor, and 60 to 80 percent for tractor and trailer. All other categories of carriers generally paid 60 to 75 percent for tractor only, and 70 to 90 percent for tractor and trailer. (The generally low percentages in household goods reflect not only the high rates per ton-mile that exist in this sector, but also the fact that it is common industry practice for owner-operators to retain up to 100 percent of charges for packing and unpacking that they perform.) It should be stressed that no conclusions may be drawn from a straight comparison of the percentage of revenue paid by one carrier with that of another. One carrier may pay a higher percentage, but pass on to the owner-operators (or require them to pay initially) various ancillary charges such as fuel taxes, tolls, base plates, insurance, and so on. the net effect on owner-operators' well-being cannot be deduced without knowing the extent of these charges and how to translate these relatively fixed annual charges to a "percentage of the revenue" equivalent (see below).

The advantages to the carrier of the percentage method of payment include ease of administration. When cost conditions necessitate a change in tariff levels, any adjustment in rates automatically provides an increase in compensation to the owner-operator. With a mileage-based payment, it would be necessary to adjust both rate levels and the mileage payment to owner-operators. The percentage method encourages the owner-operator to carry the maximum payload (especially important in bulk commodity hauling). However, it can also result in overloading if this is not carefully monitored by the carrier. The percentage method also allows the owner-operator to share the responsibility for distinguishing "good" loads from "bad" loads. With a guaranteed rate per mile, the carrier would bear all of the loss on any traffic with insufficiently high rates. (This is a strong argument in favor of mileage rates, since it is the carrier that generates the traffic and sets rate levels, and it would appear equitable that the carrier shoulder the burden of consequences of its actions.) On the other hand, mileage-based rates could have the disadvantage of removing the incentive upon the owner-operator to operate over the most efficient (that is, direct) route. This could be overcome if the payment were based not on actual mileage but upon standard mileage between the origin and destination of the shipment. Such standard mileages are available in the *Household Goods Carriers' Standard Mileage Guide*, which lists the over-the-road mileage between any two points in the Continental United States. (It should be noted, however, that there is a deep suspicion among owner-operators of the mileages given in this reference: they argue that they are often inaccurate or represent mileages using routes they would normally avoid.)

One of the strongest arguments for using the percentage method of payment is the strong desire of owner-operators to be paid that way. Until recently, Bekins Van Lines was unusual in the household-goods sector in paying its owner-operators by the mile. Executives at the van line reported great resistance among owner-operators to this method of payment because "they don't understand it. They know how to compare percentages when looking around for a good deal, but can't compare our mileage rate to a percentage. We try to show them how to do it, but they are very distrustful." As part of a general reorganization of its business, Bekins switched to the percentage basis of payment in 1979.

The Allocation of Expenses

As noted above, financial arrangements between carriers and owner-operators extend well beyond the basic percentage of revenue or mileage payment, since there exist a large number of expense categories (see appendix 5A) for which arrangements must be made. These arrangements may take the form of (1) requiring the owner-operator to pay for the expense directly (such as is normal for fuel cost and maintenance expenses); (2) the carrier paying initially, but charging back the expense to the owner-operator in the form of deductions from weekly or monthly settlements (such as might be used for base plate license fees); or (3) the carrier paying for and bearing the expense.

Which of these the carrier elects to choose for a particular expense category is a key element of management decision. The decision is affected only in part by the influence it will have on the net revenues of the owner-operator, since a carrier that elects to bear the costs of many of these expense items will be less able to pay a higher percentage of revenue. (This argument was made with some force during the ICC proceedings which led to the revision of leasing rules. Carrier groups argued that an attempt to help the owner-operator by requiring the carrier to bear the cost of certain expenses would inevitably lead to a lowering of the basic percentage of revenue, thus potentially leaving the owner-operator no better off.)

It is therefore best for the carrier to view its payment system decisions in two stages: (1) what (annual) net revenues should the carrier aim to provide its owner-operators, and (2) what is the best mix of payment system elements (percent of revenue, employ mileage payments, allocation of expense categories) to achieve this goal?

Decisions in this area will be influenced by the following factors. First (and possibly foremost) is the importance of perception: how the owner-operators will view a given package. There is a common belief among many carrier managers that owner-operators are relatively unsophisticated in their process of choosing a carrier, and tend to focus extensively on the percentage of revenue rather than other elements of the compensation package. Consequently, carriers tend to aim to keep the gross percentage high, and either allocate most expense categories to the owner-operator directly, or charge them back in the form of deductions. An additional perception consideration is that carriers believe owner-operators to be suspicious and resentful of too many deductions appearing on settlement statements, and thus will tend to have owner-operators pay various expenses directly, or (better) absorb the cost themselves and make suitable adjustments in the basic percentage rate.

Owner-operator perceptions are an important consideration but should not be allowed to dominate the decision on how to treat expenses. Apart from the dangers of being accused of misrepresentation (advertising a high percentage of revenue with less emphasis on what may come to be termed "hidden charges") a large number of other factors are relevant.

An important factor derives from consideration of the role of the carrier as franchisor. Part of the service that carriers (should) provide to their owner-operators is the facilitation of the owner-operators' tasks. This will include (1) assisting in obtaining various forms and permits; (2) helping to finance the "up-front" costs of permits, insurance, and the like; (3) helping the owner-operators budget their cash and make provisions for such items as health insurance, pension plans, and so on. Consideration of the carrier's responsibility in this area ("helping the owner-operator succeed") suggests that carriers should avoid having the owner-operator pay for such items directly, and should instead offer to arrange for and finance as many expense categories as possible. Whether or not these categories are subsequently charged back is a separate decision dependent upon the other factors described here: the fact that the carrier will *assist* in these areas is of importance in and of itself.

Also of relevance to how to deal with expense categories is the ability of the carrier to perform the functions represented by the expense categories more efficiently, or to use its size to obtain discounts on the prices of these items. Many items may be considered eligible here: obtaining license fees; purchasing fuel, vehicles, or ancillary equipment; arranging insurance, health, and pension plans; and so forth. Rather than requiring the owner-operator to pay for these items directly, economies of scale and efficiency at the carrier level (one of the justifications for the owner-operator system) would dictate that the carrier at least make available its services to arrange and finance these activities.

If a carrier has decided to arrange and (initially, at least) pay for certain expense items, it must consider other factors in deciding whether to recoup this cost either directly in the form of "chargebacks" or indirectly through a lower percentage of the revenue. One consideration in this regard is the required incentive upon the owner-operator to operate efficiently. A good example of this is provided by fuel taxes.

It is a requirement in most states that a trucker (or trucking company) purchase in that state all the gasoline used in operations in the state, or (failing to do this) to pay fuel taxes on any shortfall. Efficient operations therefore dictate careful planning of fuel purchases in order to avoid having to pay double taxes (once where the fuel was purchased and once as a penalty for buying insufficient fuel in another state). If the carrier were to absorb all fuel tax costs (and particularly penalties), then the owner-operator would have no incentive to plan fuel purchases efficiently. The whole rationale of the owner-operator system dictates that the owner-operator be either directly responsible for (or "charged back" for) any expense items she or he can control. It should be noted that, in some states, *excess* purchases of fuel in a given state (that is, more than was used in operations in that state) allow a carrier to claim a rebate on fuel taxes. Since fuel tax settlements with the states are almost exclusively performed by the carriers, not the owner-operators (a fact largely dictated by state officials, not the carriers), equity would seem to dictate that, as well as charging back fuel tax penalties, carriers should pass back any fuel tax rebates. This is often not the case. In some instances (in New Jersey, for example) this may be that, in order to obtain the fuel tax rebate, the carrier must establish a permanent office in the state. In general, however, good contractor relations would seem to indicate the wisdom of passing back rebates (particularly as the amounts involved are usually small).

A predominant influence in deciding whether or not to charge back expense items is the potential impact this may have on the owner-operator's "employee or independent contractor" status (see chapter 8). If the carrier absorbs the cost of a large number of expense items, then it is likely that the National Labor Relations Board (or some other relevant jurisdiction) will rule that the owner-operator bears "insufficient risk" (opportunity for profit or loss) to be ruled an independent contractor. This would suggest that the carrier should charge back as many expense items as possible. (The inherent paradox between *helping* the owner-operator by absorbing business risk and the desire to preserve independent contractor status by *not* absorbing risk is again apparent.)

It should be noted that the allocation of operating costs and (more importantly) business risk to the owner-operator can be taken too far. Even if these are more than compensated for by a very high percentage of the revenue (thus avoiding claims of trying to rip off the owner-operator), the carrier may leave itself exposed to charges of an illegal lease of operating rights. For example, if all expense items in appendix 5A (including insurance) are paid for by, or charged back to, the owner-operator, and the carrier's contract includes a clause indemnifying the carrier for deductible payments, then there can be some question of whether the carrier is adequately bearing its responsibility to the public under the terms of its operating authority. Unless the carrier bears a reasonable proportion of the business risk, it can be charged with illegally leasing its operating rights.[16]

It may be seen that there are many influences upon the carrier's decisions about the payment structure of its contract. No one solution exists for all carriers. However, there is one overriding principle that should guide efforts in this regard, and that is one of *comprehendability*. The ICC's recent action has made full disclosure a matter of law: it was always sound business practice for any carrier concerned more with its long-term contractor relationships than with short-term recruiting needs. As such, the carrier should not only ensure that all relevant elements of the payment structure are itemized in the lease (as the ICC now requires) but that the contractors fully understand the structure.

This is not an idle recommendation. Since leases are likely to become more complex because of the full-disclosure provisions of the regulations, carriers will need to be better able to explain the consquences of their payment structure to owner-operators, particularly in their recruiting efforts.

As we have noted, comparison of contracts will increasingly involve the owner-operator in tradeoffs of an increased percentage of the revenue for the responsibility of (ultimately, at least) paying for various expense categories.

It is, in principle, not impossible to establish such a comparison with the uses of broad averages. For example, consider license charges. Most carriers will require the owner-operator to pay the charges for a home-state base plate, but many do not require him or her to pay for license extensions to other states. How much would this be worth to an owner-operator if he or she is trying to decide whether to go with a carrier that does require him or her to pay for such extension? Suppose that the cost of license proration is $800 (an arbitrarily chosen figure). Suppose further that the average owner-operator in the fleet runs 100,000 loaded miles in a year hauling loads averaging freight charges of 90 cents per mile. On average, therefore, an annual cost of $800 would represent just less than 1 percent of the annual revenue from the loads hauled. To compensate for bearing these (license extension) charges, the owner-operator would need to receive an extra 1 percent of the revenue.

This example is a relatively straightforward illustration: the annual costs of license extension can be reasonably well established with some certainty. Others are not so easy to identify. For example, what is the "equivalent percentage of the revenue" for the owner-operator having to bear the maintenance charges on a company-provided trailer? Actual maintenance costs cannot be predicted with a small margin of error, and hence may be difficult for the owner-operator to estimate.

It is noteworthy that the information necessary for the conversion of fixed charges to a percentage of the revenue equivalent is likely to be held by the carrier. It is the carrier, not the owner-operator, that knows that number of loaded miles that the owner-operator can expect to run in a year in the carrier's operation. Similarly, it is the carrier that can best estimate the average revenue per mile represented by the traffic that the carrier obtains. Finally, it is the carrier that has (or should have) most ready access to historical statistics on the relatively unpredictable expense items such as trailer maintenance. This suggests that while, indeed, it is possible to translate these expense items into equivalent percentages, it is the *carrier* that can best do this, not the owner-operator.

It might be of some benefit for carriers to perform these calculations for themselves. More than one carrier complained to me that it was losing owner-operators to other carriers who appeared to offer better deals which the original carrier was convinced did not, in fact, provide greater net revenues. These carriers reported that it was difficult to demonstrate the "disadvantage" of the competing contract to the owner-operators. For any carrier that is convinced that it "has a good deal," it would be worth estimating (and disseminating among its owner-operators) a series of "percentage equivalents" for various expense items. The general formula for this calculation, as illustrated above, is relatively simple:

$$\text{Percent equivalent} = \frac{\text{expected annual value of expense item}}{\text{expected annual loaded miles} \times \text{average revenue per mile}}$$

It is recognized that this formula is heavily dependent upon many uncertainties, and subject to much variation. However, performing this calculation might assist the carrier in establishing or modifying its contract terms by setting appropriate ranges for particular items.

Other Contract Terms

The lease contract is only in part a document concerning payment systems. It also should delineate the rights and responsibilities of the two parties with regard to all aspects of their business dealings. As noted at the beginning of this chapter, an effort in this direction *can* make the contract excessively complex. A normal (and sensible) way out of this dilemma is to establish a rules and procedures manual and to include as part of the contract agreement a clause to the effect that adherence to policies and procedures contained in the manual is considered integral to the contract agreement. When designing such a manual, the carrier should bear in mind the legal requirements of independent contractor status. If such a system is used, however, then the carrier has a legal responsibility to allow contractors (and, if necessary, their lawyers) to inspect a copy of the procedures manual before the contract is signed.

The desire to establish the owner-operator as an independent contractor (rather than an employee) is reflected in most carriers' contracts. Many (if not most) explicitly include a statement that "the parties intend to create by this agreement the relationship of carrier and independent contractor and not an employer-employee relationship. Neither party is the agent of the other and neither party shall have the right to bind the other by contract or otherwise except as herein specifically provided." Such phrases clearly establish the "intent of the parties," which is one component to be taken into account by, for example, the NLRB.

To support this statement of intent, many contract clauses clearly have their basis in the desire to establish independent contractor status, in that they specifically itemize those aspects of operations to be controlled by the owner-operator. The following is typical:

> The CONTRACTOR shall determine the means and methods of the performance of all transportation services undertaken by the CONTRACTOR

under the terms of this agreement. The CONTRACTOR has and shall retain all responsibility for selecting, purchasing, financing and maintaining the equipment; selecting all routes within the scope of the operating authority within which he travels; and paying all operating expenses, all expenses of fuel, oil and repairs. . . .

It may be seen that the language here has been carefully chosen to correspond to that used by the NLRB and IRS in determining contractor status (see chapter 8).

McGuire has written of franchise contracts that they are "usually quite explicit in defining the franchisee's responsibilities. By contrast, they are sometimes rather vague about the specific contractual responsibilities of the franchiser."[17] The same may equally be said of motor-carrier lease contracts. Few contracts lay binding obligations on the carrier, although some do contain language such as the following:

> The carrier agrees to make commodities available from time to time for transportation by the contractor and the carrier shall exercise every reasonable effort to make sufficient commodities available so that the contractor shall be able to keep the equipment in reasonably regular use under the terms of this agreement, although this shall not be construed as an agreement by the carrier to furnish any specific number of loads or pounds of freight for transportation by the contractor at any particular time or any particular place.

One lawyer with whom I discussed this lack of carrier obligation made the remark that "there is such an absence of consideration in many of these contracts that they can hardly be considered contracts at all in the legal sense of that word."

The absence of carrier responsibilities from the contract is troublesome in more than a legal sense. The example cited above, wherein the carrier offers to exercise every reasonable effort, has the virtue that it is a fair representation of the carrier's side of the bargain: it describes accurately what the carrier does and does not promise to do. Van Cise has written of franchise contracts:

> Following the execution of such a contract, some franchisees have asserted that erroneous representations by the franchisor had been made with respect to the assistance which the franchisee was to receive and the profits he was to earn. Moreover, such assertions on occasion have been found to be justified. If proven, any such franchisees would have actionable claims for deception and failure of consideration against their franchisor. The franchise agreement therefore might reduce to writing any representations which had been made to the franchisee in order to induce his execution of this document, and contain an acknowledgement from the franchisee that no others had been made either orally or in writing.[18]

Such advice is probably also sound for motor-carrier managers. The opportunity to describe accurately the responsibilities of the carrier (even if these are only on a "best efforts" basis) not only adds to the "balance" of the contract, but would also constitute a fair disclosure of what the owner-operator can expect from the carrier and how the carrier will behave. To the extent that this accurately describes the role of the carrier (see the discussion of role theory in chapter 3), the contract may then be used as a means of preventing future conflict in contractor relations. Disappointment or dissatisfaction are determined primarily by the measuring of events against expectations. To the extent that the contract can be used to create appropriate expectations, it can be used as a major component of the carrier's owner-operator management system.

Appendix 5A
Sample Expense Items
to be Allocated
between Owner-
Operator and Carrier

Maintenance of tractor
Maintenance of trailer
Repairs
Inspection fees
Base plate
Licenses
Permits (overweight, overlength, and so on)
Fuel
Fuel taxes
Tolls
Road taxes
Withholding taxes
Social security
Workmen's compensation
Fines (if owner-operator negligent)
Fines (if carrier negligent)
Telegrams (for advances, dispatching, and so on)
Telephone calls (for dispatching)
Identification of carrier on truck (required by ICC)
Painting (or other identification of carrier) on trailer
Removal of identification upon termination of contract
Loading and unloading expenses
Detention charges
Pickup and delivery expenses
Expenses incident to transfer and delivery (in event of breakdowns)
Cargo insurance
Collision insurance
Bodily injury insurance
Property damage insurance
Bobtail coverage
Claims (or deductible portion) for cargo, tractor, trailer, driver, public
Credits for unused portions of license plate fees upon termination
Credits for unused portions of permit fees upon termination
Trip-lease revenues
Ancillary equipment (for example, dollies in household goods, hooks
    for meat hauling)
Empty mileage.

6 Operations

Introduction

If, as Wyckoff has demonstrated,[1] the key to successful management of a regular-route common carrier of general freight is control of terminal expenses, then it is equally true that the key to successful management of an irregular-route carrier of special commodities is control of *line-haul* expenses. As we show in chapter 9, and as Eads has noted,[2] line-haul expenses account for very large proportions of the total expenses of most irregular-route special commodity carriers.

For the typical LTL common carrier of general freight, operating over regular routes, controlling line-haul costs is a relatively straightforward matter, since tractors move over well-defined routes between fixed terminals. Apart from the obvious need to control out-of-pocket operating costs connected with line-haul (fuel, maintenance, and labor), the main determinant of line-haul costs for such a carrier is its ability to raise the load factor on interterminal runs, that is, to ensure that as much LTL traffic as possible is carried on the truck that is due to depart anyway. The role played by the dispatcher in such a company is a relatively minor one: his main decision is whether to delay the departure of a given (partially loaded) truck while waiting to accumulate more traffic for the purpose of raising the load factor. Such decisions are fairly routine, and most carriers have well-established policies to follow in such cases. Similarly, the assignment of individual (employee) drivers to specific runs is normally a routine function, determined largely by terms of the collective bargaining agreement which provide for "bidding" by drivers, usually according to seniority rules.

Control of the line-haul function in an irregular-route carrier is markedly different from this, and is a task that is simultaneously more important and more complex than for the general freight LTL carrier. Inherent in the nature of irregular-route operations is the prospect of "empty backhaul," the danger that there may not be a return haul from the destination point of an outbound shipment. In consequence, discretion must be exercised both in the decision on whether to accept a given load (or, since most irregular-route carriers are common carriers and must meet their common-carrier obligation, whether to solicit given loads), and in the assignment of loads to individual drivers. Note that whether the carrier uses employee drivers or owner-operators, this problem of assignment remains. Because of the lack of fixed routes, even collective bargaining rules concerning dispatching will be more complex and difficult to implement for the irregular-route carrier than for the regular-route carrier.

For most regular-route carriers, a given vehicle "trip" will be relatively simple, usually involving an outbound journey and a return along the same route (that is, between fixed terminals). Such routings can be planned well in advance. The same would not be true for the irregular-route carrier, for whom there would not necessarily be a return load to the point of origin. Its vehicles may need to be dispatched to a third or fourth (and sometimes higher) point before being returned to the "home base." It is therefore necessary for the irregular-route dispatcher to attempt to "plan" routings involving successive loads to numerous points, and to perform this planning on a "real-time" basis.

The final important difference is operations control between regular-route and irregular-route carriers is that the "supervisory" or "monitoring" task is inherently more difficult for the latter. A driver for an LTL general freight carrier departs from a carrier terminal and terminates at a carrier terminal. His or her time in transit is easily measured and controlled, and he or she has no interface with the customer. In contrast, an irregular-route driver departs from a shipper's dock, terminates at the consignee's dock, and may never physicially turn up at any of the carrier's locations. Monitoring of the driver's time in transit, dealings with the customers, and all other aspects of his or her performance must be conducted at a distance, usually via telephone communications. Most irregular-route carriers require their drivers to call in every day to report their location, check that there are no problems, and, in the case of some carriers, such as transporters of perishable commodities, to report on the condition of the load. The monitoring function thus becomes more difficult, and, it should be noted, more explicit.

These functions of operations control in an irregular route carrier are illustrated in figure 6-1. Of necessity, this description is somewhat idealized in that we have, so far, only referred to irregular-route carriers generally. For some types of irregular-route carriers, one or more of these separate functions will take on a greater or lesser importance. For example, a *radial* irregular-route carrier will have a different load-planning problem than will a non-radial carrier, since all of its trip assignments will tend to be of the "there-and-back" kind (due to the nature of its authority) and route planning will be a less complex task. Because of this, the monitoring function will also usually be simpler. In contrast, a household-goods carrier will have a complicated route-planning task because of the extreme variability in origins and destinations required by household-goods shipments and because of the need to assemble three or more individual shipments to make up a full truckload. Carriers working in market sectors that require high

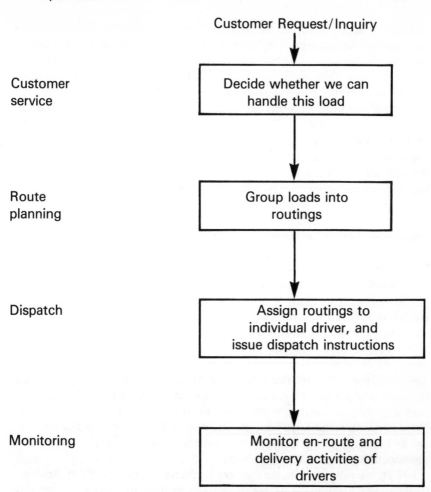

Figure 6-1. Elements of Operations Control in an Irregular-Route Carrier

transit-time reliability (such as refrigerated products) will need to give greater importance to the monitoring function than will carriers working in sectors that do not have high transit-time reliability requirements (such as steel).

In many, if not most, carriers the functions described in figure 6-1 are all performed by the same individual: the dispatcher. In such cases, the dispatcher's job is a high-pressure, multi-faceted task that bears a large part of the responsibility for the financial success of the carrier. As one carrier put it, "a constant sales effort and a consistent level of service are the things that keep a motor carrier in business. . . . The working level for both sales and service is in the dispatch office."[3] The sales effort of the dispatchers (that is, the customer-service function of figure 6-1) should not be forgotten. As the same carrier went on to observe, "whether most dispatchers realize it or not, they probably do as much to make sales by talking to shippers on the telephone as any road salesman can."[4] Indeed, this carrier had adopted a policy of requiring its dispatchers to make a certain number of sales trips per month, on the theory that dispatchers make good salespersons; they have the contacts and know-how for operational feasibility. In addition, drivers will appreciate dealing with dispatchers who have visited the customers' docks and will thus have obtained a better understanding of physical loading and unloading realities at particular locations.

Dispatching Owner-Operators

So far in this chapter we have described the tasks of operational control/dispatching for irregular-route carriers generally. We must now introduce the owner-operator. Although the dispatching function we have already described is a complex task, the use of owner-operators by a carrier serves to increase both the difficulty and importance of the dispatcher's job. The first and most important point to note is that in the vast majority of cases, the dispatcher is the single person in the carrier's organization that deals with the owner-operator on a regular basis. Owner-operators may be recruited and trained by others, but once this is accomplished their daily contact with the carrier is through the dispatcher. Even their regular payments (trip settlements) are usually mailed to them rather than picked up, and in many companies it is the dispatcher who first learns if the owner-operator has any problems in this area.

Next, we observe that the element of figure 6-1 labeled "dispatching" (that is, the assignment of routings to individual drivers) is completely transformed by the use of owner-operators. A carrier that wishes to preserve his owner-operators as independent contractors rather than employees cannot *require* an owner-operator to accept a load or routing assignment, that is, use what is termed a "forced dispatch" system (see chapter 8). The owner-operator must retain the right to refuse a load; a right, we might note, that, regardless of the carrier's desires, the owner-operator jealously guards as a mark of much-valued independence. (It should be noted, however, that in the course of this research, a number of carriers that do use force dispatch for their owner-operators were encountered.)

The lack of forced dispatch means that the dispatcher must convince the owner-operator to take either the individual load or, in some cases, complete route assignment. This task makes demands upon the dispatcher's interpersonal skills, and the development of a personal working relationship between the owner-operator and the dispatcher is the one essential element of any successful program of owner-operator fleet management. Owner-operators' refusal of loads is, by a large margin, the most commonly reported disadvantage in utilizing owner-operators rather than a company-owned fleet. Refusals mean that the carrier can plan less well, and, as we have seen, operational planning is a difficult task for any irregular-route carrier because of the "real-time" nature of planning required of such carriers.

Determining why individual owner-operators turn down specific loads is one of the more difficult problems that a dispatcher faces. Some aspects of the problem are obvious: there are loads which may clearly be seen to be "good" or "bad" by everyone. An obviously "bad" load would be one that was low-rated (that is, for which the revenue per mile was low) or one that terminated at a location from which it was well known that the carrier had difficulty in generating return loads. Other aspects may be equally obvious for carriers of specific commodities: some commodities may be notoriously difficult to handle and take care of (for example, strawberries); some customers or towns may be notoriously difficult to get unloaded at quickly. For such loads the dispatcher must depend upon appeals to friendship, fairness ("everyone has to take a bad load once in a while"), future compensating dispatches ("take this one and I'll find you a good load next time"), or the prospect of a good load waiting at the destination ("just get there and there's a real doozy of a load waiting for you").

However, on top of this problem is the fact some (all?) owner-operators will occasionally turn down what appear to be "good" loads for reasons that are purely personal and sometimes impenetrable: "I just don't want to go there this week." It is one of the tasks of the dispatcher to get to know his or her owner-operators sufficiently well to become aware of each driver's individual desires, needs, and quirks. Some carriers, in somewhat sexist but nevertheless effective fashion, utilize women for the dispatching task (or at least that part of it that involves communications with the driver), in the hope that this will facilitate the development of a friendly relationship between dispatcher and driver. Such a device might be particularly effective where a carrier has a high proportion of "bad" loads that require the sort of appeals described in the previous paragraph.

It should be noted that the need to "sell" loads to owner-operators can, if not carefully policed, lead to undesirable results. For example, there might develop what could be termed "the rich get richer and the poor get poorer syndrome," whereby the older, more experienced owner-operators are more aware of what the bad loads are, where the bad destinations are, and so on, and hence turn them down. On the other hand, the new, inexperienced owner-operator will accept bad loads, either from ignorance or a willingness to please. Since the new, inexperienced owner-operator is the one who is most likely to have pressing financial requirements, this is an unfortunate situation. It tends to reinforce itself because the more low-paying loads owner-operators get, the more pressing their financial position, and the more likely they are to be willing to accept any load offered in order to keep rolling and keep cash flow up.

A similarly unfortunate conflict may develop between "cooperative" and "uncooperative" owner-operators, in that the latter will uniformly turn down bad loads and not be responsive to appeals to "help us out this time." This forces the dispatcher to give the cooperative owner-operator an unfairly high proportion of the bad loads. One carrier made this point by observing that "the dispatcher gets screwed by the bad guys, so he rescues himself by screwing the good guys."

Even a strict first-in-first-out dispatching rule can become problematical if experienced owner-operators feel they have a prior claim to better loads. Unless strict control is exercised, such a system can fail if there are too many examples of owner-operators that call in to say they are empty and ready to load, when in fact they are not, but are attempting to "beat the system" in order to have a wider choice of loads.

Qualities of a Good Dispatcher

It will be clear from the previous discussion that the qualities required of a good dispatcher are many and various. One carrier summarized it well:

> The key men in any operation are the dispatchers. To drivers they are the company. The should have the patience of Job, the wisdom of Solomon, and a damned good sense of humour. We expect them to be the driver's buddy and father confessor all rolled up into one.[5]

However, even this statement fails to capture the full range of qualities that a good dispatcher requires. It will help in understanding the dispatcher's job in more detail if we discuss some of the more important qualities.

First, the dispatcher must be able to work under pressure. The dispatcher spends her or his day on the telephone talking with customers wishing to ship their goods, drivers who want loads, wish to report a delay or other problem, or make a complaint. It is not uncommon for a single dispatcher to be responsible for forty or fifty owner-operators on her or his "board" (dispatch board). Dispatchers will also, in most companies, handle inquiries from consignees who wish to trace their shipment (hence, incidentally, the need for regular call-ins by the owner-operator).

Second, the dispatcher must be fair and honest. We have seen that dispatchers routinely engage in making "promises" to owner-operators about future loads, and have the power to influence the financial success of the owner-operator by making available good and bad loads. Dispatchers must be sure to stick to any promises that are made. They must also treat all owner-operators with equity and not play favorites. This aspect of the dispatcher's task is one which is surrounded by controversy, and is problematical for many companies in their control of the dispatch function. The dispatcher has many opportunities for dishonesty and other, less clearly defined, "gray-area" activities. Some dispatchers have been accused of taking bribes ("kickbacks") to give an owner-operator a good load. In some companies, dispatchers will even own their own trucks (with or without the carrier's knowledge), which, naturally, receive favorable treatment in the selection of loads. Even without these examples of obvious dishonesty, every dispatcher will have a natural tendency to favor those owner operators with whom she or he has a more friendly relationship.

"Crooked dispatchers," or more generally, unfair treatment by the dispatchers, is a common complaint among owner-operators. Indeed, together with general personality conflicts with the dispatcher, it is one of the most prominent reasons for owner-operators terminating their lease contract with the carrier. As one owner-operator put it, "I don't think most drivers mind living with strict rules when they know they apply to everyone, and that the company is fair."[6] It should be noted that many irregular-route carriers use a mix of owner-operators and company trucks. This creates the natural suspicion among owner-operators that company-owned trucks will be dispatched first, and will get the good loads. In some companies, this is indeed the case, and dispatchers will have a difficult task in convincing the owner operators that the dispatching system is fair.

Third, the dispatcher must have a broad knowledge of all aspects of trucks and trucking. As the company's main contact with the driver, he must be prepared to give advice and/or to react in the case of numerous problems that the driver might face. These could include problems with the tractor or trailer, problems with the shipper or consignee in loading or unloading, matters of company policies, owner-operators' trip settlements (payments), or a host of other matters. In the final analysis, dispatchers may pass major problems on to some other officer of the company (the safety director, the general manager, the accounting department, and so on), but they must have the ability to recognize the difference between major and minor problems, and be prepared to deal with the latter themselves. Their knowledge must include regulations of the ICC, so that they will be aware of what the carrier can legally haul, and, perhaps more importantly, they must be aware of the hours-of-service regulations of the Bureau of Motor Carrier Safety so that they do not attempt to dispatch a driver for a load that the driver cannot legally haul in the available time.

Fourth, the dispatcher must understand the economics of both carrier and owner-operator. This topic covers a wide range of aspects of the dispatcher's dealings with the drivers, but two that we have not yet identified should be measured. First is the topic of advances to drivers on the revenue they will derive from the haul to cover on-the-road expenses. In many companies, it is the dispatcher who makes the decisions on how much of an advance to allow the driver (if any at all). Usually the amount of such advances are laid down by company policy ("x percent of the revenue, up to a maximum of y dollars"), but there still remain areas of discretion for most dispatchers. Such decisions often lead dispatchers into "paternal," or perhaps "fraternal," relations with the driver, in that they may counsel the driver not to take too much cash in advance to spend on the road while leaving little left over at the end of the month ("Have you sent any money home to your wife this month?"). Dispatchers in some companies also have the authority to pay allowances to the owner-operator for empty mileage. Even where they do not have this power, dispatchers must be aware of the impact this has on the carrier's and the owner-operator's costs. Indeed, the "route-planning" function of figure 6-1 is almost entirely about the minimization of empty mileage.

A fourth quality that the dispatcher must have might best be termed a sense of position. While they are the company's representatives to the owner-operator, they are also to a large extent the owner-operator's representatives to the company. Many carriers rely on their dispatchers to keep the owner-operators happy, but many owner-operators also rely on their dispatchers to resolve difficulties that they are having with the company. Indeed, some of the most successful dispatcher/driver relationships (which are one of the keys to dispatch success) derive from the fact that the dispatcher "took on" the company to resolve a problem that the owner-operator was having. For this reason, many carriers encourage, to some extent, the dispatchers' supporting their owner-operators when an interdepartmental problem arises. In addition, many (if not all) carriers are in the process of continually updating their operating practices, particularly with a view to finding ways to cut down on owner-operator dissatisfaction and hence turnover. The dispatcher is the prime source of knowledge about what aspects of the carrier's policies most irritate the owner operators and can play a very prominent role in the revision of company policies.

The final quality that we can identify as being required by a good dispatcher is that he or she should have a good memory. Demands upon dispatchers' memory come from many directions. For example, they must be able to react to an owner-operator who asserts, "You've given me nothing but bad loads for the past four weeks." They must know what loads are available at what locations, what drivers are due in, and so forth. They must remember promises they have made to owner-operators for good loads, and to act on requests from the owner-operator to talk to other officials in the company. Similarly, they must remember when the owner-operator calls to relay messages that may have come from other departments of the carrier, from shipper or consignee, or even from the owner-operator's wife and family. They must remember personal details about the owner-operator and his family, and keep careful track of such things as how much the owner-operator has been earning, when he last got home, and various other small, but important, matters.

To a large extent, of course, the dispatcher's memory can and will be aided by the record-keeping system used in the dispatch office, and it is to this topic that we now turn.

Computerized Dispatching

For many irregular-route motor carriers, the record-keeping system in the dispatch office is based on a card system, with an individual card representing either an individual shipment or an individual driver. Filing systems are set up in front of the dispatcher (or on a rotating drum) so that the key information on each card is visible. Separate columns or files are established to distinguish between shipments available to load, shipments due in today, shipments due in tomorrow, and so forth. Color coding is often employed to distinguish some other piece of information not captured by the visible portion of cards, column placement, or color codes. It is very common for the dispatcher's office to have a teletype which serves as a means of communication between different dispatch locations.

In experienced hands, this system can be remarkably effective. It is a remarkable experience to watch a busy dispatcher deal with a large number of telephone calls in a short period of time, capture and record a large volume of information, and be able to respond to a call about an individual shipment or driver with complete knowledge of all relevant details. However, such systems have their limitations.

> Several years ago, it became apparent that our existing dispatch system was reaching its limits. It was a good system, fine for fifty trucks, and fine for one hundred trucks, and it was alright for a couple of hundred; but when the figure reached two hundred and fifty trucks to three hundred trucks, we realized that it was reaching the end of the road. We had clipboards scattered around the office representing each truck. On one wall we had a little map, and we had little magnets that represented the trucks, their location and their status. The clipboards alone were enough reason for us to move into another office, just to accommodate the room that was needed for the clipboards. And, we just flat found that we were having a paper hurricane. We were always struggling to catch up, and never really had a current picture of our status.[7]

This carrier (Melton Truck Lines), and increasing numbers of growing irregular-route carriers, turned to computer-based dispatch information systems to resolve the problems of card systems. In a typical operation, each dispatcher will sit in front of a CRT-terminal with access to various information about loads, shippers and drivers. Such systems are on-line and interactive, in that the dispatcher can continually update information kept in the computer.

The essence of any computer-based dispatching system is a set of files which contain constantly updated information of certain categories. A list of the basic files in a simple system is given in figure 6-2. The files are interrelated so that when a given driver and his tractor have been assigned a trailer and picked up a load from a given shipper, these facts are recorded by "connecting" the relevant elements in each file. The computer program will usually contain internal checks so that, for example, two drivers cannot be assigned to pick up the same load (an occurrence that, while rare, can occur in a system that relies on the dispatcher's memory and his card system).

The value of the computerized system can best be illustrated by considering the separate "displays" that in a basic system dispatchers can call up onto the screen. Suppose that a driver calls in. By typing in that driver's code number (which may be an alphanumeric codenumber such as DHMAIS), the computer will display that driver's file, containing such information as name of codriver (if any), make and year of tractor, license number, registration state, and the date the driver's license and safety in-

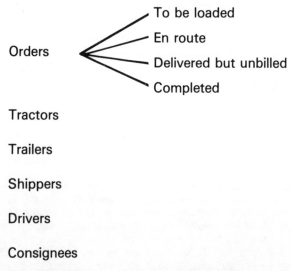

Figure 6-2. Base Files for a Computer-Based Dispatch System

spections are due. It may also give his wife's name, his birthday, the last time he was home, and other personal details. Perhaps, on a separate display, it will give details on all the loads handled in the past month, the code number of the load the driver is currently hauling, and the gross revenues received from the carrier in the past six months. It is also possible for the screen to display any messages that should be passed on to the driver, and warning signals to the dispatcher on such matters as "this driver owes us some paperwork from his last trip".

All this can be displayed and scanned by dispatchers in seconds, who would then be well informed to deal with the driver. They could then type in the code number of the load the driver is currently hauling (shown in the previous display) and get a display of all relevant information about the load: when it departed, when it was due, what is the commodity. Based on information given by the driver, the dispatcher can update this, or any other, file by typing in such items as the current location of the tractor (to assist in responding accurately to subsequent customer tracing enquiries). The "load display" will also usually contain a shipper or consignee reference number which can be typed in to call up a display of relevant information from the shipper or consignee files that can be passed on to a driver who has never visited the location before.

Other possible displays would include loads available, a list of all loads delayed, a list of all loads delivered that day, a list of tractors (and drivers) ready to load, and so on.

The costs of such a system as this can vary widely, but the following numbers are instructive. When Melton Truck Lines installed its first system in 1970, its annual revenues for the previous year were $7 million, and the cost of the system was $1,400 per month. By 1973, when annual revenues were up to $20 million, the cost of the system, through programming improvements, had risen to $6,100 per month. This supported ten CRT-terminals (display units).[8]

Another carrier, C & H Transport, which also went "on-line" in 1970, estimated in 1976 that its system averaged one on-line inquiry every six seconds. This was in a system which had eighty CRTs (and supported 1,300 tractors). C & H's system was sufficiently sophisticated that

> accurate estimates of the amount an independent contractor will earn on a given haul can be made using a formula which looks at the zipcodes of pickup and delivery points and rate per ton-mile figures. Advances to contract drivers are partially determined by this figure.[9]

The potential benefits of a computer-based system are many. Apart from relieving the pressures upon the dispatcher's memory, such a system will inevitably make the dispatching room more efficient due to the orderly and quick access to information. Communication between the dispatcher and driver is facilitated, as is communication between the dispatcher and shipper or consignee. Indeed, the use of a computer-based system allows the separation of the driver-related and customer-related functions. Whereas in a manual system it is only the dispatcher who has ready access to information concerning the status of a given shipment (and who must therefore handle customer calls), with a computer-based system it is possible to have separate personnel dealing with customer calls who can either refer to the computer screen (for tracing enquiries) or add to the data in the computer (by booking loads).

Because of the efficient structuring of information about the current state of the carrier's system (loads available, equipment ready to load), it should be possible with a computer-based system to improve service and maximize the use of equipment.

One of the greatest potential benefits of the computer system is the geographical coverage it can give. Many, if not most, irregular-route motor carriers (of all types) have centralized their dispatching process, with or without a computer, to one or a few dispatching locations. Centralization can be beneficial in allowing the efficient control of the entire operations of the carrier from a single location. It also has benefits for the management of owner-operators in that, under such a system, a driver can be assigned to a single dispatcher no matter where the driver is. This will facilitate the development of the personal relationship described above and avoid such problems as an owner-operator's entering a new dispatching area and receiving (or claiming to have received) conflicting dispatching instructions from two dispatchers in different areas.

The computer, by assisting in the feasibility of centralized dispatching, can greatly assist in the route planning function identified in figure 6-1 in that it will permit rapid display of loads available in a few days' time at various distant locations. The dispatcher can then put together entire route assignments, rather than dispatching each load one at a time. The ability to do this will not only increase the efficiency of utilization of the fleet, but will increase the opportunity of the dispatcher to "dangle the carrot" in front of the owner operator, that is, promise good loads at the destination point of an otherwise unattractive load.

In effect, this application of the computer system serves to increase the planning horizon of the route-planning component of the dispatching system. Taken to its logical conclusion, this implies that the route-planning function (along with the customer-service function) can be separated from the dispatching function. Although the computer is not essential for this, it greatly facilitates the process.

Separation of Route Planning from Dispatching

The separation of route planning from dispatching is an increasingly common phenomenon. In the course of the research for this book, it was found most commonly among household-goods carriers (who, we have seen, generally have the most complicated route-planning problem due to regional imbalances, LTL shipments, and widely varying origins and destinations). It is being used by carrier in other sectors, but its development is somewhat limited by the fact that the order lead time (between the request for service and the date the shipment is to be transported) is generally low in most other sectors of the irregular-route trucking industry. Where such is the case, very limited amounts of load planning can take place.

When the route planner can assemble loads free from the distractions (and pressures) of direct communications with drivers and customers, the process can yield more efficient routings. There are other benefits in the fact that the dispatcher, freed from customer-service and route-planning functions, now becomes primarily a *communicator*, issuing instructions to the drivers and receiving information from them. Such dispatchers can give more attention to dealing with the owner-operator as an individual, and solving individual problems. It has the side benefit that since the dispatcher no longer assembles or assigns loads, the possibilities of underhanded dealings such as those described above between dispatcher and owner-operator are no longer possible, or at least are made much more difficult. One carrier described the separation of planning and dispatching as "the driver's safeguard."

However, the separation is not without its disadvantages. First, too much advance planning can lead to situations whereby a load to a given destination is assigned to one driver, but not yet picked up, when another driver requests a load to that destination. The second driver will be told that none is available, only to discover later that his or her "buddy" is going right where he or she wanted to go. Such situations can be an irritation to owner-operators who are otherwise satisfied that the dispatching system is fair and responsive to their individual desires.

A far more problematical disadvantage of the separation of planners and dispatchers is that dispatchers, in being reduced to communicators, now have as their main task the "selling" of loads to the owner-operator. If the owner-operator refuses to accept the assigned load, dispatchers no longer have the power to replace it with another, but must get in touch with the load planners to find a substitute. Since, in most such situations, a dispatcher is likely to be evaluated on the basis of minimizing the number of such occurrences, the exhortations used by the dispatcher to get the owner-operator to take the assigned load are likely to become more shrill and urgent. This might work against the company's desire to have the dispatcher develop a friendly, cooperative relationship with the driver.

Indeed, the position of a dispatcher in such a system is not an enviable one. The responsibility given (to keep the owner-operator happy) is not equivalent to the authority given (to switch loads). In some companies, this and other conflicts in the dispatching task are resolved by yet another separation of functions. In these companies the task of looking out for the owner-operator is shared between the dispatcher/communicator and a separate group of individuals generally known as counselors (see chapter 7).

Commission Agents

In spite of any impression that may have been created above, not all operating functions in irregular-route trucking can be centralized. There still remains the task of generating traffic, which requires a strong local presence in the communities served by the carrier. Because of the expense of maintaining sales offices in all the (distant) points served, many carriers (especially the special-commodity divisions of general freight carriers) have adopted the practice of subcontracting this task out by using commission agents. While the primary role of these individuals is to generate loads, they also perform a number of operating tasks. These may include providing pickup and delivery instructions to permanently leased owner-operators when they enter the agents' area. In many instances, they may have the power (or indeed are relied upon) to sign on new owner-operators, at least on a trip-lease basis. *Transport Topics*, a weekly trucking industry newspaper, regularly has advertisements form carriers seeking agents with "shipper and owner-operator following."

As appendix 6A (which is a typical commission agent agreement) demonstrates, agents are normally compensated on the basis of a percentage of the revenues from the loads they generate (typically 7 or 8 percent).

The use of commission agents is not without its critics. One Department of Transportation (DOT) study (which asserted that "nearly all irregular route carrier terminals are operated by agents or fleet brokers") contained the following:

> Agencies are very questionable entities. There is a strong suggestion from every level of the business that agents "buy" their business. The Chairman of the Board of a major carrier, who uses agents, uneqivocally stated that agents buy their business with payoffs to the traffic managers.[10]

Whatever the validity of this charge, it can be noted that, by the use of independent agents, the carrier distances itself even further from its customers, the shippers. Not only is the line-haul transportation being performed by independent contractors, but so are many of the carrier's other "normal" functions: traffic generation, office operations, and even recruiting owner-operators. The fact that such agents are not employees of the carrier may hinder the development of good owner-operator relations, since the carrier is less able to control the interactions between owner-operators and agents than it could between owner-operators and its own employees. Many of the problems of owner-operator "abuse" discussed in the congressional hearings referred to in chapter 2 involved activities by agents, and questions have been raised as to the degree of control that a carrier can, does, and should exercise over its agents.[11]

Closely related to the use of agents is the topic of trip leasing. As noted in chapter 1, our concern in this book has been with permanently leased owner-operators, but the practice of trip leasing deserves some recognition. As noted above, some carriers seek agents who have an owner-operator following. This refers to the fact that, through success in generating traffic (a "shipper following"), a commission agent may gain a local reputation for having loads available. Accordingly, itinerant owner-operators seeking backhauls will call the agent whenever they are in the area, even if they are not permanently leased to the carrier that the agent represents. (Under 1979 ICC regulations an agent could represent only one carrier unless he or she had a property broker's license, which few did. Property broker regulations were amended in 1979.[12]) Assuming that the owner-operator met the qualifying conditions for a legal trip lease (conditions not always honored to the letter of the law), the agent would give the load to the owner-operator, letting her or him carry it under the carrier's ICC operating authority. Unlike permanent leases, revenues to the itinerant owner-operator for trip leases are often flat rate (that is, a given dollar amount) rather than a percentage of the revenue. In markets where loads are scarce, trip-lease payments fluctuate in accordance with supply and demand for available owner-operators and available loads. Accordingly, trip-lease activities can be very profitable to the carrier (and agent) since the owner-operator may receive much less than the 75 percent of revenues typical of permanent leases. As one carrier phrased it, "trip leasing is the only way to make real money. You can pay a low percentage, have no permit or fringe costs usually associated with permanent leases, and the agent does all the work." It is not surprising that most owner-operators do not like trip leasing. Apart from the problems described above, they claim that they often have difficulty collecting revenues from companies with whom they have only a tenuous relationship.

The scenario described above relates primarily to arrangements between agents and free-agent owner-operators, that is, those not already under permanent lease to another carrier. When a trip lease is executed between an agent for one carrier and an owner-operator (or company driver) working for another carrier, it is more usual for a percentage of the revenue to be paid by the carrier generating the load to the carrier supplying the transportation. Arrangements between individual carriers vary, but typically the carrier generating the load will retain 15 to 25 percent of the revenue, paying the remainder to the transporting carrier. If the load is hauled by an owner-operator permanently leased to the transporting carrier, then the carrier will pass on the payment to the owner-operator. Practices vary, but most carriers will pass virtually all of the payment on, less a paperwork deduction. However, some carriers will pass on only a proportion of the revenue. In part, the proportion passed on may depend upon who found the backhaul trip lease. Wyckoff[13] reports that 83 percent of owner-operators under permanent lease have their backhauls arranged by the company for whom they haul.

In spite of the problems discussed above, both agents and trip leasing play a role in the efficient functioning of the trucking industry. For a carrier with a geographically widespread, irregular-route operation, it may be difficult to maintain a salesforce and operating function at all the points it is authorized to serve. Agents paid by commission offer a way to maintain a presence in a distant market without the fixed expenses of a permanent office. Similarly, trip leasing is essential in a regulated market, since without it carriers without backhaul loads would be forced to incur excessive empty mileage. Trip leasing allows a carrier with a load to be hauled to be matched up with an available (empty) truck. It is unclear to what extent trip leasing would be affected by deregulation, although this matter is discussed in chapter 10.

Summary

In this chapter we have identified the dispatcher as the key linking-pin in any owner-operator management system. Whatever policies and procedures the carrier wishes to use to deal with owner-operators, they must be implemented through the dispatchers and (for those carriers that use them) the agents. This perspective raises an important question: how can top management ensure that its philosophy of owner-operator management is being applied on a day-to-day basis? In large part, the answer lies in the way that the operations function itself is monitored and controlled. It is a basic axiom of general management in all industries that the way an individual (or group) is evaluated will determine to a significant extent the way that individual (or group) performs a given task. The establishment of appropriate appraisal and control procedures for evaluating agents and dispatchers is thus a central component of the task of managing an owner-operator system. However, it is often a neglected one. Many carriers I interviewed had few (if any) explicit criteria for appraising their dispatchers and agents. At other carriers, appraisal procedures which focused exclusively on operational efficiency and keeping shippers happy led dispatchers into behavior that caused them to "ride" the owner-operators more than may have been necessary, or desired, by top management.

A number of carriers do recognize the conflicting pressures upon the dispatchers, and explicitly include in their criteria for evaluating them the extent to which they can keep the owner-operators happy. For example, at one (large) carrier, each dispatcher is responsible for fifty specific owner-operators; and is partially appraised by the degree of turnover among his or her group. Another carrier carefully monitors statistics concerning the group of owner-operators reporting to each dispatcher: such statistics as average weight and revenue per mile and average number of line-haul miles per owner-operator per month are used. Not only averages are inspected: the statistics relevant to each dispatcher are inspected to ensure that he or she is not favoring one owner-operator above others: all owner-operators are expected to perform a minimum number of miles per month. This ensures not only that dispatchers are fair, but also that they encourage the owner-operators to keep their productivity up.

The dispatcher and the agent are the front-line supervisors of the owner-operator system. There is a wide general-management literature[14] on the problems (and techniques for dealing with problems) of these individuals: this literature is too wide to review in detail here. However, by explaining their function, this chapter has attempted to give dispatchers their rightful place at the center of the action.

Appendix 6A
Commission Agent
Agreement

This Agreement made and entered into on this __ of _____ 1977, by and between a corporation having its principal place of business at _____, _____ hereinafter called "First Party", and _____, having his principal place of business at _____, hereinafter called "Second Party."

Witnesseth:

Whereas, The First Party is a motor carrier in interstate commerce with certificated authority to transport iron, steel and other similar articles all commonly referred to as "special commodities," and desires to appoint the Second Party to act as its agent to solicit such business and to arrange for the movement by the First Party of such freight, and the Second Party desires to act as such agent.

Now, Therefore, it is Mutually Agreed Between the Parties as Follows:

1. The First Party does hereby designate and appoint the Second Party, and the Second Party does consent and agree to act as agent for the First Party in soliciting from the public such special commodities freight destined to First Party's certified points as outlined in the Interstate Commerce Commission Certificate, same to be transported by the First Party in its business as an authorized motor carrier of freight in interstate commerce.

2. The Second Party will diligently and faithfully serve the First Party as its agent to the best of his ability and undertakes that on all freight he solicits on behalf of the First Party, he will make all necessary and customary arrangements for the movement of such freight on motor vehicles operated by the First Party.

3. The Second Party is now and during the existence of this agreement shall continue to be an independent contractor, and nothing contained in this agreement shall be construed to the contrary; that the authority and powers granted to the Second Party are expressly limited by this agreement; that in the event he deems it necessary to hire employees in fulfilling his duties and services under this agreement, such employees shall be subject to the full control and direction of the Second Party at all times, and at his own expense, including but not limited to Workmen's Compensation and other employment benefits for the Second Party and all his employees.

110

Although the Second Party promises and agrees to comply with the rules, regulations and instructions of the First Party promulgated in the conduct of its business, the First Party's interest in this agreement is the accomplishment by the Second Party of the service contemplated by this agreement and not the means by which said services have been accomplished.

4. The Second Party, at his own expense, shall provide and maintain an office and truck parking lot, together with a telephone and all office supplies necessary for the services to be by him performed.

5. The Second Party shall be authorized to negotiate and enter in leases with owners of motor equipment for the lease of such motor equipment and driver to the First Party on a single trip basis only, provided, however, that terms, compensation and conditions of the lease shall be those prescribed by the First Party in its rules, regulations, policies and instructions issued by the First Party to the Second Party, and that the Second Party shall at all times observe all laws, rules, regulations enacted by the Interstate Commerce Commission, DOT, and the various States governing the leasing and operation of motor vehicles in interstate commerce by the First Party.

6. The Second Party may interview owner-drivers desiring to lease their equipment to the First Party and enter permanent employment with the First Party, subject to the approval of the First Party after receiving a written employment application, proposed equipment leases, or other information that may be requested by the First Party. The First Party reserves the right to reject any prospective employee that may be recommended by the Second Party.

7. That in consideration of the services to be rendered by the Second Party to the First Party, the Second Party shall be paid for an amount equal to seven percent (7%) of all revenue due to the First Party for all such freight so solicited by and delivered to the First Party for transportation. However, said compensation shall be increased to eight percent (8%) after Second Party generates a gross revenue of $15,000 for two successive months or $30,000 gross revenue in either of the two months mentioned above. Conversely, if Second Party drops below said $15,000 gross for two months, said compensation shall drop to seven percent (7%) which will again start the incentive cycle. It is understood and agreed that such commission or compensation shall be considered earned and due to the Second Party when shipper shall execute bill of lading and deliver such freight to the possession of the First Party for transportation and that Second Party shall not be held responsible for the payment of charges accruing to the First Party for transporting said freight, provided that the Second Party does promise and agree to exert his best efforts to assist the First Party in the collection for such charges due First Party on all freight solicited by the Second Party. All overcharge claims will be charged to the Second Party at the same percentage as commission paid.

8. The Second Party shall prepare and deliver to the First Party a weekly statement of total freight obtained for First Party, together with proper documents in support of said statement, and upon receipt of approval thereof by the First Party shall promptly remit to the Second Party its payment covering commissions due the Second Party upon such freight.

9. The Second Party agrees to protect, indemnify and hold the First Party harmless from and against any and all loss, damage, cost, expense, or claims, including attorneys fees, that may be suffered or incurred by the First Party, in performing or failing to perform any of the services or duties on the part of the Second Party to be performed under this agreement.

10. The Second Party shall permit the First Party to make all reasonable audits of his books and accounts as the First Party may desire.

11. It is understood and agreed that the First Party will furnish to the Second Party freight bills, operational forms, and/or documents and drafts entitling the Second Party to draw upon funds in the general corporate bank account of the First Party. Drafts may be drawn by the Second Party on the funds of the First Party only for the express purposes herein provided, payable to owner-operators, leased to or employed by the First Party, as operating advances and trip lease settlements (advances are not to exceed 25% of net revenue due the operator or $100 for every 500 miles of travel) for transporting freight solicited by the Second Party and Second Party shall maintain a full and complete record of all such drafts drawn upon the funds of the First Party and shall submit to the First Party daily by United States Mail, a report of all drafts issued together with two carbon copies of said drafts and that all times, the Second Party shall be liable to the First Party for all unused drafts in his possession. The Second Party further promises and agrees to reimburse and pay to the First Party all moneys wrongfully withdrawn from the funds of the First Party.

First Party reserves the right to decline party of any draft for which details have not been reported to the First Party as provided above.

12. This agreement shall become effective _____ 19__, and shall remain in effect until terminated in the manner herein provided. Either party may at any time, with or without cause, terminate and cancel this agreement by giving a thirty (30) day written notice; such notice shall be sent by certified mail, return receipt requested, and addressed to the other party at the address of said party as first above written in this agreement, or at the last known address of the party; that all computations of time pertaining to said notice shall commence upon depositing said notice properly addressed in a U. S. Mail chute or Post Office, provided that the company may immediately terminate the agreement upon Second Party's failure to perform or observe any term in this agreement. Further, upon termination for any reason, all property owned by the First Party, i.e., drafts, freight bills, forms, etc., shall be immediately returned to the First Party.

In Witness Whereof, the parties have set their hands and seals on the day and date first above written.

7 Information and Control Systems

Franchise Reporting Systems

Among the services provided by a franchisor to a franchisee (such as those listed in chapter 2), most are of greatest perceived value to the franchisee in the early months and years of the relationship. Examples of this are business training, advice on operations, location assistance, and financing. The services provided later in the relationship are often less obvious to the franchisee, and indeed are often resented. The primary function of the franchisor in a mature franchise system is the administration of the *system* as a whole. This involves ensuring that the type of markets served continue to be viable; experimenting with new services that, if successful, can be introduced on a system-wide base (consider the introduction of breakfast menus in many hamburger chains); and, above all, using the experience of individual franchisees to identify common problems and opportunities shared by all franchisees. The individual franchisee, faced with a problem, should be able to turn to the franchisor to discover how other franchisees have dealt with the problem. Efforts to overcome problems which may be beyond the powers of the individual franchisee may be possible when addressed by the franchisor on behalf of the total system. In playing this system-administration role, the franchisor need not be passive, reacting only to problems when they are reported. Indeed, most successful franchisors actively monitor the operations of each franchisee and, by comparison of operating results, are often able to identify franchisees with problems before the franchisee himself is aware of them. For example, if the sales volume of an individual outlet is lower than the system average (after correcting for such factors as regional differences), the franchisor may be able to signal this problem symptom to the franchisee before the franchisee has become aware of any difficulty. Further, the franchisor may be able to analyze the franchisees' activities, discover the source of the problem, and provide corrective advice or assistance before the problem deteriorates.

The basis of this capability is, of course, a comprehensive reporting system which allows the franchisor to monitor the activities of individual outlets and perform analyses to identify system-wide averages and deviations from these "norms." However, comprehensive reporting systems are often resented by franchisees as an intrusion into their privacy and an offense against their (semi-) independent status. Emmons has described this problem well:

> Many franchisors have established sophisticated computerized management information systems designed to provide operating data feedback to individual franchisees. The data reflects operating results on an individual, regional and national basis for comparative and diagnostic purposes. . . .
>
> Most franchise agreements legally require franchisees to prepare periodic reports and transmit them in a timely manner to the franchisor. Far too many franchisees treat this obligation in a cavalier manner. The result is often late, incomplete and inaccurate reporting of operating results to franchisor management. The franchisee frequently fails to see the benefits derived from accurate reporting, and this is most unfortunate, for the data collected often forms the basis for decisions affecting the entire franchised system.[1]

Owner-Operator Reporting Systems

As in so many other aspects, the owner-operator system in the trucking industry resembles the franchising business in the opportunity and problems of using information systems to control (and *improve*) its operations.

As in franchising, experience can be shared among operations regarding such matters as problem shippers and consignees that create loading or unloading problems, areas from which it is difficult to obtain backhauls, and so on. As in franchising, it is part of the carrier's franchisor responsibilities to address these common problems by generating traffic in problem backhaul areas and, in the case of frequent unloading problems, to negotiate with shippers on behalf of the owner operators.

Unlike most franchise systems, few motor carriers have instituted comprehensive reporting systems for their contractor operations in the form of regular reports filed by owner-operators. There are many reasons for this, but two predominate. First is the familiar difficulty that if reporting requirements are made compulsory, the motor carrier runs the risk that this element of its relationship with owner-operators may be used by the NLRB or IRS to find an employee status rather than an independent contractor status (see chapter 8). Second, as Emmons noted for franchisees, many (if not most) owner-operators resent the control that reporting requirements represent, perceiving it as a threat rather than as an opportunity. The problem is further compounded by the fact that many owner-operators do not themselves keep accurate records of their operations and hence are not capable of providing information to the carrier about their operating costs.

In spite of these problems, the appropriate use of information systems on owner-operator cost and revenue experience is probably one of the most powerful tools available to a motor carrier in the successful administration of an owner-operator fleet. Indeed, it is the very fact that many owner-operators are not capable of providing information to the carrier about their operating costs that provides the opportunity for the carrier to provide a real service to the owner-operator by assisting in the essential record-keeping vital to any business endeavor.

It is interesting to note the institutional context that has allowed (or even *forced*) the relatively slow development of carrier administrative activities in this area. Apart from the pressures of the NLRB and IRS referred to above, the ICC has also played a role in failing to encourage carriers accurately to monitor their owner-operators' costs of operation. The historical attitude of the ICC (now undergoing substantial change, as reported in chapter 10) was aptly captured in a 1972 proceeding called *Motor Carrier Rates—Owner Operators*.[2] In this proceeding it was confirmed that, in justifying rate applications before the ICC, a carrier that relied predominantly on owner-operators was *not* required to present evidence that the payments to owner-operators (at a percentage of the applied-for rates) were adequate to cover the owner-operators' costs. The appropriate criteria for rate applications in such circumstances had been established in a 1962 proceeding[3] which permitted a carrier employing owner-operators to prove the "compensativeness" of rates by merely showing (1) that *its* retained revenue substantially exceeded its own costs, and (2) that the amount paid to the owner-operators was "sufficient to acquire and retain their services" (that is, that the carrier had owner-operators working for similar rate levels). As a district court later pointed out concerning the second of these criteria, "the assumption that an owner-operator will hire himself out to the carrier *only* if his earnings from his operations will exceed his costs or expenses . . . is patently questionable."[4] In past decades, therefore, there has been no pressure applied by the ICC upon carriers to know their owner-operators' costs *in detail*, and to justify their rates upon an intimate knowledge of the owner-operators' revenue requirements.

In large part, the absence of this pressure is readily understandable due to the extreme variability in owner-operators' cost experience. (Indeed, it was just this argument that led the ICC to the criteria described above.) As the American Trucking Associations, Inc., has commented, "owner-operator costs may be the most elusive of all costs within the motor carrier industry. One carrier has likened this elusiveness to trying to capture air . . . costs will vary, often to extremes, with each owner-operator, often without regard to revenues, commodities, or purposeful acts of the owner-operator."[5] The extreme variability of individual owner-operator cost experience was also demonstrated by Wyckoff and Maister,[6] who showed that individual per-mile costs could vary by over 250 percent depending upon a variety of factors such as miles operated per year, year and model of tractor, commodities hauled, and so forth.

Estimating Owner-Operator Costs

In spite of this variability, or perhaps because of it, it is extremely important for carriers to keep track of owner-operators' costs. As noted above, the need is twofold. First, the carrier requires some estimate of some average, or expected, cost (per mile or per ton-mile) so that it can perform its essential function of ensuring that rates are set at an adequate level to return a reasonable income to the owner-operator. Second, it needs to be able to identify those owner-operators who experience costs higher than these norms so that it can provide corrective advice and assistance.

Naturally, the former (average) costs are easier to obtain. One common method of estimating normal operating expenses is for the carrier to operate (and maintain) its own fleet of vehicles and use its own costs to estimate those of the owner-operator. This method must be employed with some caution, since owner-operator and carrier experience with certain expense items may not be similar. For example, the carrier may be able to make use of bulk fuel purchases, while the owner-operator is usually forced to purchase fuel from retail truckstops. Other evidence on differing carrier and owner-operator expenses is provided in a survey conducted by the Motor and Equipment Manufacturer's Association, some results of which are shown in tables 7-1 through 7-5. A second method is to reconstruct the owner operator's costs. Given relatively simple (and readily available) input data such as the average price of fuel, estimated miles per gallon, purchase price of vehicles, and so on, it is possible to construct a "pro-forma" operating statement for a typical owner-operator. A methodology for doing this was developed by Wyckoff and Maister,[7] to which the reader is referred. It is a relatively simple matter to adjust the formula used there and update the input values employed. (A brief description of Wyckoff and Maister's procedures is presented in appendix 7A.)

Finally, a detailed analysis of average truck operating cost data is published on an annual basis by the Hertz Truck Division. Hertz's annual analysis estimates costs to owners operating ten-vehicle fleets with an equal number of units one to five years old. In this way, inflationary or product improvement expenses can be calculated separately from rises resulting from vehicle age and mileage factors. The double effect of rising costs due to increase in vehicle age and inflation can be demonstrated by figures from the latest available report (published in 1979), which showed that a tractor-trailer bought new in 1974 had a first-year ownership and operating cost then of 32.5 cents per mile (*excluding* drivers' payment). By 1978, in the unit's fifth year of service, the outlay was 52.4 cents per mile, an increase of 62 percent. Further detail may be obtained from tables 7-6 and 7-7. These tables amply illustrate some of the carriers' problems in the estimation of

Table 7-1
Comparison of Frequency of Overhaul of Various Systems between Owner-Operators and Fleets, 1978
(percent)

Number of Overhauls over Vehicle Life	Fleets	Owner-Operators
Engine		
0	6.2	6.1
1	45.5	42.8
2	33.8	34.3
3	11.0	12.5
4	.7	2.4
5 or more	2.8	1.8
Cooling System		
0	6.3	14.9
1	32.6	41.6
2	25.7	21.9
3	16.7	9.8
4	7.6	5.7
5 or more	11.1	6.0
Clutch		
0	6.3	6.2
1	14.6	39.5
2	25.7	31.8
3	18.7	12.0
4	13.2	6.8
5 or more	21.5	3.7
Transmission		
0	18.3	18.8
1	50.0	49.7
2	18.3	22.5
3	4.2	5.3
4	4.2	2.8
5 or more	4.9	.9
Differential		
0	26.1	24.8
1	47.2	45.8
2	14.1	19.1
3	5.6	4.1
4	3.5	3.1
5 or more	3.5	3.1
Charging System		
0	4.9	4.7
1	6.3	20.7
2	15.3	19.1
3	18.7	19.4
4	19.4	15.7
5 or more	35.4	20.4

Table 7-1 continued

Number of Overhauls over Vehicle Life	Fleets	Owner-Operators
Cranking System		
0	4.2	6.2
1	15.4	26.2
2	12.6	29.0
3	19.6	17.1
4	15.4	10.0
5 or more	32.8	11.5

Source: "Survey Pinpoints Ways Trucking Firms, 0-0's Vary in Making Major Purchases," *Transport Topics*, May 14, 1979, p. 66. Study conducted by Motor and Equipment Manufacturer's Association. Reprinted with permission.

average truck operating costs, showing the crucial dependence of the average on the age of the equipment, the purchase price, the average rate of inflation. This poses an awkward problem for the carrier in its pricing activities: upon what assumptions about the equipment of the typical owner-operator should it base its judgments of adequate rate level? If a three-year-old vehicle is chosen, and rates are set to return an adequate income to such operators, what becomes of operators with older equipment? If they keep their five-year-old tractors they will incur higher maintenance costs than the average imbedded in the rates: if they trade in, they will incur higher ownership costs. Should the carrier aim for rates based on *replacement* costs? It should, of course, be noted that the carriers' ability to press for rate increases may, in any event, be severely limited. As noted in chapter 1, the sectors of the trucking industry characterized by high owner-operator use are among the most competitive. Few refrigerated or heavy haulers belong to tariff bureaus, petroleum haulers face a concentrated customer (shipper) base, and household-goods carriers' rates are carefully monitored by the ICC as being those most directly affecting the U.S. consumer (rather than indirectly through industrial shipping costs).

In spite of these problems, the discussion above illustrates the principle that with a small degree of effort, any carrier should be able to estimate the *expected* costs of operation for an individual owner-operator without specifically requesting such information from the individual. Virtually all carriers will know the age and model of its contractors' equipment; virtually all will know the monthly payments that each contractor faces on his or her equipment. From its own records, drivers' logs, and fuel tickets, it should know each individual's total mileage and loaded mileage. It is therefore well within the capabilities of most carriers to estimate relatively accurately the expected cost experience of any individual owner-operator. As noted in the previous chapter, some carriers have computerized this calculation so that it can predict the operator's cost per mile for any given trip.

Table 7-2
Comparison of Vehicle Life and Use between Owner-Operators and Fleets, 1978.
(percent)

	Fleets	*Owner-Operators*
How many miles per year is one of your heavy duty trucks driven?		
50,000 miles and less	43.3	27.6
50,000-59,999	1.2	1.4
60,000-69,999	7.3	11.9
70,000-79,999	7.9	13.8
80,000-89,999	11.0	14.7
90,000-99,999	6.7	8.5
Over 100,000	22.6	22.1
On the average, what is maximum vehicle life in years?		
5 or less	25.0	30.0
6	7.3	11.8
7	6.7	12.0
8	14.6	9.8
9	6.1	2.0
10	28.1	23.5
Over 10	12.2	10.9
On the average, what is maximum vehicle life in miles?		
200,000 miles or less	22.2	7.4
200-299,999	8.7	8.0
300-399,999	14.1	15.2
400-499,999	12.8	13.6
500-599,999	14.8	22.3
600-699,999	9.4	10.8
Over 700,000	18.1	22.6

Source: see table 7-1. Reprinted with permission.

Monitoring Cost Experience

In spite of the carriers' ability to estimate their contractors' expected operating costs, cost estimates are not cost experience. This is amply illustrated by the following carrier's comments:

In mid-1976, the company established a committee of five individuals from various mangerial positions within the company, to look into the matter of "contractor retention." While our contractor turnover over the years has been relatively small, we had noticed an increase at this time. This committee was established to determine what the causes were for contractor turnover and make appropriate recommendations to remedy this situation. Two basic areas were studied. The first was revenue and how to increase the contractor's portion of the revenue. Areas looked into were dead-head miles, total number of miles operated, commodity rates, areas of loading and unloading, net loading weights, length of time out-of-service, and any other items which were incidental to contractors' total revenue. The second area that was studied was the operating costs of the contractor. Areas that were included in this were the cost of the power equipment, cost of fuel, the cost of licensing, the cost of repairs, the age of the truck, the number of miles per gallon or the efficiency of the truck, the payments to any hired drivers, and the type of depreciation schedules available.

As a result of this study, we implemented several new programs, especially in regard to the new contractors' cash flow problems. However, one of the most notable results of this study was the wide variances in the earnings per mile of the contractors on the fleet of International Transport. Further investigation into this area also resulted in the determination that there was a wide variance in the operating costs of various owner-operators that were

Table 7-3

Frequency of "Specing" Components on New Trucks and Trailers *(percent)*

Component	Fleets	Owner-Operators
Air deflectors	34.4	7.8
Air filters	54.5	50.6
Batteries	69.5	44.2
Brakes	71.5	63.0
Bumpers	45.0	49.6
Cab type	90.1	95.9
Clutch	78.8	66.4
Drive axles	80.8	83.2
Engine	99.0	99.0
Engine heaters	50.3	63.3
Engine shutdown units	45.7	27.4
Frame rails	54.3	57.5
Front axle	87.4	88.7
Fuel tanks	86.1	92.5
Lights (clearance & signal)	50.3	44.5
Mirrors	54.3	52.7
Mufflers	29.1	32.3
Oil filters	49.0	54.4
Radiators	43.0	48.6
Rear suspension	92.7	97.6
Temperature sensing units	43.7	52.4
Thermostatically controlled fan	70.2	53.1
Tires	88.7	91.4
U-joints	47.0	36.6
Wheels	73.5	74.0
Wheel/axle bearings	21.1	20.9
Windshield wiper motors	25.2	11.6
Wiring	20.5	15.7

Source: see table 7-1. Reprinted with permission.

Table 7-4
Frequency of Brand Specification in Replacement-Product Selection
(percent)

	Fleets	Owner-Operators
Air brake components	71.6	43.6
Air filters	74.8	63.6
Alternators & other electrical units	74.8	55.4
Axle/wheel bearings	53.8	35.6
Batteries	78.0	56.2
Bulbs (sealed beam & miniature)	35.7	22.5
Clutches	68.2	47.8
Friction material/brake blocks	52.6	37.9
Lights (clearance & signal)	61.2	38.1
Mirrors	46.7	21.0
Mufflers	39.6	38.9
Oil filters	76.9	70.5
Safety products (triangles & extinguishers, etc.)	37.3	12.1
Tires	83.1	78.6
Tools	49.6	54.6
U-joints	65.5	42.8
V belts/hoses	59.2	38.6
Wheels	59.3	42.1
Wiper blades/arms	44.0	19.9

Source: see table 7-1. Reprinted with permission.

studied. We noted that rate variance in revenue per mile to the contractor was directly related to their ability to maximize the total utilization of their trailer. Many contractors would look for LTL freight, spend the time to fit it into their loads, while others would not. In dealing with the contractor's operating costs per mile, we noticed that many, many items created the variance here. The first being the total mileage that the contractor operated during the year. Generally, the more miles the contractor could operate, the more he would reduce his fixed operating cost per mile. Then we found that there was a great variance in what a contractor felt he needed when purchasing his tractor. While some contractors could purchase a tractor in the $40,000 range, we found others buying a true luxury tractor in the $50,000-$60,000 range. We found that some stressed fuel economy when ordering their tractor and could average between 5 and 6 miles per gallon, while others stressed simply horsepower and theirs would average at best 4 miles to the gallon. There were many other items which helped to create this vast variance in operating costs per mile. A few of them which we could not accurately place cost factor on, were extended length of time out-of-service, excessive dead-head, excessive miles out of the way to get through home. Some contractors seem to feel justified in driving as much as 500 miles out of the way to get through home, where others will only go through home when it is at a reasonable cost to them.

Table 7-5
Comparison of Maintenance Services Used by Owner-Operators and Fleets, 1977-78
(percent)

	Fleets		Owner-Operators	
	1977	*1978*	*1977*	*1978*
Fleet specialist	19.7	15.3	8.4	13.7
Truck dealer	48.8	59.7	51.2	50.0
Truck stop	11.1	6.5	9.02	6.0
General repair shop	20.4	18.5	31.4	30.0

Source: see table 7-1. Reprinted with permission.

In the final analysis, we felt that a great deal of the variances were attributed to the individual contractor's business judgement. It was very hard for us to judge what was true operating costs and what should be considered personal costs of the contractor in his exercising his independence. While we were losing some contractors, we found that many contractors were adding additional equipment to the fleet, while many others decided to stay at one truck and operate it themselves, they were upgrading their equipment constantly. While we note that many owner-operators complain they are losing money, we see many contractors purchasing additional equipment and growing within our company.[8]

Few carriers are able to obtain their owner-operators' actual cost experience on a regular basis. However, it is possible to do so. One carrier has established a tradition of suggesting that each of its contractors incorporate themselves and have their accounts kept by a local firm that specializes in owner-operator record-keeping. By agreement with the contractors, the carrier has access to their accounts, and thus a detailed knowledge of every individual's financial position on an ongoing basis. The advantages of this system accrue not only to the carrier. By means of the accounting firm, the carrier ensures that the owner-operator keeps accurate records, makes provision for emergency repairs (a failure to so do being a prime cause of owner-operator bankruptcy), and generally conducts affairs in a business-like manner. By tracking the contractor's maintenance records, the carrier is able to recommend a preventive maintenance program, thus saving the contractor time and money in the form of avoided downtime costs.

Even without such access to owner-operators' individual accounts, it is possible for any carrier to keep a reasonably close watch on the relative profitability of each of its contractors. Many carriers, on a routine basis, will assemble a report which shows the total miles traveled and revenue earned by each of its contractors in the previous month. Because of its knowledge of average operating costs, the carrier is able to identify any individual that clearly earned insufficient revenue or performed an insufficient number of loaded miles per week. Having so identified the problem

Table 7-6
Estimates of 1974-78 Operating Costs for a Tractor-Trailer Purchased in 1974

Vehicle Use-Year	Tractor-Trailer @ 100,000 Miles a Year					Five-Year Average
	First	Second	Third	Fourth	Fifth	
Vehicle Cost-Year	1974	1975	1976	1977	1978	
Vehicle Purchase-Year	1974	1974	1974	1974	1974	
Depreciation	.0738	.0738	.0738	.0738	.0738	.0738
Interest	.0293	.0245	.0246	.0269	.0278	.0264
Licenses, taxes	.0120	.0121	.0121	.0123	.0140	.0125
Insurance	.0167	.0168	.0238	.0382	.0493	.0290
Garaging	.0050	.0053	.0056	.0060	.0064	.0057
Administrative	.0188	.0199	.0219	.0242	.0265	.0223
Fixed cost subtotal	.1546	.1524	.1618	.1814	.1978	.1697
Maintenance	.0247	.0442	.0969	.0819	.1312	.0758
Washes, repainting	.0030	.0032	.0065	.0037	.0039	.0041
Tires, tubes	.0158	.0290	.0304	.0326	.0345	.0285
Grease, oil	.0040	.0042	.0044	.0052	.0057	.0047
Fuel	.1225	.1250	.1289	.1378	.1513	.1331
Variable cost subtotal	.1700	.2056	.2671	.2613	.3266	.2462
Fixed & Variable Total						
Cents per mile	.3246	.3580	.4289	.4427	.5244	.4159
Dollars per year	32460	35800	42890	44270	52440	41590
5-year dollar total						207,950

Source: Hertz Trucking Division. Reprinted with permission.

Note: figures reflect "real-time" costs in each category, and in the overall totals as well, for fleets purchased in 1974 and run through 1978. Note that depreciation (at 7.38¢ on tires and tubes, for example) for all years reflects 1974 price but the 2.78¢ interest in 1978 reflects interest at 1978 rates but on the amount required in 1974 for the truck purchased then.

contractors, the carrier is able to make special efforts to discover the particular problems faced by such contractors. Some large carriers have instituted the practice of calling in the bottom ten (or so) performers each month for special consultations. (One carrier I observed made it a practice to terminate the contracts of those individuals that had the lowest total mileage each year!)

Owner-Operator Counselors

Other carriers have taken this practice one step further by the institution of formal counseling departments (referred to in chapter 5). As with many other developments in the management of owner-operators, the development of the concept of owner-operator counselors has primarily taken place among household-goods carriers.[9] (It should perhaps be said that this is not necessarily due to either virtue or wisdom on the part of such carriers, but

Table 7-7
Estimates of 1978 Operating Costs for One- to Five-Year Old Tractor-Trailers

| | Tractor-Trailer @ 100,000 Miles a Year | | | | | |
Vehicle Use-Year	First	Second	Third	Fourth	Fifth	Five-Year Average Cost
Vehicle Cost-Year	1978	1978	1978	1978	1978	
Vehicle Purchase-Year	1978	1977	1976	1975	1974	
Depreciation	.1129	.0922	.0847	.0853	.0738	.0898
Interest	.0425	.0347	.0319	.0321	.0278	.0338
Licenses, taxes	.0140	.0140	.0140	.0140	.0140	.0140
Insurance	.0493	.0493	.0493	.0493	.0493	.0493
Garaging	.0064	.0064	.0064	.0064	.0064	.0064
Administrative	.0265	.0265	.0265	.0265	.0265	.0265
Fixed cost subtotal	.2516	.2231	.2128	.2136	.1978	.2198
Maintenance	.0319	.0546	.1137	.0933	.1312	.0849
Washes, repainting	.0039	.0039	.0075	.0039	.0039	.0046
Tires, tubes	.0197	.0345	.0345	.0345	.0345	.0315
Grease, oil	.0057	.0057	.0057	.0057	.0057	.0057
Fuel	.1513	.1513	.1513	.1513	.1513	.1513
Variable costs subtotal	.2125	.2500	.3127	.2887	.3266	.2780
Fixed & Variable Total						
Cents per mile	.4641	.4731	.5255	.5023	.5244	.4978
Dollars per year	46410	47310	52550	50230	52440	49,780
5-year dollar total						248,900

Source: Hertz Truck Division. Reprinted with permission.

rather to the volume of their owner-operator needs and the complex nature of their business.) The essence of the counselor system is the establishment of a group whose sole responsibility is monitoring the financial well-being of the owner-operators in the fleet and offering advice to them concerning various aspects of the *business* of being an owner-operator.

This task is accomplished by a regular review of each owner-operator's financial performance, and by regular telephone calls between the counselor and the owner-operator. At one major household-goods carrier, a distinction is made between new owner-operators (that is, those who are relatively inexperienced) and those who have been with the company for some time. Some counselors are dedicated to dealing solely with new drivers (typically being responsible for sixty to seventy-five drivers each), and will speak to the owner-operator two or three times per week. The conversations will range from those in which the counselors are solely *reactive* ("Do you have any problems I can help you with?") to those where they are *proactive* ("Have you called your wife this week?" "Have you sent money home?"). This system can be very paternal in instructing owner-operators how to manage their finances, and, taken to its extreme, somewhat demeaning ("You're short of cash? Well, how many steak dinners have you been eating? You can't afford to stay at the Sheraton, you know!"). However, in principle, the counselor system is potentially a very important management tool in managing owner-operators, since one of the most commonly reported sources of owner-operator failure is poor cash management. By providing ongoing business advice to the owner-operator, the carrier is indeed playing an important role in justifying the owner-operator system (see chapter 2 for the discussion of similar activities in franchising operations in other industries). As we have seen, the new owner-operator is always at some disadvantage in needing to learn the tricks of the business, and the counselor system is a means of overcoming this. For experienced owner-operators, the typical counselor will deal with 150 to 175 drivers, and serve only as a troubleshooter rather than as a source of managerial advice.

Some carriers have experimented with the use of ex-owner-operators as driver counselors. This practice matches with similar experiments made in the franchising field, as reported by Emmons.[10] As he notes, such field supervisors (often described as the key element in any franchise control system) have the benefits of experience in the franchisee's (or owner-operator's) business and are thus more likely to be sympathetic to field problems, and more likely to be respected and have their advice needed. Unfortunately there are two problems with this practice. First, the counselors may be *too* sympathetic and fail to perform their function adequately. Second, the best counselors are usually from the ranks of the most successful operators, and they are making too much money to want to be counselors!

Among larger carriers it is often the counselor who must take what might be considered to be the hardest decisions in the field of owner-operator management: the decision on whether to advance a substantial sum of money to help out an owner-operator with insufficient cash to pay for an unexpected major repair. In such circumstances, the owner-operator's livelihood is often in the balance: if the loan is not forthcoming, bankruptcy may result. When making these decisions, the counselor (or, in smaller firms the owner or general manager) must play the role of venture capitalist: deciding whether or not to bet on the man or woman. The decision is not a light one, since there are often significant risks that the individual may not recover from his or her bad debts.

It should be noted that it is not necessary to establish a separate department in order to provide the counseling function. In many small carriers, the dispatcher, the operations manager, or, in some cases, the general manager of the carrier will provide counseling advice, and will often do this more effectively because of a more personal relationship than is possible with a somewhat impersonal counseling department. Even in large companies, the separate establishment of a counseling group may be avoided because of this. It should also be noted that a system of independent driver counselors is an extra cost to the carrier and thus may be hard to cost-justify to top management. Counseling departments have also been avoided by some carriers because of potential threats to the owner-operator's independent contractor status.

Performance Reviews

So far in this chapter we have discussed information systems and control mechanisms necessary to assist owner-operators. The discussion has been an overview, in that many other specific techniques are available to carriers that give thought to how assistance may be provided. As a final example, we may note that one carrier interviewed checks *all* contractor trip reports and drivers' logs in order to track down excess mileage, that is, to see whether the contractor took the most direct route between pickup and delivery. The carrier views this exercise both as a means of identifying inexperienced drivers and thus providing assistance, and as a means of quality control to identify problem drivers who fail to provide the fastest service possible. As this last example illustrates, the carriers' information system must not only identify operators in need of assistance, but also those whose performance is not satisfactory.

Driver performance reviews may take in a number of variables. An example of one system for judging the contractor is shown in appendix 7B, which gives a questionnaire used by one carrier. Such a report is completed on a periodic basis by the dispatchers. Many other carriers achieve the same result by more or less formal methods: in some circumstances, accurate records are kept of all refused loads, delayed pickup and deliveries, and so on. As in so much else concerning owner-operator management, other carriers avoid committing such facts and judgments to paper for fear of threatening the independent contractor status. Control must also be exercised over the owner-operator's safety performance. Most carriers require periodic safety inspections of contractor's equipment: one carrier has all owner-operator settlements (that is, regular payments) hand-delivered to its contractors by the safety director, so that no question concerning safety is left unresolved before payment is made! (There may be some question of the legality of this practice in the light of the 1979 revision of ICC leasing rules.) The extreme importance carriers place on safety is not just public-spiritedness: many have insurance contracts that are experience-rated, and a single accident can significantly affect a carrier's premiums.

Summary

Mockler and Easop have observed that "closer supervision is really the only solution to the problems arising from the lack of direct employee control in franchising."[11] This chapter has attempted to show how supervision and the appropriate use of information systems can assist not only in achieving control of operations, but also in bringing the full benefits of *association* to the owner-operator. Rosenberg and Bedell offer the opinion that the true keys to success in franchising are centralized control, effective franchisor-franchisee communications, and long-range planning.[12] For all of these, a well-designed information system is essential. Unfortunately, as has commonly been observed, the line between service and control in this area is a thin one. Carriers are thus faced with the challenge of winning the cooperation of their owner-operators so that the full benefits of effective communications may be realized. The task is difficult, but the experience of the franchising industries suggests that the effort is worthwhile.

Appendix 7A
Estimation of Average
Owner-Operator Costs

In *The Owner-Operator: Independent Trucker*, Wyckoff and Maister identify nine components of an owner-operator's expenses:

1. Tractor depreciation (T)
2. Trailer depreciation (where the owner-operator owns the trailer) (TR)
3. Finance charges (F)
4. Insurance (I)
5. Licenses and permits (L)
6. Drivers' payment (D)
7. Fuel (FU)
8. Maintenance (M)
9. On-the-road living expenses (OTR).

Of these nine categories, the first six may be viewed as "fixed charges," independent of the number of miles traveled or tons transported. Fuel, maintenance, and on-the-road expenses may all be taken as varying directly with the number of miles traveled (empty and loaded).

Total, *annual* owner-operator costs may therefore be expressed by the formula

$$\text{Total annual costs} = [T + TR + F + I + L + D] + [FU + M + OTR] \times P$$

where

$$P = \text{number of miles traveled per year.}$$

Tractor depreciation, trailer depreciation, and finance charges are relatively simple to estimate on an annual basis by assuming certain purchase prices, depreciation lives, and effective interest rates. Annual insurance and licensing cost data should be easily available to the carrier. Drivers' payment is, of course, residual, the amount left over from the owner-operator's revenues after all expenses are paid. However, for rate-setting and estimation purposes it is possible to attribute a reasonable figure that represents the amount of residual necessary to keep the owner-operator in business (or, rather, to ensure an adequate supply of new entrants). One method of setting this figure is to take it at some percentage (say, 85 percent) of a Teamster's average earnings, recognizing the owner-operator's price of independence. Fuel and maintenance expenses per mile are readily available from industry sources, and on-the-road expenses, while difficult to estimate accurately, can be obtained from average meal prices and hotel costs.

Having estimated total annual costs, it is possible to estimate average costs per mile by dividing the total by annual miles traveled. To estimate required revenue per mile, one may divide total annual costs by annual *loaded* miles, or simply divide average costs per total miles by the percentage of miles that are loaded. This is expressed by the formula

Required revenue per mile = average cost per mile ÷ percent loaded miles

$$= \frac{\text{total annual costs}}{\text{total miles}} \div \frac{\text{total loaded miles}}{\text{total miles}}$$

Of the factors discussed above, the major determinants of an individual owner-operator's required revenue per mile (and hence the crucial assumptions to be made) are (1) purchase price and finance charges of vehicle; (2) driver's payment; (3) total miles traveled; and (4) percent of miles loaded.

Omitted from the above calculations are some owner-operator expenses that may need recognition: these include medical and life insurance, pension contributions, workman's compensation expenses, social security contributions, and so on. However, these may be considered or included in "drivers' payment."

Appendix 7B
Owner-Operator
Control Questionnaire

Driver   Code #   Date

1. What is this driver's call-in record?

   Calls in all the time
   Calls most of the time
   Calls infrequently
   Never calls

2. Does this driver have a cooperative attitude?

   Yes_____No_____

3. When circumstances allow, is this driver reliable in meeting his preferred arrival dates?

   Always
   Most of the time
   Seldom

4. When circumstances allow, is this driver reliable in meeting his pick-up dates?

   Always
   Most of the time
   Seldom

5. Would you consider this driver dependable?

   Yes_____No_____

6. How frequently does this driver accept his assignment?

   All of the time
   Most of the time
   Seldom

7. Would you select this driver to handle a key assignment?

   Yes_____No_____

8. Overall, how would you rate this driver?

   Excellent
   Good
   Fair
   Poor

8 Independent Contractors, Employees, and Unions

In *The Owner-Operator: Independent Trucker*, Wyckoff and I presented a discussion of the legal status of the owner-operator as an employee or independent contractor. We concluded that "the resolution of the problem of the owner-operator's exact status is not a simple one."[1] That (understated) conclusion remains valid today. However, there are a number of reasons for examining this topic once more. First, there has been (and continues to be) sufficient activity in this area in the past five years that additional evidence is available on precisely what conditions and practices appear to influence the determination of legal status. Second, no book on management of owner-operators can afford to give anything but the highest priority to this topic. If the stress given in previous chapters on the role of labor cost in leading carriers to choose the owner-operator method of operation is correct, then the future growth of system will be predominantly influenced by the issues addressed in this chapter.

The Legal Basis

The historical basis for distinguishing in law between employees and independent contractors derives from the common law of agency, which grew up around attempts to determine when an individual was or was not acting as an agent of some other individual or company. The legal significance of the distinction was (and is) that a person is legally responsible for the acts (legally, the torts) of his or her employees but not for those of any independent contractors he or she hires.

The modern *Restatement of the Law of Agency* contains the following language:

> While an employee acts under the direction and control of the employer, an independent contractor contracts to produce a certain result and has full control over the means and methods which he shall use in producing the result. He is usually said to carry on an independent business.[2]

It may be seen that the *central* criterion employed is the power to control the *means* (or method) of production (rather than the end result). However, behind this simple sentence lies a wealth of confusion concerning what specific tests should be aplied to determine the degree of control of means that might exist in an individual situation.

133

The *Restatement of the Law of Agency* provides ten criteria by which such a situation is to be judged:

(a) the extent of control which, by the agreement, the master may exercise over the details of the work;

(b) whether or not the one employed is engaged in a distinct occupation or business;

(c) the kind of occupation with reference to whether, in the locality, the work is usually done under the direction of the employer or by a specialist without supervision;

(d) the skill required in the particular company;

(e) whether the employer or the workman supplies the instrumentalities, tools, and the place of work for the person doing the work;

(f) the length of time for which the person is employed;

(g) the method of payment, whether by the time or by the job;

(h) whether or not the work is a part of the regular business of the employer;

(i) whether or not the parties believe they are creating the relation of master and servant; and

(j) whether the principal is or is not in business.[3]

As may be clearly seen, these criteria continue to be quite vague, covering a multitude of possible situations. This, in itself, is not surprising, since the question of independent contractor status may arise in a wide variety of different industries, including, it appears, the case of go-go dancers working in neighborhood pubs![4]

While the law of agency is the foundation of the legal distinction between employees and independent contractors, it does not stand alone. The employer-employee status has implications not only for the law of torts, but also for determining the rights of employees to protection under the National Labor Relations Act, the freedom to bargain collectively under the Taft-Hartley Act, the responsibilities of the employer to the Internal Revenue Service and to state workers' compensation boards, and many other matters. Accordingly, one of the early (and important) cases on this issue concerned the applicability of the law of agency, and, more importantly, who was to apply it.

The National Labor Relations Board

In 1944 (in *NLRB* v. *Hearst Publications*)[5], the U.S. Supreme Court ruled that Congress had given to the National Labor Relations Board the right to determine whether workers were employees or independent contractors for the purposes of matters relative to the National Labor Relations Act. The court judged that the standard expressed in the law of agency did not provide a simple, uniform, and easily applicable test and did not constitute a technical legal classification. Instead, the application of the test was to be performed by the NLRB and not the court. " . . . In reviewing the Board's ultimate conclusions, it is not the court's function to substitute its own in inference of fact for the Board's, when the latter [has] support in the record."[6] The significance of this decision lies in the great power it places in the hands of the NLRB, since, in effect, it significantly limits judicial review of board decisions. It should be noted that this view has not been unchallenged. In a 1968 case, the Supreme Court acknowledged that " . . . there is no doubt that we should apply the common-law agency test,"[7] although yet another decision indicated that the approach of the 1944 decision was not totally discredited.[8]

In the application of common law tests to owner-operators in the trucking industry, a complicating factor is introduced. This is the fact that ICC and Department of Transportation regulations *require* the motor carrier to exercise a significant degree of control over the owner-operator's *means* of operation. For example, driving logs must be completed and returned to the carrier. In its decisions, the NLRB has tended to resolve this problem by ruling that carrier controls mandated by the ICC, DOT, or state regulations do not play an important role in the determination of employee/contractor status.[9]

Such was not always the case. Aitken claims that "the Board found that owner-operators were employees in nearly every case it considered during the 1960's. To a great extent, the Board relied upon the control that the carrier is required to exert by reason of the Rules and Regulations of the Interstate Commerce Commission and the Motor Carrier Safety Regulations of the Department of Transportation."[10] In particular he cites the 1971 *Deaton* case, where, in a strong dissent, then NLRB Chairman Miller noted that virtually all of the carrier's controls were required by the ICC, and argued, "In any given case, therefore, it becomes necessary to examine beyond this point and to explore and analyze what degree of control is retained and exercised beyond that required by the law of transportation."[11] In spite of this dissent, the majority ruled that an employee condition existed.

It should be noted that in many of the recent decisions turning on this matter, the board has been divided. In *George Transfer*, two board members (in dissent) declare, "George, and George alone, not the individual driver or owner of leased equipment is legally and operationally responsible for the critical means whereby freight entrusted to George is moved from shipper to consignee. . . . It is irrelevant, in our view, that some of the rules enforced by George emanate from the Interstate Commerce Commission, the Department of Transportation, or other government agencies. For, surely, as the record shows, the drivers controlled by George are not under the aegis of those agencies but under the complete and operative authority of George."[12] This reasoning, as Harter[13] points out, would seem to imply that all trucking owner-operators leased to carriers must be declared employees because of the carrier's ICC-mandated "exclusive possession, *control* and use of the equipment."

However, as Harter further points out, the two board members "have not followed through with this reasoning. Instead they have joined the majority in pointing to specific practices and conditions to show that the carriers exercised enough control over operations to be considered employers and the owner-operators to be considered employees. They have joined their colleagues in pointing to indica which might lead either to an independent contractor status or to an employee status and then striking a balance. Each of the indica is considered but no individual one is controlling."[14]

This task of "striking a balance" among many indica (some of which are given in appendix 8A) must, of necessity, lead to ill-defined criteria. Chief Judge Bazelon summed up the situation well: " . . . I find myself in a maze of precedents with few standards for decision discernible. . . . How great a degree of control must exist, how that control is to be quantified, and how various incidents of control are to be weighed comparatively are questions left unanswered by Congress and the Board in its various efforts in this area."[15]

Judge Bazelon's remarks were made in the context of two 1974 decisions by the NLRB that have been widely discussed. In *Molloy Brothers Moving and Storage, Inc.*,[16] the board ruled that owner-operators under lease to Molloy, a household-goods carrier, were employees. In *Santini Brothers, Inc.*,[17] a case decided only one day previously, the board ruled that the owner-operators working for Santini Brothers, also a households-goods carrier, were independent contractors. The *Santini* decision was appealed by Local 814 of the IBT,[18] and remanded for reconsideration by the board because of the seeming similarity of the conditions at Molloy and Santini. The board argued that it had reached opposite conclusions at the two carriers because of the following conditions.[19] First, Molloy's training program for its owner-operators was compulsory, while Santini only "offered" a training program. Molloy, in an attempt to control its contractors, used "discipline" for infraction of the carrier's (non-government-mandated) rules, while Santini did not. Molloy Brothers paid for their owner-operators' health insurance while the owner-operators working for Santini paid for their own. Molloy paid trip advances (and "bore the risk of default by a customer") while Santini did not. Molloy's owner-operators participated in a profit-sharing plan and had access to loans from Molloy for a variety of purposes. Also of relevance was the fact that Santini had its own operating authority from the ICC, while Molloy did not. (See criterion j in the *Restatement of the Law of Agency* given above.)

As is so often the case, the board's decision on *Santini Brothers* was not unanimous. The dissenting members argued even though Santini did not impose the controls used by Molloy, Santini's owner-operators were still substantially controlled by the carrier. Of great importance to the dissenting members of the board was the "lack of opportunities" for making entrepreneurial decisions. They felt that the owner-operators' expenses were too uniform to be substantially controlled (!), and that their earnings were controlled almost entirely by Santini.

The real significance of the *Molloy* and *Santini* decisions lies in consideration of the factors cited above that the NLRB used to distinguish the two situations. As may be seen, many of the indicators used by the board to find an employee status at Molloy correspond to the elements of good management discussed elsewhere in this book. Molloy was very active in training its owner-operators. It paid for their health insurance. It helped them with loans and offered a profit-sharing plan. Rather than *control* (a word with overtones of discipline and an adversary relationship), it would appear from the record that Molloy was very *supportive* of its owner-operators, assisting them in many ways. This perspective suggests an important and inherent conflict in carrier/owner-operator relationships. If, as we have argued, the secret of success in running a franchiselike owner-operator system is helping your franchisees succeed in spite of themselves, many (if not most) actions that a carrier could take toward this goal will only serve to increase the likelihood that as employee status will be found, thus removing what has been, until now, a major (if not predominant) reason for using owner-operators in the first place!

It is not clear whether there can be any resolution of this catch-22. To some extent, certain procedures are available. In the first place, carriers will need, as much as possible, to make their various forms of assistance to owner-operators optional rather than compulsory, although this fine line will still be subject to the interpretations of individual NLRB members. Second, some carriers may wish to adopt a practice employed by one (very successful) carrier that suggests its operators incorporate themselves. The carrier then enters into a contract with the corporation and not the individual. In such a circumstance, the chances of an employee relationship being found are lessened. This procedure can have many other benefits, in that the act of incorporation may, in and of itself, help promote a more businesslike attitude on the part of the owner-operator. It is also possible for a carrier to establish separate subsidiaries to provide selected services (such as purchased supplies, accounting and record-keeping, and maintenance), thus assisting the owner-operator without establishing too strong a bond between the carrier's business and the owner-operator's. Naturally, any such services should be only optional.

However, in spite of the availability of such tactics, there remains a central problem due to the interpretative powers of the NLRB. For example, even though most carriers are careful to avoid forced dispatch, giving their owner-operators the right to refuse loads, some NLRB members have expressed the opinion that this right is illusory since if the owner-operator exercises it too frequently, his or her contract will be terminated. This argument could be used to find an employee status.

The paradox presented to carriers in establishing the appropriate forms and degrees of control and assistance for its owner-operators derives in large part from a paradox within the NLRB. As the *Hearst* case showed, the resolution of the employee/independent contractor situation is not (or should not be) a technical legal distinction, but one that reflects the remedial intents of the National Labor Relations Act. As such, it would appear that an important distinction could and should be made between carrier practices designed to increase control and those designed to *assist* the owner-operator. As the evidence of the *Molloy* case shows, the board does not currently make this distinction. It would also appear that the board is failing in its responsibilities to establish (or, at least, *evolve*) a more readily understandable and reliable set of criteria for the resolution of the owner-operator status. With over 4,000 carriers using this method of operation, there have been and will continue to be numerous such cases before the board, and such a volume would seem to warrant the effort of special attention. This is particularly true since the relevance of the carrier's responsibilities to the shipping public, the ICC, and the DOT still constitutes ambiguous areas.

It is only with slight exaggeration that one could make the observation that the trucking industry as a whole might be better off if *all* owner-operators were ruled employees than to continue the current uncertainty. While there would be, inevitably, a substantial reduction in the total number of owner-operators employed, the core of the system would remain. Carriers could then proceed to improve their owner-operator management systems without the constant fear that they would suddenly become subject to the substantial competitive disadvantage of having *their* owner-operators ruled employees while their competitors continued to enjoy the benefits of an independent contractor status. In the interim, however, carriers should adopt the (wise) practice used by one major van line that makes *no* change in any aspect of its dealings with owner-operators without first checking with its lawyers.

The Internal Revenue Service

The NLRB is not the only body with jurisdiction over the legal status of owner-operators. While an NLRB decision will influence the rights of the owner-operators to bargain collectively, and the rights of the International Brotherhood of Teamsters to represent them (a distinction, it should be noted, that is not an idle one), collective bargaining is not the only reason why carriers wish to avoid employee status. Employee status will also influence various payroll taxes, such as Social Security, workers' compensation, and various IRS-mandated withholding taxes. For each possible consequence, a separate body of law is relevant, since decisions, in line with the *Hearst* ruling, are meant to reflect the specific remedial purposes of the applicable legislation and not only the common law of agency. For example, the famous *Harrison* v. *Greyvans, Inc.*,[20] case in 1947 was resolved by the courts within the context of the Social Security Act. Other (nontrucking) cases have involved the Fair Labor Standards Act[21] and the Occupational Safety and Health Act.[22] However, the two most important jurisdictions apart from the NLRB are the IRS and the worker's compensation boards of each state.

The guidelines used by the Internal Revenue Service to determine the tax status of independent contractors were developed in 1973 as a consequence of the appeal of several cases to the National Office of the IRS by various carriers.[23] At stake was the tax liability of common carriers for the accruing Federal Insurance Contributions Act (FICA) taxes, the Federal Unemployment Tax Act (FUTA) taxes, and federal withholding taxes.

The guidelines used are shown in appendix 8B. It may be seen that they do not differ substantially in principle from the NLRB criteria, focusing primarily upon the financial independence of the owner-operators, their opportunity for profit or loss, and the degree of control exercised by the carrier.

Since these guidelines were issued, there has been much activity concerning the tax status of owner-operators. In 1976 the IRS issued Revenue Ruling 76-226,[24] which clarified the criteria shown in appendix 8B. In particular, it recognized that "the elements of control implemented as a response to government regulations binding on the trucking company are insufficient here to reach this result [that the owner-operators were employees]."

In 1977 the Joint Committee on Taxation of the U.S. Congress released a General Accounting Office study which examined the general question of tax treatment of employees and self-employed persons.[25] It noted the recurrent problems faced by the IRS in dealing with employee/contractor disputes in many industries. In particular it identified an important reason why many businesses were unhappy with the current law. Upon a finding of an employee status, an employer can be retroactively assessed employment taxes for the past three years. (Many motor carriers I interviewed cited this as one of their greatest fears in relation to employee/contractor disputes in spite of the fact that in 1978 Congress wiped out most of the potential tax liabilities from previous years.) The report also presented twenty rules that the IRS had adopted to guide it in reaching decisions (appendix 8C).

The GAO recommended that Congress should amend section 3121 of the Internal Revenue Code to exclude separate business entities from the common law definition of employee in those instances where they (1) have a separate set of books and records which reflect items of income and expenses of the trade or business; (2) have the risk of suffering a loss and opportunity of making a profit; (3) have a principal place of business other than at a place of business furnished by the persons for whom he or she performs or furnishes services; and (4) hold themselves out in their own name as self-employed and/or make their services generally available to the public.[26] It further recommended that if an independent contractor could not meet at least three of these criteria, then he or she should be considered an employee. In the owner-operator field, it should not be difficult to meet criterion 1, although owner-operators are reputedly poor at keeping formal books. Criterion 2 should be easily satisfied, while 3 could be problematical, since it is difficult to determine an itinerant trucker's place of business. Criterion 4 could *not* be met if it refers to a single instant in time, since ICC regulations require "exclusive possession and control" of the equipment.

The Treasury and the IRS objected to the GAO's recommendations on the grounds that the change in the law would probably increase the number of self-employed taxpayers and result in lost tax revenues, since self-employed taxpayers are reputed to have a low compliance rate in reporting income earned. (This reputation is not without foundation: I have met owner-operators who cite this as one of the benefits of being an independent contractor. The same is often said of trip-lease revenues.)

This concern surfaced again in 1979 when the Treasury Department asked Congress to require withholding by companies for their workers who were independent contractors. Officials claimed that almost half of all independent contractors (in all industries) were failing to pay federal income taxes, and close to two-thirds were not paying Social Security taxes.[27] However, in hearings before the House Ways and Means Subcommittee, nineteen industry groups (including the American Trucking Associations, Inc.) opposed this measure (and disputed the statistics), while only the IRS and the AFL-CIO supported it.[28] Instead, most groups (including the ATA) supported a new bill proposed by Rep. Richard Gephardt (D-Mo.) which would establish more definite standards for determining who gets independent contractor status. In particular, the Gephardt bill would require independent contractors to meet all of five criteria: (1) the individual must control the total number of hours scheduled and worked; (2) the individual maintains a principal place of business; (3) the individual has a substantial investment in equipment; (4) the individual must perform a service according to a contract which shows employment tax responsibility; and (5) the person for whom service is performed must file information returns.[29] (It may be seen that these criteria are similar in spirit to those proposed by the GAO.) However, Duncan McRae, Jr., speaking for the ATA, expressed concern over whether independent truck drivers would be able to meet all of the tests. In November 1979, the House voted to block the administration's efforts to change the tax treatment of independent contractors, thus delaying any action on this matter.

Workers' Compensation Boards

The liability of a carrier for injury to a contractor driver under workers' compensation statutes is a matter adjudicated by the relevant boards and courts of each state. As Nevins writes, this area illustrates well how "the common law definition of an independent contractor has been altered by modern social legislation."[30] Generally, most courts rule that owner-operators *are* covered by the applicable workmen's compensation statutes, since apart from the right-to-control test, an additional test is applied to determine independent contractor status. This is the relative-nature-of-work-test.[31] If the workers' activities are *integral* to the employer's activities (as indeed they are in the case of trucking owner-operators) then the courts are inclined to rule that the workers are employees for the purposes of workers' compensation. A large number of citations to support this conclusion are provided by Corber.[32]

The International Brotherhood of Teamsters

In spite of tax, Social Security, and workers' compensation implications of the employee/contractor distinction, many carriers wish to preserve their owner-operators' independent contractor status largely "to keep out of the hands of the Teamsters." It is therefore appropriate to review briefly the (somewhat stormy) history of Teamster attitudes toward owner-operators and the carriers that use them.

It is not surprising that the underlying basis of Teamster attitudes toward owner-operators has, historically, been one of distrust and competition. Union leaders have tended to look upon owner-operators (quite appropriately) as substitutes for Teamster labor and have tried to limit the scope of their operations. However, beyond this basic antipathy, there have also been occasions when the Teamsters' actions have served (directly or indirectly) to improve the lot of at least some owner-operators. Dave Beck, a prominent IBT leader, applied great pressure in the 1920s to force Seattle employers to stop using owner-operators in the retail distribution trades such as the dairy, laundry, and bakery industries. He forced companies to guarantee their driver-salesmen a minimum income, thus inducing the companies to reduce the number of driver-salesmen capable of earning this guarantee. Prior to this, companies had been inclined to flood the market with driver-salesmen, especially when using owner-operators working on straight commission. It is a matter of debate as to whether this should be viewed as a pro- or anti- owner-operator action. On the one hand it forced a number of owner-operators out of business, while on the other, it probably improved the revenues of those that remained. In 1948, when the Interstate Commerce Commission first proposed regulations to control owner-operator leasing, the Teamsters were the principal (almost the sole) supporter of the Commission's proposals.

The union's attitudes as to whether it welcomes owner-operator members have varied over the years. Seidenberg writes, "The question of whether owner-operators should be eligible to join the Teamsters' union almost caused the young union in 1903 to founder, because locals, especially in the larger cities, maintained the drive toward higher wages and better conditions would never succeed if owner-operators were permitted to become union members. Gradually, over the years, owner-drivers were permitted to join, basically as a measure of self-preservation."[33] A number of court cases were necessary to determine whether the union could act for owner-operators.[34] In some cases, the union engaged in strong tactics to force owner-operators into the union, in order to mitigate their competitive threat.

However, as Garnel observed, "the problem of the owner-operator . . . was too acute to be solved by the relatively simple process of forcing him into the union. . . . Furthermore, they proved so unreliable as members that they were as much a menace inside the union as they were outside."[35] The reasons for this unreliability as members is easy to identify. An owner-operators' outlook is one of a small businessperson attempting to become a large businessperson. Owner-operators might have been organized through the use of coercion, but historically they have tended to revert to nonunion status as soon as the coercive pressure is removed. Owner-operators, in the drive to increase their revenues, work long hours, sleep on highways, grease and repair their own vehicles, none of which Teamster members wish (or have) to do. Most importantly, the owner-operators' loyalty in the event of a Teamster-led strike has proven transitory, as the owner-operators continued to run in order to make their monthly payments.

In spite of these problems, there are today many owner-operators in the Teamsters union: Frank Fitzsimmons estimates 20,000.[36] Certain Teamster jurisdictions are still largely characterized by owner-operators. These include the taxicab industry; log, agricultural, steel, and livestock hauling; and most furniture movers within the union. It is therefore of interest to examine how the Teamsters have acted with respect to owner-operators in their collective bargaining.

In 1939 Farrell Dobbs, who had established what was to become the Central States Drivers Council, had negotiated a single (two-year) contract for over 300 Chicago-based motor carriers. This contract marked the beginnings of area-wide collective agreements, on the way to what was to become, under James Hoffa's direction, a nationwide National Master Freight Agreement (NMFA), the first of which was concluded in 1964.

The 1939 agreement, which won a 9 percent wage increase for the drivers in each of its two years, also covered the areas's owner-operators, who were represented during the negotiations by the Chicago Independent Truck Drivers' Union. The issue of whether the owner-operators were employees or independent contractors was a factor in these negotiations, and there already existed a union distrust of carriers' use of owner-operators. Dobbs later wrote:

> Firms holding carrier rights issued by the government employed many of these independents, paying them flat rates by the mile, ton, or trip for the rig and driver. It was truly a cut-throat setup. Diverse methods were used to heap inordinate trucking costs upon the owner-operators, thereby shaving down their earnings as drivers. At the same time, devious patterns were woven to confuse the true nature of the employer-worker relationship and turn the individuals in an anti-union direction.[37]

Muldea, in his (overtly adversary) study of the Teamsters Union,[38] reports that "many carriers who had signed the CSDC agreement began to cheat their owner-drivers." He cites David Lipman, chairman of the Chicago Truck Owners and Operators Association:

> The International Brotherhood of Teamsters has sought . . . to correct [the problems of owner-operators] by placing employment responsibility where it rightfully belongs—on the shoulders of the operating company, which is now held responsible for the driver's wages, social security tax, compensation insurance, etc., regardless of whether he is employed by the operating company or through a small fleet owner.

> Not least in importance in the general problem is the driver who is given a paper title to the truck by the operating company, usually on a deferred payment plan, and is then paid as an individual owner-operator, not as a legitimate business relationship, but as subterfuge to escape the payment of the union wage scale.[39]

By the end of this first contract, Muldea reports, union attitudes toward owner-operators had changed.

> Although Dobbs pledged to continue helping the owner-operators, other Teamster leaders changed to a policy of refusing to "negotiate a profit for equipment," claiming that "owner-operators complicate the bargaining process." In other words, the IBT abandoned the owner-operators' interests.[40]

It should be noted that, under the National Labor Relations Act, it would have been (and is) unlawful for the Teamsters to attempt to negotiate a profit for equipment, since this is outside the scope of permissible collective bargaining agreements. However, Muldea quotes a Hoffa associate as saying, "After the war, Jimmy really turned against the owner-operators in that he didn't want anyone to be one. Everyone should work for a certified carrier and use his equipment. Of course, this made the owner-operators mad at the union and turned them against us."[41]

The owner-operator sections of the 1949 Central States Over-the-Road Agreement, which was negotiated by Hoffa, required that the owner-operator was to be an employee of the leasing carrier, and to have seniority as though he were a regular driver. Compensation for wages and working conditions were to be in "full accordance" with all provisions of the contract and separate checks for wages and equipment rental were to be issued by the carrier. The contract specifically required the leasing carrier to pay for any "road or mile tax, social security tax, compensation insurance, public liability, and property damage insurance, bridge tolls, fees for certificates, permits and travel orders, fines and penalties for inadequate certificates [and] license fees." It also required compensation to the owner-operators "for loss of driving time due to waiting at state lines, and also cargo insurance." It stipulated minimum rental rates to be paid for the leased equipment. All grievances were to be administered through the regular joint grievance procedure.

However, in spite of these protective provisions, the contract also acted to restrict the carrier's use of owner-operators. It provided that carriers were to use their own available equipment, plus all existing leased equipment before hiring any extra equipment at all. It prevented the engaging of any owner-operator who owned three or more pieces of equipment, although certain allowances were made for such operators as existed at the time of the agreement.

By 1957, these stipulations had been extended to many other over-the-road agreements, with the noticeable exceptions of the Western and Northeastern States. However, the union's right to negotiate these provisions was challenged by a group of Ohio-based carriers, and in 1955 the Ohio lower court ruled that the Central States' owner-operator articles were illegal, a decision upheld by the Ohio Supreme Court. Two main grounds were given: (1) it violated Ohio antitrust laws and (2) it represented "a remote and indirect approach to the subject of wages." The union appealed the decision to the U.S. Supreme Court, and in 1959 the Court ruled in the union's favor.[42] It argued first that the Ohio court did not have jurisdiction, since trucking was an interstate activity, and proceeded to disagree with the Ohio court on the issue of whether the union's owner-operator clauses were to be viewed as *wage*-related or attempts to fix prices on behalf of independent contractors. With this issue resolved, the owner-operator language was soon extended to virtually all IBT agreements.

As may be seen from appendix 8D, which shows the 1979-82 owner-operator clauses of the NMFA, the intent and language of these clauses has hardly changed from that described above for the 1949 Central States Contract. Teamster drivers (and other workers) in the trucking industry are covered generally by the NMFA, then more specifically by a variety of supplemental agreements or riders, particular to a geographical area or commodities hauled. With respect to owner-operators (as in many other matters) variations among these supplemental agreements are small.

In spite of the fact that the union has so many owner-operator members, there have been constant assertions that the union fails to represent adequately the interests of these members. In a report on the owner-operator sector, the ICC reported: "Of the two carriers [interviewed] who are parties to the Teamster's National Master Freight Agreement (N.M.F.A.), only one indicated that owner-operator grievances were represented by union officials." It also reported that none of the owner-operator association leaders it interviewed "believed that the owner-operator's interests were represented by the Teamsters: similarly, none believed that their members were active participants in union affairs."[43]

The Steel Industry

Relationships between the IBT and owner-operators have been particularly stormy in the steel industry, as was discussed in some detail in Wyckoff and Maister.[44] Since that book was written, there have been few improvements in this relationship, and indeed some decline. The steel haulers were particularly incensed about a "blunder" made in the IBT's 1976 contract covering them which, they claimed, led to a pay *cut* from previous levels. The key element which led to this result was a contract provision which called for a 7 percent increase in owner-operator earnings over 1975 level and additional 6 percent rises in 1977-78 and 1978-79. Unfortunately these raises were tied to the April 1976 rates for hauling steel, so that when rates on this traffic subsequently increased by more than 10 percent, the owner-operators were no longer receiving 75 percent of the revenues from these loads. Instead, they received 75 percent of the April 1976 rate plus the negotiated annual percentage increases. In effect, the owner-operators would not benefit from further ICC-approved rate increases.

In the winter of 1978-79, Bill Hill, president of the Fraternal Association of Steel Haulers, led a wildcat strike in the steel industry with the explicit objectives of seeking relief from these provisions and achieving decertification of the Teamsters on the bargaining unit for steel haulers.

However, when threatened with a prison sentence by a federal judge, Hill advised the steel haulers to return to work.[45] The unrest appeared to have some effect, since the 1979 Steel Rider to the National Master Freight Contract corrected the "blunder" in the previous contract and restored the 75 percent rule as the basis of payment for owner-operators in that sector. The 75 percent was broken down into the following categories: 26 percent for wages, 33 percent for the lease of the tractor, 13 percent for the trailer, and 3 percent for vacation, holiday, funeral leave, and sick leave. The contract also stipulated that the carrier would pay any additional cost for license plates over the base plate costs of the owner-drivers' state of residence, as well as receive payment for detention time after two hours (at $13.50/hour).[46]

To my knowledge, only in the steel industry are there union contracts negotiated by an owner-operator organization: the Fraternal Association of Special Haulers (FASH). This organization is not unrelated to the Fraternal Association of Steel Haulers. The FASH contract is interesting, since it potentially represents a guide to the ways in which an owner-operator union might differ in its goals from the Teamsters Union.

Like the Steel Rider of the NMFA, the FASH contract assures a union shop by requiring all employees to be members of the union and all owner-operators to be employees. Like the NMFA, FASH requires a copy of all lease agreements to be filed with the union. The FASH compensation package totals 74.5 percent: 39 percent for lease of the tractor, 10 percent for lease of the trailer, and 25.5 percent for the driver.[47] As may be seen, this differs from the Teamster-negotiated packages in its allocation. Anthony[48] reports that FASH believes their division reflects "operating realities," since many owner-operators do not own their own trailer and since the largest portion of equipment-operating costs are attributable to the tractor.

Both the NMFA and FASH agreements require carrier contributions to union health, welfare, and pension funds. Under both agreements the carrier is required to pay social security, unemployment compensation, workers compensation, as well as tolls, license and permit fees, state highway use taxes, state tax plates, and public liability and property damage insurance. Under the FASH agreement there is one seniority list for all drivers; under the NMFA a separate seniority list for owner-drivers and company drivers is kept. We may conclude from this brief review that few *significant* differences (as far as a carrier may be concerned) exist between the bargaining goals of Teamsters and owner-operator unions.

"Sweetheart" Contracts

In the course of my research, I heard reports of a substantial number of "sweetheart" contracts between carriers and the IBT involving the owner-operators. The most common form of such deals were that while all leased operators would be required to join the Teamsters Union, and thus contribute dues collected by the carrier and passed on to the union, the union would not attempt to represent those owner-operators in grievances with the carrier. In addition, or alternatively, the union would not interfere with the carriers relations with the owner-operators, allowing the carrier to impose (or negotiate directly with the owner-operators) any operating practices it wished. In some cases, it was reputed that restrictions on the use of the NFMA would not be enforced, thus allowing the carrier greater flexibility. From the reports that I heard, it would appear that such sweetheart agreements are strictly *local* affairs, agreed to by individual IBT locals, rather than a reflection of policy from higher up in the union's hierarchy. "As long as the local gets the dues," one carrier reported, " they leave use alone. Where those dues go, the Lord only knows."

In a letter to John Shenefield, assistant attorney general in the Anti-Trust Division of the Department of Justice, Frank Fitzsimmons responded to the charges that the union failed its owner-operators. Fitzsimmons repeated his judgment that "unless all owner-operators are considered employees of regulated carriers and allowed to bargain collectively, efforts to alleviate their economic problems will not be successful."[49] However, strains of IBT opposition to owner-operators showed through Fitzsimmons's reactions to the claim that owner-operators were more productive than employee drivers: "If owner-operators not represented by the Teamsters' Union drive 4,000 to 5,000 hours per year, as suggested by [a Justice report], of course they would have higher utilization of equipment than company drivers and Teamster owner-operators who obey the maximum hours of services and speed regulations of the DOT. It is a false measure of productivity or efficiency if one fails to consider and thereby seems to condone the true social costs of illegal speed and hours"[50]

Reacting to charges that the "owner-operators are denied effective access to union grievance procedures and that union benefits, especially pensions, are not available," Fitzsimmons pointed out that the Iron and Steel and Special Commodity Rider to the Central States Over-the-Road Supplement to the National Master Freight Agreement provided for a special committee to hear grievances. "Since the Rider covers operations which presently are predominantly performed by owner-operators," he wrote, "I can assure you that we process hundreds of grievances monthly for owner-operators. . . . As employees, Teamster-represented owner-operators receive the same group insurance and pension benefits as company drivers."[51]

Appendix 8A
Summary Checklist of Questions Relevant to the Determination of an Employer-Employee Relationship

Control over owner-operator's opportunity for profit

1. Does the lease agreement provide for exclusive use of the leased equipment by the lessee?
2. Is the owner-operator prohibited from soliciting business from other companies?
3. If the owner-operator may solicit other business, must the lessee first approve the transaction?
4. Does the lessee unilaterally determine the owner-operator's compensation and customer charges?
5. May the lessee unilaterally adjust shipping charges so as to cut an owner-operator's compensation after the trip has been completed?
6. Does the lessee hire the owner-operator's helpers, select the owner-operator's route or determine the owner-operator's hours of work?
7. Is the owner-operator prohibited from rejecting undesirable assignments?
8. Does the lessee pay for operation costs, maintenance costs, insurance, taxes, tolls, license fees, or registration fees?

Control exercised over the owner-operator's means of work

1. Does the lease agreement provide for the lessee's exclusive control and supervision of the use, operation, maintenance, or possession of the leased equipment?
2. Does the lessee control consignor-consignee customer relations?
3. Does the lease agreement provide for termination of the lease by either party upon a fixed number of days notice?
4. Does the lessee require that the owner-operator file an operator's log or maintenance reports?
5. May the lessee terminate the owner-operator's lease for failure to obey company regulations?
6. Does the lessee hire a safety service to make on-the-road safety checks?

Source: "Owner-operators; Employees or Independent Contractors," prepared by Robert H. Sayers, American Truckers Association, 1969. Reprinted with permission.

7. Does the lessee pay a bonus to owner-operators who meet the company's safety standards?
8. Does the lessee give the owner-operator cash advances to meet trip expenses and equipment payments?
9. Does the lessee's dispatcher make assignments, specify delivery destination or the type of commodity to be handled?
10. May the lessee discipline an owner-operator who refuses to take a load?
11. Is the date, time, and place of delivery of a shipment controlled by the bill of lading furnished by the lessee?
12. May the lessee veto the selection of a driver made by the owner-operator?
13. Does the lessee provide the owner-operator with a helper and pay his expenses?
14. Does the lessee unilaterally set rates for the owner-operator's backhauls when the lessee's trailer is used?
15. Does the lessee require backhual contracts to be made in the lessee's name?
16. Does the lessee prohibit the owner-operator from taking backhauls from competing companies?
17. Does the lessee provide employment application forms or medical forms for the owner-operator?
18. Does the lessee's mechanic inspect or repair the owner-operator's equipment?
19. Does the lessee determine the order of loading trailers?
20. Does the lessee sublease the leased equipment without the owner-operator's consent?
21. Does the lessee make charges on the owner-operator's account without his consent?

Intent of the parties

1. Does the lease agreement provide that the owner-operator is to be an employee rather than an independent contractor?
2. Does the lessee have a contract with a third party describing the lessee's relationship with the owner-operator as an employment relationship?
3. Does the lessee have a contract with a third party, the terms of which imply an employment relationship?

Nature of ownership

1. Does the lessee retain any legal interest in the leased equipment?
2. Does the lessee provide the owner-operator with any assistance, financial or otherwise, in obtaining the leased equipment?

3. Was the leased equipment purchased on a conditional sales contract from the lessee?

Miscellaneous

1. Is the lessee's name and certification number displayed on the leased equipment?
2. Does the lessee give the owner-operator a Christmas bonus?
3. Does the lessee furnish the owner-operator with work clothes bearing company insignia?
4. Does the lessee maintain fuel facilities for use by the owner-operator on a credit basis?
5. Does the lessee maintain a company parking lot which he requires the owner-operator to use?
6. Does the lessee provide bunkroom facilities, sheets, and a janitress?

Comparison with employer-employee relationship

1. Is the owner-operator paid on the same basis as the regular employees of the lessee?
2. Does the owner-operator perform the same tasks as regular employees?
3. Does the lessee pay the owner-operator's social security tax and withhold income taxes?
4. Does the lessee contribute towards unemployment compensation for the owner-operator?
5. Is the owner-operator included in carrier contributions for workmen's compensation?
6. Is the owner-operator included within company pension and welfare plans?
7. Are the carrier's hiring practices for owner-operators (job applications, medical examinations, testing procedures, etc.) the same as for regular employees?

Appendix 8B
Technical Guidelines
for Disposition of
Employment-Tax Cases

[Copy furnished Sutherland, Asbill & Brennan by Internal Revenue Service pursuant to request made under Freedom of Information Act.]

(1) The issue of whether contract operators of trucking equipment are independent contractors or employees of a carrier for purposes of the Federal Insurance Contributions Act (FICA), the Federal Unemployment Tax Act (FUTA), and the Collection of Income Tax at Source on Wages (WT), will, under present law, be decided in favor of an independent contractor relationship where the facts are substantially similar to those in the cases of *United States* v. *Mutual Trucking Co.*, 141 F. (2d) 655 (6th Cir., 1944) and *United States* v. *Silk* and *Carter H. Harrison* v. *Greyvan Lines, Inc.*, 331 U.S. 704; CT. D. 1688, 1947-2, 167.

(2) The factual situation in the cases indicated that no control over the contract operators was contemplated by the agreement or, generally, was practiced in the performance thereof beyond those elements of control made necessary through governmental regulations and through the need to adequately establish or set out the result to be accomplished. Revenue Rulings 55-593, C.B. 1955-2, 610, and 56-453, C.B. 1956-2, 687, involve these principles. Revenue Rulings 70-441 and 70-602, C.B. 1970-2, pages 210 and 225, respectively, are distinguishable.

(3) The combined effect of the above is to create a strong inference that a contract operator is an independent contractor when the following six factors are present:

(a) He owns the equipment or holds it under a bona fide lease arrangement;
(b) He is responsible for the maintenance of the equipment;
(c) He bears the principal burdens of the operating costs, including fuel, repairs, supplies, insurance, and personal expenses while on the road;
(d) He is responsible for supplying the necessary personal services to operate the equipment;
(e) His compensation is based upon a division of the gross revenue or a fee based upon the distance of the haul, the weight of the good, the number of deliveries, or combination thereof; and

Source: Taken from the Internal Revenue Manual, as quoted in *Heavy Specialized Carrier Conference Newsletter*, July 6, 1973.

151

(f) He generally determines the details and means of performing the services, in conformance with regulatory requirements, operating procedures of the carrier and specifications of the shipper.

(4) The factors in (3) (a) through (e) above give contract operators substantial opportunity for profit and loss and the risks of enterprise, which are indications of independent contractor relationships. Economic factors alone, however, are not conclusive when the company meaningfully controls the details and means used by the contractor operators. Such controls do not include those which a carrier imposes upon his drivers in order to direct them as to the results to be achieved. For instance, a company rule that drivers report regularly or frequently in a prescribed manner to receive work assignments should not be considered significant. In addition, operating requirements imposed by governmental regulatory agencies upon carriers are also not significant. As an example, governmental regulations require that a carrier's name appear on the operator's equipment; and, therefore, such identification is not evidence of company control.

(5) Where one or more of the factors in (3) (a) through (c) above are missing or they are all present together with meaningful company controls, the total situation must be considered. If the matter cannot be resolved at the district level, request for technical advice under IRM 4550 procedures should be considered.

(6) Where an employer-employee relationship is determined, the period of delinquent or additional tax adjustment will depend upon the facts of each case. For delinquent tax cases, see IRM 4682.31 (4) through IRM 4682: (5), to be issued as 521 of IRM 4960, Audit Tolerance and Criteria Handbook. In additional tax cases, the period of adjustment will generally be within the audit cycle for the employer's income tax return.

Appendix 8C
The Common-Law
Rules—Factors

1. *Instructions*. A person who is required to comply with instructions about when, where, and how he is to work is ordinarily an employee. Some employees may work without receiving instructions because they are highly proficient in their line of work and can be trusted to work to the best of their abilities; however, the control factor is present if the employer has the right to instruct. The instructions may be oral or may be in the form of manuals or written procedures which show how the desired result is to be accomplished.

2. *Training*. Training of a person by an experienced employee working with him, by correspondence, by required attendance at meetings and by other methods is a factor of control because it is an indication that the employer wants the services performed in a particular method or manner. This is especially true if the training is given periodically or at frequent intervals. An independent contractor ordinarily uses his own methods and receives no training from the purchaser of his services.

3. *Integration*. Integration of the person's services into the business operations generally shows that he is subject to direction and control. In applying the integration test, first determine the scope and function of the business and then whether the services of the individual are merged into it. When the success or continuation of a business depends to an appreciable degree upon the performance of certain services, the people who perform those services must necessarily be subject to a certain amount of control by the owner of the business.

4. *Services Rendered Personally*. If the services must be rendered personally it indicates that the employer is interested in the methods as well as the results. He is interested not only in getting a desired result, but also in who does the job. Lack of control may be indicated when an individual has the right to hire a substitute without the employer's knowledge.

5. *Hiring, Supervising, and Payment of Assistants*. Hiring, supervising, and payment of assistants by the employer generally shows control over all the men on the job. Sometimes one worker may hire, supervise, and pay the other workmen. He may do so as the result of a contract in which he agrees to provide materials and labor and under which he is responsible only for the attainment of a result, in which case he is an independent contractor. On

the other hand, if he does so at the direction of the employer, he may be acting as an employee in the capacity of foreman for or representative of the employer.

6. *Continuing Relationship.* The existence of a continuing relationship between an individual and the person for whom he performs services is a factor tending to indicate the existence of an employer-employee relationship. Continuing services may include work performed at frequently recurring though somewhat irregular intervals either on call of the employer or whenever the work is available. If the arrangement contemplates continuing or recurring work, the relationship is considered permanent, even if the services are rendered on a part-time basis, they are seasonal in nature, or the person actually works only a short time.

7. *Set Hours of Work.* The establishment of set hours of work by the employer is a factor indicative of control. This condition bars the worker from being master of his own time, which is a right of the independent contractor. Where fixed hours are not practical because of the nature of the occupation, a requirement that the worker work at certain times is an element of control.

8. *Full Time Required.* If the worker must devote his full time to the business of the employer, the employer has control over the amount of time the worker spends working and impliedly restricts him from doing other gainful work. An independent contractor, on the other hand, is free to work when, and for whom, he chooses.

Full time does not necessarily mean an 8-hour day or a 5- or 6-day week. Its meaning may vary with the intent of the parties, the nature of the occupation, and customs in the locality. These conditions should be considered in defining "full time."

Full-time services may be required even though not specified in writing or orally. For example, a person may be required to produce a minimum volume of business which compels him to devote all of his working time to that business, or he may not be permitted to work for anyone else and to earn a living he necessarily must work full time.

9. *Doing Work on Employer's Premises.* Doing the work on the employer's premises is not control in itself; however, it does imply that the employer has control especially where the work is of such a nature that it could be done elsewhere. A person working in the employer's place of business is physically within the employer's direction and supervision. The use of desk space and of telephone and stenographic services provided by an employer places the worker within the employer's direction and supervision unless the worker has the option as to whether he wants to use these facilities.

The fact that work is done off the premises does indicate some freedom from control. However, it does not by itself mean that the worker is not an employee. In some occupations the services are necessarily performed away from the premises of the employer. This is true, for example, of employees of construction contractors.

10. *Order or Sequence Set.* If a person must perform services in the order or sequence set for him by the employer, it shows that the worker may be subject to control as he is not free to follow his own pattern of work, but must follow the established routines and schedules of the employer.

Often, because of the nature of an occupation, the employer does not set the order of the services or sets them infrequently. It is sufficient to show control, however, if he retains the right to do so.

11. *Oral or Written Reports.* If regular oral or written reports must be submitted to the employer, it indicates control, in that the worker is compelled to account for his actions.

12. *Payment by Hour, Week, Month.* An employee is usually paid by the hour, week, or month; whereas, payment on a commission or job basis is customary where the worker is an independent contractor. Payment by the job includes a lump sum which is computed by the number of hours required to do the job at a fixed rate per hour; it may also include weekly or monthly payments if this method of payment is a convenient way of paying a lump sum agreed upon as the cost of doing a job.

The guarantee of a minimum salary or the granting of a drawing account at stated intervals with no requirement for repayment of the excess over earnings tends to indicate the existence of an employer-employee relationship.

13. *Payment of Business and/or Traveling Expense.* Payment by the employer or the worker's business and/or traveling expenses is a factor indicating control over the worker. Conversely, a lack of control is indicated where the worker is paid on a job basis and has to take care of all incidental expenses.

14. *Furnishing of Tools, Materials.* The furnishing of tools, materials, etc., by the employer is indicative of control over the worker. Where the worker furnishes the tools, materials, etc., it indicates a lack of control but consideration must be given to the fact that in some occupational fields it is customary for employees to use their own hand tools.

15. *Significant Investment.* A significant investment by a person in facilities used by him in performing services for another tends to show an independent status. On the other hand, the furnishing of all necessary facilities by the employer tends to indicate the absence of an independent status on the part of the worker.

Facilities include, generally, equipment or premises necessary for the work but not tools, instruments, clothing, etc., that are provided by employees as a common practice in their particular trade.

16. *Realization of Profit or Loss.* A person who is in a position to realize a profit or suffer a loss as a result of his services is generally an independent contractor, while the individual who is an employee is not in such a position. Opportunity for profit or loss may be established by one or more of a variety of circumstances, e.g.:

A. The individual hires, directs, and pays assistants.

B. He has his own office, equipment, materials, or other facilities for doing the work.

C. He has continuing and recurring liabilities or obligations and his success or failure depends on the relation of his receipts to his expenditures.

D. He agrees to perform specific jobs for prices agreed upon in advance and pays expenses incurred in connection with the work.

17. *Working for More Than One Firm at a Time.* If a person works for a number of firms at the same time, it usually indicates an independent status because in such cases the worker is usually free from control by any of the firms. It is possible, however, that a person may work for a number of people or firms and still be an employee of one or all of them.

18. *Making Service Available to General Public.* The fact that a person makes his services available to the general public is usually indicative of an independent contractual relationship. An individual may hold his services out to the public in a number of ways. He may have his own office and assistants, he may hang out a "shingle" in front of his home or office, he may hold business licenses, he may be listed in business directories, or he may advertise in newspapers, trade journals, magazines, etc.

19. *Right to Discharge.* The right to discharge is an important factor in indicating that the person possessing the right is an employer. He exercises control through the ever-present threat of dismissal which causes the worker to obey his instructions. An independent contractor, on the other hand, cannot be fired as long as he produces a result which measures up to his contract specifications.

Sometimes an employer's right to discharge is restricted because of his contract with a labor union. Such a restriction does not detract from the existence of an employment relationship.

20. *Right to Terminate.* An employee has the right to end his relationship with his employer at any time he wishes without incurring liability. An independent contractor usually agrees to complete a specific job and he is responsible for its satisfactory completion or is legally obligated to make good for failure to complete the job.

Appendix 8D
Owner-Operator
Clauses of the
1979-1982 National
Master Freight
Agreement

Article 22

Section 1. Owner Operators. Owner-operators (See Note), other than certificated or permitted carriers shall be affiliated by lease with a certificated or permitted carrier which is required to operate in full compliance with all the provisions of this Agreement and holding proper ICC and state certificates and permits. Such owner-operators shall operate exclusively in such service and for no other interests.

(Note: Whenever "owner-operator" is used in this Article, it means owner-driver only, and nothing in this Article shall apply to any equipment leased except where owner is also employed as a driver.)

The provisions of Article 22 will apply to a signator Employer whether or not such signator Employer is a "certificated or permitted carrier" under applicable law and regulation.

Section 2. This type of operator's compensation for wages and working conditions shall be in full accordance with all the provisions of this Agreement. The owner-operator shall have seniority as a driver only.

Section 3. Certificate and title to the equipment must be in the name of the actual owner.

Section 4. In all cases, hired or leased equipment shall be operated by an employee of the certificated or permitted carrier. The performance of unit work by owner-operators shall be governed by the provisions of this Agreement and Supplements relating to owner-operators. The Employer expressly reserves the right to control the manner, means and details of, and by which, the owner-operator performs his services, as well as the ends to be accomplished.

Section 5. Certificated or permitted carriers shall use their own available equipment, together with all leased equipment under a permanent lease with a minimum thirty-(30) day cancellation clause, on a rotating board, before hiring any extra equipment. The hiring of such extra equipment shall be subject to the provisions of Article 32 (Subcontracting).

Section 6. Separate checks shall be issued by the certificated or permitted carriers for driver's wages and equipment rental. At no time shall the equipment check be for less than actual miles operated. Separate checks for drivers shall not be deducted from the minimum truck rental revenue. The driver shall turn in time direct to the certificated or permitted carrier. All monies due the owner-operator may be held no longer than two weeks, except where the lease of equipment agreement is terminated and in such case all monies due the operator may be held no longer than thirty (30) days from the date of the termination of the operation of the equipment.

Section 7. Payment for equipment service shall be handled by the issuance of a check for the full mileage operated, tonnage or percentage, less any agreed advances. A statement of any charges by the certificated or permitted carrier shall be issued at the same time, but shall not be deducted in advance.

Section 8. The owner-operator shall have complete freedom to purchase gasoline, oil, grease, tires, tubes, etc., including repair work, at any place where efficient service and satisfactory products can be obtained at the most favorable prices.

Section 9. There shall be no deduction pertaining to equipment operation for any reason whatsoever.

Section 10. The Employer or certificated or permitted carrier hereby agrees to pay road or mile tax, Social Security tax, compensation insurance, public liability and property damage insurance, bridge tolls, fees for certificates, permits and travel orders, fines and penalties for inadequate certificates, license fees, weight tax and wheel tax, and for loss of driving time due to waiting at state lines, and also cargo insurance. It is expressly understood that the owner-driver shall pay the license fees in the state in which title is registered. All tolls, no matter how computed, must be paid by the Employer regardless of any agreement to the contrary.

All taxes or additional charges imposed by law relating to actual truck operation and use of highways, no matter how computed or named, shall be paid by the carrier, excepting only vehicle licensing as such, in the state where title is registered.

Section 11. There shall be no interest or handling charge on earned money advanced prior to the regular pay day.

Section 12. (a) All certificated or permitted carriers hiring or leasing equipment owned and driven by the owner-operator shall file a true copy of the lease agreement covering the owner-driven equipment with the Joint Area Committees. The terms of the lease shall cover only the equipment owned and driven by the owner-operator and shall be in complete accord with the minimum rates and conditions provided herein, plus the full wage rate and supplementary allowances for drivers as embodied elsewhere in this Agreement.

(b) The minimum rates for leased equipment owned and driven by the owner-operator, the minimum guarantees for tractors and trailers, and other conditions are set forth in the Area Supplement attached hereto.

Section 13. Driver-owner mileage scale does not include use of equipment for pick-up or delivery at point of origin terminal or at point of destination terminal, but shall be subject to negotiations between the Local Union and Employer. Such negotiations shall be only for the purpose of protecting the wage rate of the driver only as an employee. Failure to agree shall be submitted to the grievance procedure.

Section 14. There shall be no reductions where the present basis of payment is higher than the minimums established herein for this type of operation. Where owner-operator is paid on a percentage or tonnage basis and the operating company reduces its tariff, the percentage or tonnage basis of payment shall be automatically adjusted so that the owner-operator suffers no reduction in equipment rental or wages, or both.

Section 15. It is further understood and agreed that any arrangements which have heretofore been entered into between members of this Union, either among themselves or with the Employer or with the aid of the Employer, applicable to owner-operator equipment contrary to the terms hereof, shall be dissolved or modified within thirty (30) days after the signing of this Agreement so that such arrangements shall apply only to equipment of the owner-operator while being driven by such owner-operator. In the event that the parties cannot agree on a method of dissolution or modification of such arrangement to make the same conform to this Agreement, the question of dissolution or modification shall be submitted to arbitration, each party to select one member of the arbitration board, and the two so selected to choose a third member of said board. If the two cannot agree upon the third within five (5) days, he shall be appointed by the Joint Area Committee. The decision of said board is to be final and binding.

Section 16. It is further agreed that the intent of this clause and this entire Agreement is to assure the payment of the Union scale of wages as provided in this Agreement and to prohibit the making and carrying out of any plan, scheme or device to circumvent or defeat the payment of wage scales provided in this Agreement. This clause is intended to prevent the continuation of or formation of combinations or corporations or so-called lease of fleet arrangements whereby the driver is required to and does periodically pay losses sustained by the corporation or fleet arrangement, or is required to accept less than the actual cost of the running of his equipment, thus, in fact, reducing his scale of pay.

Section 17. It is further agreed that if the Employer or certificated or permitted carrier requires that the owner-operator sell his equipment to the Employer or certificated or permitted carrier, directly or indirectly, the owner-operator shall be paid the fair true value of such equipment. Copies of the instruments of sale shall be filed with the Union and unless objected to within ten (10) days shall be deemed satisfactory. If any question is raised by the Union as to such value, the same shall be submitted to arbitration, as above set forth, for determination. The decision of the arbitration board shall be final and binding.

Section 18. It is further agreed that the Employer or certificated or permitted carrier will not devise or put into operation any scheme, whether herein enumerated or not, to defeat the terms of the Agreement, wherein the provisions as to compensation for services of and for use of equipment owned by owner-operator shall be lessened, nor shall any owner-operator lease be cancelled for the purpose of depriving employees of employment, and any such complaint that should arise pertaining to such cancellation of lease or violation under this Section shall be subject to the discharge and grievance provisions of the Area Supplement.

Section 19. (a) The use of individual owner-operators shall be permitted by all certificated or permitted carriers who will agree to submit all grievances pertaining to owner-operators to joint Employer-Union grievance committees in each respective state. It is understood and agreed that all such grievances will be promptly heard and decided with the specific purpose in mind of:

(1) protecting provisions of the Union Agreement;

(2) prohibiting any and all violations directly or indirectly of Agreement provisions relating to the proper use of individual owners;

(3) prohibiting any attempts by any certificated or permitted carrier in changing his operations which will affect the rights of drivers under the terms of the Agreement, and generally the certificated or permitted carriers agree to assume responsibilitiy in policing and doing everything within their power to eliminate all alleged abuses in the use of owner-operators which resulted in the insertion of Section 19 (Article 33) in the original 1945-47 Central States Area Agreement;

(4) owner-operator operations to be terminal-to-terminal, except where no local employees to make such deliveries or otherwise agreed to in this Agreement;

(5) the certificated or permitted carriers agree that they will, with a joint meeting of the Unions, set up uniform rules and practices, under which all such cases will be heard;

(6) it shall be considered a violation of this Agreement should any operator deduct from rental of equipment the increases provided for by the 1976 Amendments or put into effect any means of evasion to circumvent actual payment of increases agreed upon effective for the period starting April 1, 1976 and ending March 31, 1979.

(b) No owner-operator shall be permitted to drive or hold seniority where he owns three or more pieces of leased equipment. This provision shall not apply to present owner-operators having three or more pieces of equipment under lease agreement, but such owner-operator shall not be permitted to put additional equipment in service so long as he engages in work covered by this Agreement or holds seniority. Where such owner-operator drives, he can hold seniority where he works sixty (60) per cent or more of the time.

Section 20. All leases, agreements or arrangements between carriers and owner-operators shall contain the following statement: The equipment which is the subject of this lease shall be driven by an employee of the lessee at all times that it is in the service of the lessee. If the lessor is hired as an employee to drive such equipment, he shall receive as rental compensation for the use of such equipment no less than the minimum rental rates, allowances, and conditions (or the equivalent thereof as approved by the Joint Area Committee), established by the then current appropriate Area Over-The-Road Motor Freight Supplemental Agreement, for this type of equipment, and, in addition thereto, the full wage rate and supplementary allowances for drivers (or the equivalent thereof as approved by the Joint Area Committee).

The lessee expressly reserves the right to control the manner, means and details of, and by which the driver of such leased equipment performs his services, as well as the ends to be accomplished.

To the extent that any provision of this lease may conflict with the provisions of such appropriate Area Over-The-Road Motor Freight Supplemental Agreement as it applies to equipment driven by the owner such provision of this lease shall be null and void and the provisions of such Agreement shall prevail.

The carrier shall make available to the Union upon request all documents and reports relating to service by owner-operators which are required to be maintained by law.

9 The Economics of Owner-Operator Use

In previous chapters, we have attempted to understand the owner-operator system by examining the individual components of the system: why owner-operators are used, the activities necessary to support such a system, and the legal context within which the system operates. In this chapter, our attention turns to the *results* of the system. We shall attempt to discuss such questions as

1. Are carriers that use owner-operators more profitable than those that do not?
2. What are the levels of costs incurred by carriers in supporting owner-operator operations?
3. What does the available evidence suggest about the "equitability" of current divisions of revenues between carrier and owner-operator?

It should be recognized that interest in these questions is not only managerial ("Are we efficient in our owner-operator support activities?") but also derives from public policy concern, as evidenced by the phrasing of the third question given above. In the course of the investigations of the owner-operator system by the ICC, Congress, and others, it has been suggested that the percentage of revenue from shipments retained by carriers might be "excessive" in some sense, at a level above that justified by the costs incurred by the carrier in supporting line-haul operations. In particular, it has been noted that, whereas in the regulated sector of the trucking industry a carrier might retain up to 25 or 30 percent of the revenue from a given load, in the unregulated (exempt) sector the brokers who arrange loads for itinerant owner-operators will typically retain only 5 or 10 percent of the revenues. It has therefore been suggested that at least some portion of this difference is due to the fact of regulation, that is, to carriers in some way exploiting their operating authority and capturing what economists would term "economic rent" from their certificates.

Whether or not there is any validity to this assertion, it is clear that there are great difficulties in deriving any conclusions from a comparison between the activities or brokers in the exempt sector and carriers in the regulated sector, since their methods of operation are vastly different. In serving different (commodity) markets they will incur different marketing, billing, and collecting costs. Most brokers are fixed-base, local operations, whereas carriers usually operate networks and incur appropriate administrative costs. Further, the range of services provided by certificated carriers to owner-operators usually far exceeds those typical of the broker.

Because of these problems, the analyses presented in this chapter will attempt to compare the operating costs of carriers operating in similar markets, and attempt to detect differences in the operating and financial results between those that use owner-operators extensively and those that do not. The data employed were the annual reports of regulated carriers filed with the ICC, as published by the American Trucking Associations, Inc., under the title, *Motor Carrier Annual Reports*.

Carrier Support Activities

In July 1977 the Common Carrier Conference—Irregular Route, an industry association of (predominantly refrigerated) carriers relying heavily on owner-operators, issued a booklet entitled *Allegations and Answers about Independent Truck Drivers*. In this booklet, the conference listed the support activities of carriers:

> With the load revenue remaining after paying the independent contractor, regulated trucking companies perform these services. Securing state licenses and permits. Providing trailers and refrigerated units in many cases. Preparing, publishing, filing and defending of tariffs. Compiling a mass of reports required by federal and state governments. Complying with licensing and other legal requirements, including defending their interests in court. Billing and collecting from customers. Maintaining safety departments, performing safety inspections and complying with other government safety regulations. Purchasing cargo insurance. Negotiating claims settlements. Purchasing insurance to protect the public. Providing and maintaining offices, terminals and equipment. Maintaining the sales force that solicits the loads carried by independent contractors.[1]

To this list we may also add other activities (and consequent costs) that have been identified in previous chapters: recruiting, training, and counseling of owner-operators. It should also be noted, however, that items in the list such as purchasing insurance do not necessarily imply that the carrier bears the full cost of the insurance (which may be charged out to the owner-operator), but may indicate that the carrier bears the administrative cost of obtaining the insurance, and, in some cases, finances this expense by bearing the initial cost and allowing the owner-operator to make repayments by means of deductions from hauling revenues due from the carrier. Indeed, it may be seen that many of the costs of supporting an owner-operator fleet fall into the general and administrative category. As such, they are often difficult to identify and cost on a per-trip, per-ton, or per-mile basis.

It would appear, in theory, that many of the carriers' expense items are relatively fixed in nature. Once office procedures for obtaining licenses, filing fuel taxes, and so on have been established, there is often only small marginal cost in adding another (individual) owner-operator to the system. The same may also be true of such activities as billing and collecting: there is a substantial fixed component for the costs of these activities. This suggests that, at least in the short-to-medium term, there may be some economies of scale in running owner-operator fleets. This theory is largely supported by my researches, which revealed that underutilization of administrative resources such as licensing, billing, and computer-based dispatching systems is a prime concern among managers of such operations. However, it should be noted that many administrative activities are fixed-cost only with a relatively short horizon. The licensing activities of small-scale carriers (often only a part-time activity performed by low-level office administrators or "supersecretaries") clearly do not compare with the sophisticated full-time departments found at larger carriers. At one carrier, for example, a department of forty-two people exists solely to handle fuel taxes and licensing for 7,000 vehicles per year. Over the longer term, therefore, administrative costs are likely to behave as a step function, remaining relatively constant as size increases until more sophisticated procedures (and added fixed costs) are suddenly required.

It is likely that expenses for soliciting freight (that is, "traffic and sales") will have a relatively small fixed component, and be more completely variable, that is, rising and falling in relation to the volume of traffic generated. Indeed, as discussed above, many irregular-route carriers (and special-commodity divisions of regular-route carriers) have institutionalized this relationship by the use of commission agents.

The Costs of Support Functions

Because of the large number of distinct administrative activities performed by carriers, and the disparate nature of these activities between carriers of different types, it is difficult to establish standard costs for individual functions. For example, billing and collecting activities may vary widely between carriers as their size of customer, traffic mix, geographical diversity, and other factors vary. Furthermore, many other administrative functions do not appear as distinct items in carriers' accounts. Without extensive original research, it is not possible to estimate, for example, claims settlement costs (per ton handled, perhaps), dispatching costs (per dispatch), licensing costs (per owner-operator per year), or any of a large number of cost standards that might be of both managerial and public policy interest.

In their reports to the ICC, carriers divide their expenses into nine categories: line haul; pickup and delivery; billing and collecting; platform;

terminal; maintenance; traffic and sales; insurance and safety; and general and administrative. Table 9-1 shows these expense items as percentages of revenues for carriers of different types. It may be seen that this classification of accounts is most suited to general freight carriers, since other carriers typically do not make great use of pickup and delivery, platform, and terminal activities. The reader should also note that there is some degree of arbitrariness in the allocation of some carrier expenses to different cost categories.

For the purposes of our inquiry, the items of particular interest are (1) billing and collecting; (2) traffic and sales; (3) insurance and safety, and (4) general and administrative costs. These are the cost items normally borne by the carrier that supports an owner-operator fleet. Line-haul and maintenance costs are borne by the owner-operator (although these accounts may in the case of some carriers include some dispatching costs); separate pickup and delivery, platform, and terminal activities are normally avoided in the (typically) truckload operations that are characteristic of the owner-operator sector.

Not surprisingly, the (generally less-than-truckload) general freight carrier devotes a noticeably greater percentage of its revenues to billing and collecting and traffic and sales activities than do the other (truckload) sectors. This is due to the fact that it takes a larger amount of sales activity, and consequent paperwork, to fill a truck with separate LTL shipments than to sell a single truckload movement. However, with the possible exception of heavy-machinery haulers, there is much more homogeneity among the non-general-freight carriers, with billing and collecting averaging between 0.2 and 0.4 percent of revenues; traffic and sales averaging 0.5 to 1.5 percent; insurance and safety 0.5 to 0.9 percent; and general and administrative 4.3 to 5.7 percent.

It is notable that line-haul expenses appear to run at levels close to, or in excess of, 80 percent of revenues for most carrier groups. Few owner-operators are paid such a percentage: 75 percent is a more usual percentage for an owner-operator to receive. Such a comparison may, however, be deceptive. The figures shown in table 9-1 are industry-wide averages, including carriers of many types, some using owner-operators and some using company equipment. The significance of these distinctions was illustrated in table 1-13, where it was shown that carriers which are predominantly users of owner-operators (90 to 100 percent) tend to haul different types of traffic than those using predominantly company equipment (0 to 5 percent owner-operators). For example, it is clear for all four types of carriers shown in table 1-13 that revenues per ton-mile were lower for the owner-operator carriers. With the exception of refrigerated carriers, revenues per mile were also lower. Carriers using owner-operators have longer average hauls than "company equipment" carriers. Given these differences, we should beware of industry-wide "percentage of revenue" figures, since these mask percentages of widely different traffic types.

Table 9-1
Functional Costs as a Percent of Revenues, Various Carrier Groups, 1978

Expense Category	General[a] Freight	Heavy Machinery	Petroleum Products	Refrigerated Products	Agricultural Products	Motor Vehicles	Building Materials	Other Commodities
Line haul	39.5	78.9	82.0	81.2	81.9	78.3	82.3	79.1
Pickup and delivery	23.6	0.5	2.2	2.8	2.1	0.0	0.3	2.7
Billing and collecting	2.5	0.1	0.3	0.3	0.4	0.2	0.3	0.3
Platform	13.0	0.0	0.1	1.0	0.4	0.0	0.0	0.3
Terminal	6.5	2.4	1.6	2.2	0.4	8.8	2.3	2.5
Maintenance	1.5	1.0	2.5	1.2	4.1	1.8	2.0	1.8
Traffic and sales	3.0	2.8	1.0	1.5	0.8	0.5	1.3	1.5
Insurance and safety	0.8	0.7	0.6	0.9	0.5	0.6	0.9	0.8
General and administrative	3.8	5.7	3.5	4.3	5.2	5.5	5.1	5.4
Net Operating Income	5.5	7.7	5.8	4.2	3.8	3.9	5.2	5.2

Source: adapted from *1978 Motor Carrier Annual Reports* (Washington, D.C.: American Trucking Associations, Inc., 1979).

Note: columns may not sum to 100 because of rounding.

[a]All general-freight carriers.

A more interesting and potentially more useful set of statistics may be created by looking at individual functional costs on a per-ton, per-mile, or per-ton-mile basis. This is done, for various carrier groups, in tables 9-2 through 9-6.

It will be seen that, in these tables, three estimates of carrier costs are given: low, median, and high. The low estimate is that value exceeded by 75 percent of the carriers in the data base; the median, the value exceeded by 50 percent; and the high estimate, the value exceeded by 25 percent of the carriers. The use of these estimates (rather than, say, the more conventional arithmetic mean and standard deviation) has been selected since the statistics filed with the ICC by some carriers are very unreliable. Many have internal inconsistencies (the more blatant of which are excluded from the data base), and others, particularly the carrier's estimates of total miles traveled per year and total ton-miles carried, are often only guesstimates. For this reason, the extreme values discovered in the data base are best ignored.

Table 9-2 shows total operating expenses. It may be seen that, on both a per-mile and on a per-ton-mile basis, carriers that use owner-operators

Table 9-2
Total Operating Expenses per Ton, per Mile, and per Ton-Mile, Various Carrier Groups, 1977

Degree of Owner-Operator Use[a] and Level of Estimate[b]	Negligible (0-5%)			Predominant (90-100%)		
	Low	Median	High	Low	Median	High
Heavy-Machinery Carriers						
Cost per ton ($)	21.52	30.08	47.05	36.09	48.46	55.7
Cost per mile	89.85	123.72	213.63	77.42	94.09	113.7
Cost per ton-mile	6.81	8.42	20.17	5.88	6.82	7.3
Petroleum-Products Carriers						
Cost per ton	4.07	5.39	8.26	3.69	5.88	7.9
Cost per mile	82.58	97.40	119.09	68.02	77.81	106.8
Cost per ton-mile	5.63	7.14	8.43	2.94	5.96	9.7
Refrigerated-Products Carriers						
Cost per ton	26.98	36.04	52.01	36.78	41.90	54.6
Cost per mile	69.95	92.69	114.51	69.84	79.55	91.0
Cost per ton-mile	4.85	6.94	17.98	3.56	4.41	6.1
Building-Materials Carriers						
Cost per ton	8.00	10.62	17.44	10.70	20.44	26.9
Cost per mile	69.34	84.59	104.67	63.01	68.79	92.3
Cost per ton-mile	4.76	6.35	9.98	3.14	4.40	5.9

Source: derived from *Motor Carrier Annual Reports*, ATA, 1978.

[a]Measured by miles rented with driver.

[b]Low estimate is that value exceeded by 75 percent of carriers in data base; high estimate is exceeded by 2 percent of carriers; 50 percent of carriers are above the median and 50 percent below.

Table 9-3
Line-Haul Expenses per Ton, per Mile, and per Ton-Mile, Various Carrier Groups, 1977

Degree of Owner-Operator Use[a] and Level of Estimate[b]	Negligible (0-5%)			Predominant (90-100%)		
	Low	Median	High	Low	Median	High
Heavy-Machinery Carriers						
Cost per ton ($)	17.53	24.06	38.63	30.63	38.29	46.03
Cost per mile	77.89	100.95	173.35	65.08	83.45	87.81
Cost per ton-mile	6.02	7.37	17.44	5.09	5.64	6.31
Petroleum-Products Carriers						
Cost per ton	3.57	4.56	6.97	3.16	5.36	6.59
Cost per mile	66.28	83.56	100.97	64.52	69.59	96.79
Cost per ton-mile	4.67	5.97	7.16	2.53	5.23	9.11
Refrigerated-Products Carriers						
Cost per ton	21.51	28.76	38.00	30.31	38.40	47.26
Cost per mile	61.19	73.88	96.08	60.13	69.77	78.70
Cost per ton-mile	3.44	5.35	12.08	3.16	3.77	5.49
Building-Materials Carriers						
Cost per ton	6.88	8.66	14.66	10.43	18.17	22.90
Cost per mile	59.07	72.13	85.98	55.90	59.19	78.71
Cost per ton-mile	3.83	4.99	8.01	2.55	3.58	4.48

Source: derived from *Motor Carrier Annual Reports*, ATA, 1978.
[a]Measured by miles rented with driver.
[b]Low estimate is that value exceeded by 75 percent of carriers in data base; high estimate is exceeded by 25 percent of carriers; 50 percent of carriers are above the median and 50 percent below.

predominantly (as measured by the percent of total miles rented with driver) have lower total operating costs than carriers that make negligible use of owner-operators. However, the degree of variability that exists in the data base is significant. For example, any attempt to read significance into the difference between the average (median) per-ton-mile cost of petroleum carriers that do and do not use owner-operators should be approached with much caution. While the owner-operator carriers' cost (5.96 cents per ton-mile) appears lower than the non-owner-operator carrier's cost (7.14 cents per ton-mile), the former group experiences per-ton-mile costs ranging between 2.84 and 9.72 cents.

Table 9-3 shows line-haul expenses. Again, there appear to be consistent differences between the average (median) estimates of line-haul costs per mile and per ton-mile of the two groups, although these differences are relatively small in comparison to the wide variations that exist within the groups. It is not clear to what extent this extreme variability is due to either (1) the existence of wide performance characteristics among the carriers (due, perhaps, in part to significantly different types of operation) or to (2) extreme unreliability of the data. It should be noted that, in all cases,

Table 9-4
Traffic and Sales Expenses per Ton, per Mile, and per Ton-Mile, Various Carrier Groups, 1977

Degree of Owner-Operator Use[a] and Level of Estimate[b]	Negligible (0-5%)			Predominant (90-100%)		
	Low	Median	High	Low	Median	High
Heavy-Machinery Carriers						
Cost per ton ($)	15.400	50.660	84.070	84.170	153.80	188.80
Cost per mile	0.835	1.564	4.361	1.989	2.533	4.115
Cost per ton-mile	0.060	0.135	0.436	0.155	0.215	0.294
Petroleum-Products Carriers						
Cost per ton	1.090	5.340	9.850	2.770	7.800	9.430
Cost per mile	0.133	0.873	1.875	0.045	0.328	0.863
Cost per ton-mile	0.011	0.057	0.140	0.002	0.028	0.057
Refrigerated-Products Carriers						
Cost per ton	3.800	21.700	56.880	16.240	45.880	82.940
Cost per mile	0.061	0.656	1.456	0.338	0.874	1.842
Cost per ton-mile	0.019	0.048	0.205	0.023	0.059	0.090
Building-Materials Carriers						
Cost per ton	0.300	7.050	21.650	7.630	16.480	29.020
Cost per mile	0.083	0.480	2.280	0.333	0.924	1.400
Cost per ton-mile	0.001	0.031	0.155	0.028	0.041	0.096

Source: derived from *Motor Carrier Annual Reports*, ATA, 1978.

[a]Measured by miles rented with driver.

[b]Low estimate is that value exceeded by 75 percent of carriers in data base; high estimate is exceeded by 25 percent of carriers; 50 percent of carriers are above the median and 50 percent below.

predominant users of owner-operators experience higher *per-ton* costs than negligible users of owner-operators. This result derives directly from the longer average hauls of owner-operator fleets. Since the distance traveled is greater, the cost to transport a ton is greater.

Table 9-4 shows the traffic and sales cost experience of the two groups. The variability exhibited here within each group is even more striking. For example, among petroleum carriers that do not use owner-operators, traffic and sales expense per ton varies from 1.09 cents to 9.85, a multiple of nearly 9 between the low and high estimates: and these estimates exclude the lowest and highest 25 percent of carriers! Except for petroluem-products carriers, traffic and sales expense appears to be higher for "owner-operator" carriers, although these differences are not statistically significant in the face of wide variability.

The same results are discovered for insurance and safety costs, as shown in table 9-5. (Billing and collecting costs per ton, per mile, and per ton-mile are not shown here. As table 9-1 illustrated, billing and collecting costs are a very small proportion of carrier expenses. When divided by the total number of miles or tons, insignificantly small values result. In theory, no differences should be expected between the billing and collecting costs of

Table 9-5
Insurance and Safety Expenses per Ton, per Mile, and per Ton-Mile, Various Carrier Groups, 1977

Degree of Owner-Operator Use[a] and Level of Estimate[b]	Negligible (0-5%)			Predominant (90-100%)		
	Low	Median	High	Low	Median	High
Heavy-Machinery Carriers						
Cost per ton ($)	1.740	3.820	57.570	3.740	31.360	57.480
Cost per mile	0.103	0.430	1.230	0.080	0.515	0.893
Cost per ton-mile	0.005	0.016	0.101	0.009	0.048	0.098
Petroleum-Products Carriers						
Cost per ton	0.276	2.590	5.946	0.000	1.696	2.988
Cost per mile	0.029	0.371	0.941	0.004	0.215	0.518
Cost per ton-mile	0.005	0.029	0.067	0.002	0.017	0.041
Refrigerated-Products Carriers						
Cost per ton	1.640	12.190	41.190	17.260	29.550	53.010
Cost per mile	0.048	0.304	1.093	0.345	0.610	1.390
Cost per ton-mile	0.010	0.022	0.098	0.017	0.033	0.067
Building-Materials Carriers						
Cost per ton	0.225	1.620	10.840	0.000	14.520	19.510
Cost per mile	0.277	0.829	1.069	0.000	0.006	0.936
Cost per ton-mile	0.003	0.014	0.040	0.000	0.027	0.050

Source: derived from *Motor Carrier Annual Reports*, ATA, 1978.

[a]Measured by miles rented with driver.

[b]Low estimate is that value exceeded by 75 percent of carriers in data base; high estimate is exceeded by 25 percent of carriers; 50 percent of carriers are above the median and 50 percent below.

carriers that use owner-operators and those that do not, except insofar as this difference represents different types of traffic served.)

As noted above, the most significant category of costs borne by the carrier using owner-operator fleets is the "general and administrative." These are shown in table 9-6. In general, the variability in these values is a little less than for other cost categories. However, as an example, a multiple of 5 still separates the low and high cost per mile for non-owner-operator refrigerated-products carriers. With the exception of petroleum carriers, general and administrative costs per ton appear to be slightly higher for owner-operator carriers, but smaller on a per-ton-mile basis.

The data in tables 9-3 through 9-7 are, of course, only a broad overview. The extreme variability in the estimates may derive from the fact that many other factors, besides the degree of owner-operator use, will affect, for example, the carrier's general and administrative cost per ton. Among these might be the region in which the carrier operates (and hence the average wage rate), the size of the carrier (measured either by total revenues or total miles), the type of traffic hauled (and consequently the type of customers), and many others.

An attempt to take these factors into account was made by performing

Table 9-6

General and Administrative Expenses per Ton, per Mile, and per Ton-Mile, Various Carrier Groups, 1977

Degree of Owner-Operator Use[a] and Level of Estimate[b]	Negligible (0-5%)			Predominant (90-100%)		
	Low	Median	High	Low	Median	High
Heavy-Machinery Carriers						
Cost per ton ($)	1.112	2.166	3.120	1.917	2.975	4.466
Cost per mile	1.830	3.840	7.880	4.120	5.950	10.080
Cost per ton-mile	0.362	0.468	1.589	0.308	0.370	0.643
Petroleum-Products Carriers						
Cost per ton	0.220	0.379	0.573	0.073	0.159	0.445
Cost per mile	4.280	6.650	10.340	1.420	3.830	5.860
Cost per ton-mile	0.308	0.428	0.663	0.131	0.215	0.459
Refrigerated-Products Carriers						
Cost per ton	1.040	1.65	3.630	1.723	2.545	3.227
Cost per mile	2.370	4.22	12.950	2.840	4.430	6.500
Cost per ton-mile	0.157	0.397	1.302	0.153	0.231	0.342
Building-Materials Carriers						
Cost per ton	0.289	0.706	1.239	0.479	1.235	1.920
Cost per mile	3.180	5.210	7.950	2.570	4.450	6.210
Cost per ton-mile	0.172	0.378	0.687	0.218	0.286	0.392

Source: derived from *Motor Carrier Annual Reports*, ATA, 1978.

[a]Measured by miles rented with driver.

[b]Low estimate is that value exceeded by 75 percent of carriers in data base; high estimate is exceeded by 25 percent of carriers; 50 percent of carriers are above the median and 50 percent below.

a regression analysis on various functional costs for various categories of carriers. Since the statistical details of this analysis will be of limited interest to the general reader, they are deferred to the appendix. The results seem to suggest that line-haul costs per mile are higher for owner-operator-based carriers than for negligible users of owner-operators, in the refrigerated-products and "other specialized" category! (This surprising result is discussed in the appendix.) No statistically significant difference could be found for heavy machinery carriers, petroleum haulers, or building-materials carriers between the line-haul costs per mile of owner-operator users and non-owner-operator users. In the case of refrigerated-products carriers, the non-owner-operator group had line-haul costs per mile that were 93 percent of those of the owner-operator group. The equivalent percentage for "other specialized" carriers was 90 percent.

No differences could be detected in the average traffic and sales cost per ton for negligible and predominant users of owner-operators, or for insurance and safety cost per mile. The use of owner-operators did not appear to affect general and administrative costs per ton.

The net result of these analyses appears to be that there is so much variability in the cost experience of carriers that (with limited exceptions) no *significant* differences can be detected between the overhead costs (billing, collecting, insurance, traffic and sales, general and administrative) of carriers that use owner-operators and those that do not.

Given such a conclusion, it is of some interest to examine the *industry-wide* structure of costs for the carriers groups under examination. This is done in tables 9-7 through 9-9, which give the industry-wide average costs per mile, per ton, and per ton-mile. These were obtained by dividing the total industry costs by (respectively) total industry miles, tons, and ton-miles. It should be noted that while the revenues and costs shown refer to total carrier activities, the miles, tons, and ton-miles used to divide referred only to intercity operations. However, the degree of error thus introduced should be small, since the percent of total industry revenues from nonintercity (that is, local) operations of these carrier groups does not exceed 3 or 4 percent.

Some interesting conclusions may be drawn from inspection of these tables. Line-haul costs per mile vary significantly among the carrier groups, from a low of 62.90 cents for agricultural carriers to a high of 89.56 cents for liquid-petroleum carriers. In part, this may be due to higher average load weight for the former group, but, as table 9-9 shows, agricultural carriers also have the lowest line-haul cost on a per-ton-mile basis. This corresponds to their low revenues per ton-mile. (Owner-operators beware!) Insurance and safety costs per mile (mileage being the most appropriate basis for comparison) appear to be roughly similar across carrier groups, at 0.8 cents. The exceptions are not surprising, since agricultural products and building materials are likely to be less prone to cargo damage than commodities such as heavy machinery or refrigerated perishables, and not as hazardous as petroleum. For an examination of the other components of owner-operator support cost (billing and collecting, traffic and sales, and general and administrative), it is probably best to compare the expenses on a per-ton basis, as they are less likely to vary by the length of haul. Billing and collecting costs are lowest (at 5 to 7 cents per ton) for heavy-machinery and building-materials carriers, and particularly low (3 cents per ton) for petroleum haulers. This latter result possibly reflects the limited number of shippers that petroleum haulers typically work for. At the other extreme, refrigerated-products and agricultural haulers often deal with large numbers of small farmers, and this is reflected in high (18 cents per ton) billing and collecting costs.

Traffic and sales cost per ton show extreme variations between carrier groups, running from 9 cents for petroleum haulers to $1.29 for heavy-machinery haulers. Similarly wide variations may be found for general and administrative costs per ton, although variations in this category of cost on a per-ton-mile basis are less extreme.

Table 9-7
Average Industry Expenses per Mile, Various Common-Carrier Groups, 1978
(dollars)

	Heavy Machinery	Liquid Petroleum	Refrigerated Products	Agricultural Products	Building Materials	Other Specialized Carriers
Revenue	112.91	109.17	87.93	76.80	84.88	102.16
Line haul	89.15	89.56	71.44	62.90	69.89	80.85
Pickup and delivery	0.57	2.50	2.49	1.62	0.24	2.81
Billing and collecting	0.18	0.43	0.34	0.32	0.29	0.37
Platform	0.05	0.14	1.92	0.35	0.00	0.35
Terminal	2.73	1.81	1.95	0.37	1.96	2.55
Maintenance	1.13	2.76	1.13	3.19	1.76	1.89
Traffic and sales	3.18	1.16	1.33	0.67	1.18	1.62
Insurance and safety	0.79	0.67	0.82	0.43	0.82	0.85
General and administrative	6.49	3.90	3.86	4.05	4.33	5.60
Total operator expense	104.28	102.94	84.28	73.89	80.49	5.26
Operator profit	8.62	6.23	3.65	2.91	4.38	5.26
Average load (tons)	13.18	13.95	17.01	16.39	16.79	13.60
Average haul (miles)	535	107	922	511	300	250

Source: derived from data given in *1978 Motor Carrier Annual Reports* (Washington, D.C.: American Trucking Associations, 1979).

Table 9-8
Average Industry Expenses per Ton, Various Common-Carrier Groups, 1978
(dollars)

	Heavy Machinery	Liquid Petroleum	Refrigerated Products	Agricultural Products	Building Materials	Other Specialized Carriers
Revenue	45.85	8.40	47.60	23.97	15.16	18.77
Line haul	36.20	6.89	38.67	19.63	12.48	14.85
Pickup and delivery	0.23	0.19	1.35	0.50	0.05	0.52
Billing and collecting	0.07	0.03	0.18	0.10	0.05	0.07
Platform	0.02	0.01	0.50	0.11	0.00	0.06
Terminal	1.11	0.14	1.06	0.11	0.35	0.47
Maintenance	0.46	0.21	0.61	1.00	0.31	0.35
Traffic and sales	1.29	0.09	0.72	0.21	0.21	0.30
Insurance and safety	0.32	0.05	0.44	0.13	0.15	0.16
General and administrative	2.64	0.30	2.08	1.27	0.77	1.03
Total operator expense	42.35	7.92	45.62	23.06	14.38	17.80
Operator profit	3.50	0.48	1.98	0.91	0.78	0.97
Average load (tons)	13.18	13.95	17.01	16.39	16.79	13.60
Average haul (miles)	535	107	922	511	300	250

Source: derived from data given in *1978 Motor Carrier Annual Reports* (Washington, D.C.: American Trucking Associations, 1979).

Table 9-9
Average Industry Expenses per Ton-Mile, Various Common-Carrier Groups, 1978
(dollars)

	Heavy Machinery	Liquid Petroleum	Refrigerated Products	Agricultural Products	Building Materials	Other Specialized Carriers
Revenue	8.567	7.828	5.165	4.687	5.055	7.499
Line haul	6.765	6.422	4.196	3.839	4.162	5.935
Pickup and delivery	0.043	0.179	0.146	0.099	0.016	0.206
Billing and collecting	0.014	0.031	0.020	0.020	0.017	0.027
Platform	0.004	0.010	0.054	0.021	0.001	0.026
Terminal	0.207	0.130	0.155	0.022	0.116	0.187
Maintenance	0.086	0.198	0.066	0.196	0.105	0.139
Traffic and sales	0.242	0.083	0.078	0.041	0.070	0.119
Insurance and safety	0.060	0.048	0.048	0.026	0.049	0.062
General and administrative	0.493	0.280	0.227	0.247	0.258	0.411
Total operator expense	7.913	7.381	4.950	4.509	0.794	7.113
Operator profit	0.654	0.447	0.215	0.178	0.261	0.386
Average load (tons)	13.18	13.95	17.01	16.39	16.79	13.60
Average haul (miles)	535	107	922	511	300	250

Source: derived from data given in *1978 Motor Carrier Annual Reports* (Washington, D.C.: American Trucking Associations, 1979).

By multiplying the costs per ton-mile by the average haul (in miles) and by the average load (in tons) it is possible to construct a profile of the average industry-wide costs per load. This has been done in table 9-10. The virtue of this calculation is that it allows us to estimate a dollar amount for the overhead costs of supporting an owner-operator fleet. For example, if we examine refrigerated carriers, we can observe that the total cost of supporting an owner-operator operation can be estimated as the sum of billing and collecting ($3.14 per load), traffic and sales ($12.23), insurance and safety ($7.53), and general and administrative ($35.60), for a total of $58.50 per load. With an allowance of 4.2 percent of gross revenue for profit ($33.72 per load), this means that the average carrier must obtain at least $92.22 per load after paying the owner-operator. The merit of this calculation lies in the fact that while these expenses are averages for a load of 17.01 tons and an average haul of 922 miles, the estimates should not be *too* affected by different loads or average length of haul. For example, billing and collecting costs should not vary by size of load or average length of haul, nor should traffic and sales cost or general and administrative. (Insurance costs may change with increasing average length of haul.)

Naturally, the experience of individual carriers may (and does) vary from this. First, some carriers may incur additional expenses in supporting their owner-operator fleets that the average carrier does not (for example, in paying for health and welfare schemes). Second, there may be economies of scale for some of the overhead costs (such as general and administrative: see appendix), so that larger carriers will have lower support costs than will smaller carriers.

Owner-Operator Use and Profitability

In this section we turn our attention to the relative profitability of predominant users of owner-operators in comparison to negligible users of owner-operators. We might begin by noting that the average profitability of those carrier groups that tend to use owner-operators is relatively modest when examined as a percentage of revenue. For example, in the case of refrigerated products (where over 60 percent of miles are traveled by owner-operators), we may see from table 9-10 that the average operating profit (before interest payments) for the industry is $33.72 per load. In comparison to total revenue of $810 per load, and line-haul costs of $658 per load, this is a relatively small amount. If an owner-operator were to be paid 75 percent of the total revenue, or $608, then receiving the total carrier profit would only increase his revenues by 5.5 percent. If the industry-wide average may be applied to the owner-operator subsector, then there is little

Table 9-10
Average Industry Expenses per Load, Various Common-Carrier Groups, 1978
(dollars)

	Heavy Machinery	Liquid Petroleum	Refrigerated Products	Agricultural Products	Building Materials	Other Specialized Carriers
Revenue	604.08	116.84	810.04	392.55	254.62	254.97
Line haul	477.02	95.86	658.07	321.53	209.64	201.79
Pickup and delivery	3.03	2.67	22.90	8.29	0.81	7.00
Billing and collecting	0.99	0.46	3.14	1.68	0.86	0.92
Platform	0.28	0.15	8.47	1.76	0.05	0.88
Terminal	14.60	1.94	18.04	1.84	5.84	6.36
Maintenance	6.06	2.96	10.35	16.33	5.29	4.73
Traffic and sales	17.06	1.24	12.23	3.43	3.53	4.05
Insurance and safety	4.23	0.73	7.53	2.18	2.47	2.11
General and administrative	34.76	4.18	35.60	20.69	13.00	13.97
Total operator expense	557.97	110.17	776.32	377.64	241.47	241.84
Operator profit	46.12	6.67	33.72	14.91	13.15	13.12
Average load (tons)	13.18	13.95	17.01	16.39	16.79	13.60
Average haul (miles)	535	107	922	511	300	250

Source: derived from data given in *1978 Motor Carrier Annual Reports* (Washington, D.C.: American Trucking Associations, 1979).

evidence that the owner-operator's financial condition could be vastly improved merely by a redivision of the profits between the carrier and the owner-operator. In other words, there is little evidence of sizeable "economic rent" or rip-offs from this evidence. (The same conclusion holds true for other carrier groups.) This conclusion has been based on industry-wide averages. However, as discussed in the appendix, statistical analysis failed to find any significant differences between the operating ratio (or, by extension, the operating profits) of negligible and predominant users of owner-operators in any of the carrier groups.

A similar conclusion was reached by Dr. Leland Case of the Association of American Railroads, who examined thirty-nine western irregular-route common carriers that used owner-operators almost exclusively. The results of his analysis, shown in table 9-11, indicate that from 20 to 30 percent of total revenue is being used to pay for administrative functions. Case concludes, "If monopoly profits exist it is apparent that they must be of a small magnitude, perhaps less than 1 percent of truckload revenue."[2]

Table 9-11
Average Operating Expense as a Percent of Total Revenue, Selected Western Carriers, 1977

	Revenue Class ($ Millions)						
	1	*1-2.5*	*2.5-5*	*5-10*	*10-25*	*25+*	*All*
Carriers in Sample[a]	7	8	9	10	3	2	39
General expenses & supplies	3.0	2.6	2.4	3.5	2.9	3.8	3.4
Operating taxes & licenses	1.3	1.1	1.0	1.7	1.2	2.2	1.7
Insurance	2.5	3.1	2.5	3.5	3.4	1.9	2.7
Communication & utilities	1.6	1.1	1.4	1.4	1.8	1.9	1.7
Depreciation & amortization	2.2	2.3	2.2	2.3	2.2	2.2	2.2
Building & office rents	2.7	1.3	0.9	1.3	1.2	0.6	1.0
Misc. expenses	1.4	0.9	1.1	1.2	0.7	0.04	0.6
Total nonwage expenses[b]	14.7	12.5	11.6	15.1	13.4	12.6	13.3
Wages of officers	6.3	4.7	2.5	2.2	1.3	1.1	1.8
Other wages (clerical & supervisory)	9.0	6.4	6.2	6.6	7.9	6.8	6.9
Total wages (including fringes)	15.3	11.1	8.7	8.8	9.2	7.9	8.7
Total wage & general expenses	30.0	23.6	20.3	23.9	22.6	20.5	22.0
Operating ratio	100.4	99.6	96.3	96.2	95.4	94.0	95.4

Source: L.S. Case "Examination of Competition in the Truckload Intercity Motor Carrier Freight Industry," *TRF Proceedings, 1979*. Reprinted with permission.

[a]Reports to State Regulatory Commission for 1977. Insofar as possible, those carriers were selected which were exclusive users of owner-operators for providing line-haul services.

[b]Totals in this line item may not tally with the details due to aggregation and rounding of figures.

In spite of the apparent lack of any difference in operating profit as a percentage of revenue due to the use of owner-operators, it may nevertheless be the case that the owner-operator method of operation may be financially attractive. This can be so because carriers that use owner-operators can have little or no investment in transport equipment. Consequently, a predominant user of owner-operators may receive a higher return on equity than a negligible user of owner-operators. This proposition was also examined using statistical analysis (see appendix), with surprising results. The coefficient for owner-operator use was not statistically significant for any of the commodity groups. Furthermore, the sign of the coefficient seemed to suggest that, if anything, carriers that were predominant users of owner-operators had *lower* returns on equity than those that were negligible users! It should be stressed, however, that the differences between the groups was not statistically significant.

How might we explain this result? First, it should be noted that this result refers to industry *averages*. It is a simple matter to review the pages of *TRINC's Blue Book* or *Motor Carrier Annual Reports* and uncover individual carriers that own no tractors or trailers and achieve returns on equity of over 40 percent per year. However, analysis suggests that such cases are exceptions. A possible explanation might lie in the following. First, we note that carriers that rely on owner-operators exclusively tend to haul lower-rated traffic than those that use them hardly at all. While lower investment is necessary by the carrier, lower profits are available for the same volume of traffic. The owner-operator, providing a more economical method of operation than unionized employees, allows a carrier to compete for traffic it would not otherwise haul. While this is not universally true, it is this line of argument that has led many general freight carriers to establish their special commodity divisions (and, not coincidentally, persuaded the union to permit their establishment). It would appear, therefore, that if the owner-operator is sacrificing income to preserve independence, it is not the carrier that reaps the benefit in the form of higher profits, but the shippers in the form of lower freight rates.

10 The Future of the Owner-Operator System

This book has been written at a time when significant public attention has been directed toward the trucking industry in general, and the owner-operator system in particular. We have already referred to the congressional hearings on owner-operator problems that took place in 1977 (chapter 2), and the subsequent revision of the ICC's leasing regulations (chapter 5). However, these actions were only the first of a series of government actions that have affected the owner-operator system and are likely to affect it substantially more in the foreseeable future. In this concluding chapter we shall briefly review the events of the past two years and discuss some of the other trends taking place that will shape the management task of administering owner-operator fleets in the 1980s.

The Events of 1977 to 1979

The attitude of public policy officials in the late 1970s toward the owner-operator system was accurately captured on June 1, 1977, when the ICC established its Small Business Administration Office (SBAO), whose primary task was to assist owner-operators by answering questions and dealing with their complaints. In the two years since that date, the ICC has justified its chairman's comment that "at the Commission, you [the owner-operators] have been given priority status."[1] In March 1979 the director of the SBAO, Bernard Gaillard, asked 192 motor carriers to designate high-level officials who could help the ICC informally resolve disputes involving owner-operators, with the SBAO acting as intermediary. Mr. Gaillard was quoted as saying that although "most carriers want to be helpful, efforts are frequently hampered by difficulties in communication,"[2] and attributed this to the fact that his office (and the owner-operators) must deal with many different people associated with a single carrier. The complaints brought to the SBAO by owner-operators generally involved payment for services, final settlement of accounts, pertinent tariff provisions, loading and unloading problems (lumpers and detention), lease interpretation, claim liability, or interpretation of the application of company policies not covered under the lease agreement.

Another owner-operator problem upon which there has been public policy action is that of "lumpers": individuals located at certain produce markets and consignee destinations who extract a fee for loading and unloading an owner-operator's truck. There were numerous and convincing reports that certain lumping rackets existed whereby owner-operators were forced to pay extortionate amounts of money in order to get loaded or unloaded. This matter was the subject of an inquiry by the House Committee on Small Business,[3] and of action by the ICC, which stiffened its fines for such practices.[4] However, the FBI, which conducted an investigation into this matter, experienced some difficulty in accumulating sufficient evidence to bring prosecutions.[5]

A related problem was that of detention: owner-operators had complained that, while most carrier tariffs required the collection of charges from shippers who excessively delayed the loading or unloading of vehicles, some carriers were reluctant to bill shippers for detention for fear of losing a shipper's account. Alternatively, they argued, carriers collected detention charges but did not pass them on to the owner-operator, who bore the expenses (in the form of reduced truck utilization) incurred by detention. In 1978, the ICC revised its detention rules, and, through its Process of Enforcement and SBAO, investigated claims of abuse in this area.[6]

The most significant event in the owner-operator system in the late 1970s was the owner-operator shutdown of June-July 1979. To a remarkable extent, this shutdown was a replay of that of 1974 (described in detail in Wyckoff and Maister[7]). The immediate causes of the shutdown, the lack of availability and the rise in price of diesel fuel, were identical. The owner-operator's demands, allocation of more fuel, uniform weight laws, and an increase in speed limits, were also the same. After the all-too-familiar incidents of violence and disruption of the economy, the shutdown was again negotiated to an end by federal officials, with the most obvious gain by the owner-operators being the imposition of fuel surcharges on freight rates for truckload commodities (as in 1974). Initially at 6 percent, these surcharges had risen by September 1979 to 9.5 percent on truckload-rated and owner-operator-hauled shipments. The ICC monitored fuel prices continuously and made weekly adjustments in the fuel surcharge. It estimated that diesel prices has risen by 57.6 percent between January 1, 1979, and September 7, 1979.[8]

Following the negotiated end of the owner-operator's shutdown in July 1979, President Carter directed the administration to work actively with representatives of the owner-operators to find solutions to their problems, particularly those arising from the energy crisis and the inflation in fuel prices. Accordingly, an interagency group consisting of representatives of the Department of Agriculture, the Department of Transportation, the ICC, the Department of Justice, and the Federal Trade Commission was established. In a letter to the president on September 10, 1979, they summarized their progress in two months.[9] This included the continual updating of the program for fuel surcharges. The ICC investigated several hundred carriers to ensure compliance with these regulations that the surcharge be passed on directly to the owner-operator. The Department of Transportation and Energy established a mechanism for locating fuel supplies and directing truckers to them. Legislation was introduced in both House and Senate to give the president authority to mandate uniform size and weight standards on the interstate system during periods of fuel shortages. The problems of exempt owner-operators were addressed by weekly USDA bulletins on rates paid to truckers for hauling produce, and a monthly report on the cost per mile of operating refrigerated trucks. The USDA was also preparing legislation to standardize hauling contract provisions for unregulated (exempt) commodity hauls, while the ICC was considering permitting owner-operators to trip lease in their own names, in order to gain greater revenues.

The federal task force also planned a series of seminars (to be held at truckstops throughout the nation) to teach owner-operators how to run their businesses (!). The package of seminars would include a training program which the ICC's Small Business Assistance Office would use to instruct owner-operators about compliance with ICC regulation and procedures, while the DOT would tutor the owner-operators on safety regulations and the Small Business Administration (SBA) would instruct them on how to maintain a business. According to an official of the SBA, the idea for the seminar grew out of a need to make owner-operators more palatable to the SBA for loans.[10] Another SBA official noted that "a lot of owner-operators are going bankrupt every day, and the SBA is becoming somewhat of a graveyard for repossessed equipment."[11] He commented that many of these failures could be traced to poor business decisions like purchasing equipment with exorbitant interest rates, poor initial selection of equipment, and a distorted conception of operating costs.

A further development was a proposal by the ICC that it require the filing of a special report by carriers that operated leased vehicles with drivers in excess of 5 million miles per year.[12] This report, composed of fifty-seven questions, would provide information on many of the carriers' owner-operator-related activities, such as the type of traffic hauled, the method by which owner-operators were compensated, the location and title of carrier employees or agents responsible for the preparation of owner-operator settlements, and so on. The objective of the reports appeared to be to allow the ICC to monitor carriers' compliance with leasing regulations and allow the ICC to keep a closer watch on the owner-operator sector. As of this writing, no final decision has been taken as to whether or not this reporting requirement would be instituted.

The events recounted here give a strong indication of a substantial revision of the legal and institutional framework surrounding the owner-operator system. The changes instituted are clearly an attempt to redress the imbalance of bargaining power between the owner-operator and the carrier, and to use the power of government to improve the lot of the owner-operator. There is every reason to believe that, in the immediate and foreseeable future, there will continue to be an activist government sector concerned with the plight of the owner-operator.

Deregulation

In spite of the possible impact of the changes described above, none has the significance possessed by another potential change that appears a more likely occurrence with each passing day: deregulation of the motor-carrier industry. While legislative action on this matter appears slow in coming, the ICC itself has been engaging in a series of decisions that effectively remove many of the regulatory constraints surrounding the industry. Of most interest to this work is the notice of a proposed rule-making issued by the ICC on September 5, 1979,[13] to change the system of regulation for twelve (truckload) specialized trucking groups, including all major carrier groups that use owner-operators (for example, haulers of heavy machinery, refrigerated products, household goods, building materials). The new system proposed would effectively deregulate these industries by barring collective rate-making and issuing "master certificates" in place of specific route-operating authority, thus, in effect, allowing licensed carriers to operate wherever they wish. Entry into these industries (that is, the obtaining of master certificates) would presumably be made relatively liberal. At the time of writing it appeared likely that the ICC would implement some version of these proposed changes in the near future.

What impact will deregulation have upon the owner-operator sector? I have argued above (chapter 2) that I believe that the owner-operator system will continue to exist. While many owner-operators will, at least initially, attempt to operate as one-person operations (that is, without subcontracting to a carrier), I would predict that many will seek the franchising services that the carriers have to offer. From a managerial level, more carriers will be forced explicitly to recognize their franchisor obligations to the owner-operator, as owner-operators are given greater freedom of choice to subcontract or operate independently. Carriers may well find that the need for business training of owner-operators will be accentuated by any deregulation, since those owner-operators with the most business acumen are the very ones most likely to make a success of operating independently. The less sophisticated will be more likely to remain with (or return to) the carriers, and be more dependent upon the carrier's training and guidance.

Some individual carriers are likely to be significantly affected by deregulation. A distinction should be made, for example, between those carriers that establish long-term relationships with owner-operators and those that currently rely on them heavily for trip leasing. The trip-leasing business will be affected dramatically by any deregulation. While owner-operators *may* still be dependent upon carriers or brokers to generate return hauls, they will no longer need the carrier's operating authority to haul loads. Accordingly, where franchisorlike services are absent, as in trip leasing, the owner-operators' services will not be forthcoming, except for a substantially larger percentage of the revenues from the loads. The carriers most likely to be affected by deregulation will be those heavily dependent upon commission agents. Primary among the franchisor services the carrier can provide is the generation of loads: where the carrier has passed this activity on to *another* independent contractor (the agent), it is likely to find that neither the owner-operator nor the agent "needs" the carrier any longer. This will be particularly true for those carriers that currently use agents to conduct much of their interaction with the owner-operator.

Will deregulation be good for the owner-operators themselves? This is a difficult question to answer, and it must be stated that no doubt some will flourish while others will be adversely affected. However, it must be stressed that if (as many believe) the major problem facing the owner-operator system in the late 1970s was the failure of freight rates to keep pace with rising trucking costs, then deregulation, by increasing competition in the industry and keeping rates low, is likely to affect the owner-operators adversely and worsen their economic health, at least on an aggregate basis. It is somewhat ironic that, during the 1977 congressional hearings, the owner-operator system was criticized because carriers "controlled" freight rates while owner-operators bore the major proportion of operating costs. It was argued then that carriers were keeping rates too low and failing to recognize the revenue needs of the owner-operators. Any deregulation would totally remove any power the carriers did have to correct this problem. Deregulation may or may not be to the benefit of the shipping public: however, it is clear that it cannot benefit both shippers in the form of lower rates and owner-operators in the form of higher rates. (Of course, one can argue that both these can be achieved if one believes that the carrier's percent of revenue is a monopoly profit and not warranted by services performed: the evidence of this book would suggest that this is *not* a tenable position on an industry-wide basis).

Other Trends

The activities of the ICC, the USDA, and other branches of government reported above all contribute to a sense of crisis in the owner-operator system. How real is this crisis? I believe that the crisis *is* real, but the factors contributing to it are not those discussed so far in this chapter. Other trends have been taking place in the trucking industry and in society at large that are likely to affect the management of owner-operators (if they have not already begun to do so) as profoundly as any governmental action.

The first of these is the fact that, as shown in chapter 1, more and more carriers, in more and more sectors of the trucking industry, are moving to the use of owner-operator fleets. In part, this trend has been caused by the increasing success of the Teamsters Union in winning attractive wage rates for their members. (This success is indicated in Wyckoff's survey,[14] which showed that only 2 percent of Teamster members believed their standard of living to be below average.) The increasing demand for the services of owner-operators will be accentuated by any deregulation, as carriers seek to offset increased price competition through the lower wage rates represented by owner-operators, and as they seek to avoid investment in equipment in an uncertain market. This increased competition for owner-operators (already a very competitive market) will tax the resources of carriers' recruiting departments: they will be faced with the problem of trying to find ways to make *their* company attractive, and to recruit and (more importantly) retain a higher proportion of good operators.

In contrast to this increased demand for owner-operators, the supply of owner-operators is probably declining. A number of factors contribute to this conclusion. The most obvious is the economic one: given the inflation in truck purchase prices, fuel, and other expenses, the expected returns from an independent driving career are becoming increasingly unattractive. Unless the trucking industry can provide returns commensurate with opportunities elsewhere in the job market, the supply of owner-operators is likely to diminish or, at least, fail to keep pace with the increased demand. This point cannot be overstressed. We have seen that some carriers justify their use of owner-operators because of the reduced labor cost they represent. While this may be possible because of relatively high union pay-scales, the pursuit of low labor cost must not be taken to extremes if a supply of willing labor is to be obtained.

The economic factors are supported by various sociodemographic factors in suggesting that the supply prospect for owner-operators is not healthy. The (probably valid) conventional wisdom about the "typical" owner-operator of previous years is that he was a rural boy who grew up around farm machinery, perhaps obtained a high-school diploma, and "hit the road" for a few years in his youth, lured by the romance of the road. This conventional wisdom is becoming increasingly a romantic vision itself. The baby boom is over, and the average age is rising: fewer youths will be entering the marketplace for careers. Those who do will increasingly come from urban environments, and even the rural children in modern society no longer have the mechanical background that was once associated with farm life (there is a widely reported shortage of truck mechanics, too). American society is becoming increasingly educated and increasingly affluent (inflation notwithstanding), and thus the life-style and career expectations of the modern job seeker are changing. The romance of the road has faded. Finally, we may note that the military, traditionally the source of many of the best owner-operators, no longer graduates as many people as it once did.

These trends suggest that the motor-carrier industry will have to put a great deal of effort into matching up the increasing demand for owner-operators with a static or declining supply. More than in the past, efforts will need to be directed to driver training by the carriers and, more importantly, financing the equipment of new entrants. This shift will, in turn, require carriers to take a longer-term view of their relationships with owner-operators and dedicate more resources and efforts to the problems of reducing turnover. In this effort, the advantage will lie with those carriers that are large and can support both extensive training and financing programs and the other activities necessary to keep owner-operators happy. The advantage will also lie with those carriers whose motivations for using owner-operators are long-term rather than "opportunistic": those that seek greater productivity and efficiency rather than a quick way to grow or a way to offset short-term fluctuations in the marketplace.

It is appropriate at this point to remember our franchising analogy. In chapter 3 we talked of the life-cycle of the *franchisee*: how his or her attitudes, needs, and goals change over the life of the franchising relationship. It has also been commonly observed that there is a shift in the attitudes, needs, and goals of the *franchisor* over the life of the franchise.[15] One of the predominant characteristics of this life-cycle is the practice of mature franchisors beginning to buy back their franchises, that is, convert to a higher proportion of company-owned outlets. This has occurred in the case of McDonald's, Wendy's Old-Fashioned Hamburgers, and other prominent chains. The rationale for this behavior is clear: where a franchise is young, rapid growth and external capital are prime requirements. When it matures, increased profits come not from adding more units, but from greater productivity and profitability of existing units. The tighter control that company-owned units provide allows this more easily than does a franchised system.

The same life-cycle effect may occur in the trucking industry. At least one carrier I interviewed was becoming increasingly disillusioned with its owner-operator divisions. While it had successfully used owner-operators to grow, it was not finding that its company equipment was being more productive than that of its owner-operators. It attributed this to the tighter control over scheduling and the use of the two-person operations that company equipment allowed! If this carriers' experience is any guide, we may see some current owner-operator operations convert to company equipment as carriers better establish themselves in the marketplace, build balanced networks, and can use sophisticated managerial controls in place of a heavy reliance on entrepreneurial incentive.

The Teamsters

There is considerable evidence that the Teamsters' attitudes toward the owner-operators and toward carriers' use of owner-operators is undergoing substantial change. Between 1965 and 1976, the amount of freight moved in truckload quantities rose 30 percent, while the volume of less-than-truckload freight rose only 3 percent.[16] In part, general freight carriers responded to this shift by establishing their own special commodity divisions, with IBT agreement, largely based upon the use of owner-operators. However, a key negotiator for the Teamsters, Roy L. Williams, has been quoted as saying that "we think their book on special commodities is thick enough,"[17] suggesting further union concessions for growth in this area are unlikely.

One cause of this shift is that the number of drivers represented by the union has declined substantially. It has been estimated that truck-driver membership in the IBT at the time of the 1979 negotiations was some 25 percent below the level that existed a decade previously.[18] In large part this has been the consequence of the shift in the mix of freight from the (unionized) LTL sector to the nonunionized truckload sector. It might be expected that the union will seek to restore its position in the industry by "going after" the truckload carriers.

An important component of any such campaign would be dealing with the distrust that many owner-operators feel for the Teamsters Union. Here, too, there are signs of a shift in the attitudes of the union. It was noticeable that, in the early days of the 1979 owner-operator shutdown, it was the Teamsters Union that was among the first to call for a fuel surcharge on traffic hauled by owner-operators, and for guarantees that this surcharge would be passed directly to the owner-operators. Such actions suggest that the union may be abandoning its historical position of trying to neglect (or even limit) the owner-operator sector, and may instead have recognized the inevitability of the continued existence of an owner-operator sector. Certainly, if the shift from LTL to TL traffic continues (and one could confidently predict such shifts, especially if deregulation leads to lower TL rates and higher LTL rates, as many believe) then the future growth for the Teamsters Union clearly lies in organizing the irregular-route sector of the trucking industry.

While it may be difficult for the Teamsters to succeed in this area, given the historical context of poor owner-operator relations, it is not beyond the reach of imagination to see how they could adapt their own internal organization to better recognize the particular needs of the owner-operators. Certainly, in the NLRB's power to declare owner-operators to be employees, the union has a powerful tool to help in this effort. This should be seen as a disquieting trend by many carriers. It would appear from my research that there exist a number of carriers that have relied on keeping a low profile in order to avoid organization battles. With a new aggressive mood on the part of the Teamsters, such defenses may be insufficient and more considerable attention will need to be given to labor relations and NLRB and IRS criteria in ruling on employee status.

The Independent-Contractor Problem

It will not have escaped the reader's attention that throughout this book we have had to refer to the problem of the owner-operator's legal status as independent contractor or employee. In virtually every aspect of owner-operator management, and hence in every chapter of this book, the threat to independent-contractor status has been a major consideration. This preoccupation is a reflection of the concerns of management that I discovered during my research.

The "independent contractor" problem presents a paradox to every manager who might be considering applying the ideas expressed in this book. We have argued at some length that successful owner-operator management requires carriers to be increasingly involved in the affairs of the owner-operator: to consider his or her needs, to recognize his or her goals; to promote feelings of "belongingness"; to provide services to ensure financial success; to establish information systems and controls so that advice and assistance may be given at appropriate moments; to counsel and advise; to use the power of the carrier to obtain discounts on bulk purchases and solve the individual's problems.

All of these are the prime tools developed and applied by the most successful franchisors to operate networks of independent contractors. But they are also the prime tools that the NLRB and the IRS look for in determining independent-contractor status. Why franchisors like McDonald's, Speedy Muffler King, and Kentucky Fried Chicken do not face this problem is somewhat of a paradox: at first sight it would appear to be because of the greater financial investment that their franchisees make. Yet, with the escalation in tractor and trailer prices, the investment of today's owner-operator is far from trivial.

To apply the lessons of the franchising industries, the motor-carrier industry must run the risk of losing independent-contractor status for its owner-operators. How serious would this be? One carrier has estimated the total cost of workers' compensation, employment tax, health and welfare payments, and unemployment insurance payments at between 4.1 and 4.5 cents per mile. Accordingly it pays its owner-operators an additional 4 percent of the revenue if they are independent contractors rather than employees. In principle, employee status for owner-operators would not be a devastating result (though it might be an expensive one) for those carriers that seek to use owner-operators for rapid growth, capital risk avoidance, or the opportunity for greater productivity. However, for those carriers that seek lower labor cost, the managerial advice that this book contains can only be applied with the greatest caution.

We have seen that the owner-operator system offers many benefits to motor-carrier management. However, the contents of this and previous chapters suggest that the system brings not only benefits but also significant management problems and challenges. The prospect for the future is not necessarily golden: the task of managing owner-operators is likely to become more difficult in the years ahead rather than easier.

The carriers that succeed will be those that not only recognize their partnership with the owner-operator, but think carefully how they can best act upon it. But if the carrier succeeds in serving the individual owner-operators well, then the system (and more importantly the *carrier*) will survive.

Appendix: Regression Results

In this appendix we shall discuss the application of regression analysis to the operating and financial results of individual carriers in the attempt to discover whether any statistically significant differences exist between carriers that are negligible users of owner-operators (0 to 5 percent of intercity miles) and carriers that are predominant users of owner-operators (90 to 100 percent of intercity miles).

The model employed in the analysis is of a log-log form, with the following specification:

$$\text{Log}\,(y) = a + \sum_{i=1}^{4} b_i \log(X_i) + \sum_{i=5}^{15} X_i$$

where

X_1 = total intercity miles (a measure of carrier size).
X_2 = average revenue per ton-mile.
X_3 = average haul (in miles).
X_4 = average load (in tons).
X_5 = a dummy variable for "owner-operator use," equal to 1 if the use is a negligible user and 0 if a predominant user of owner-operators. (Note that the base case is predominant users. A negative coefficient would then indicate that negligible users had a lower value of the dependent variable than predominant users.)
X_6 = a dummy variable for the type of operation, equal to 0 if nonradial and 1 if radial.
X_7 = a dummy variable set equal to 0 if the carrier derives more than 50 percent of its revenues from common carriage (rather than contract) and equal to 1 otherwise.
X_8-X_{15} = 8 dummy variables to distinguish the 9 ICC geographical regions (see figure 1-1). Region 9 is the base case.

Six different dependent variables were used:

1. Log of line-haul cost per mile.
2. Log of traffic and sales cost per ton.
3. Log of insurance and safety cost per mile.
4. Log of general and administrative cost per ton.
5. Log of operating ratio.
6. Log of return on equity.

191

The analyses were performed for five carrier groups:

1. Heavy machinery.
2. Petroleum products.
3. Refrigerated products.
4. Building materials.
5. Other specialized haulers (category 17).

The results of these analyses are shown in tables A-1 through A-6. The notation used in these tables is as follows:

P_F = probability that the F-statistic is not significantly different from zero.
β = estimated value of coefficient.
P_t = probability that the estimated coefficient is not significantly different from zero.

It should be noted that since the log-log form is used, the coefficients should be interpreted with care. For the dummy variables, such as "no-owner-operator use," the effect on the *real* dependent variable of interest (that is, the natural value rather than its log) can be derived by calculating e^β where β is the estimated coefficient and $e = 2.718$. Thus, in the case of line-haul cost per mile for refrigerated carriers, the estimated coefficient shown is -0.070. Since $e^{-0.070}$ is 0.932, this means that the line-haul costs per mile for carriers that are negligible users of owner-operators are, on average, 93.2 percent of the line-haul costs per mile of carriers that are predominant users of owner-operators.

For the nondummy (continuous) variables, the β coefficients represent "elasticities." For example, the coefficient for log (average revenue) in the regression of line-haul costs per mile for refrigerated carriers is 0.794. This means that for every 100 percent increase in average revenue, the average line-haul costs per mile increase by 79.4 percent.

It is clear from table A-1 that the major determinant of line-haul cost per mile is the average revenue per ton-mile of the carrier's traffic. When this is high, line-haul costs are high: when it is low, carriers are forced to use cheaper methods of line-haul operation. The values of the coefficients shown in table A-1 are interesting. For example, the log of average revenue per ton-mile for heavy-machinery, refrigerated, and "other specialized" carriers has a coefficient close to 0.78 in all three cases. Because of the log-log form of the regression equation, this can be interpreted to mean that as average revenue per ton-mile increases by 1 percent, average line-haul costs per mile increase by approximately 0.78 percent. This corresponds closely to the average line-haul costs as 75 to 80 percent of revenues, an indication that rates (revenue per ton-mile) are closely tied to operating costs for these

Table A-1
Regression of Log of Line-Haul Cost per Mile, Various Carrier Groups, 1977 Data

	Heavy Machinery		Petroleum Products		Refrigerated Products		Building Materials		Other Specialized	
	β	P_t	β	P_t	β	P_t	β	P_t	β	P_t
Intercept	-0.177	0.71	0.223	0.39	0.071	0.78	0.039	0.90	-0.403	0.08
Log (miles)	-0.001	-0.96	0.001	0.94	-0.007	0.61	-0.020	0.30	0.029	0.05
Log (average revenue)	0.777	0.00	1.025	0.00	0.794	0.00	0.959	0.00	0.793	0.00
Log (average haul)	-0.012	0.87	-0.016	0.55	-0.019	0.55	-0.020	0.51	-0.085	0.00
Log (average load)	0.812	0.00	0.924	0.00	0.790	0.00	1.019	0.00	0.911	0.00
Radial	0.075	0.35	-0.047	0.13	0.046	0.21	0.002	0.96	-0.012	0.74
Contract	0.070	0.65	-0.054	0.26	0.028	0.44	-0.044	0.31	0.127	0.00
Region 1	0.044	0.81	-0.154	0.20	-0.099	0.30	-0.030	0.77	-0.017	0.84
Region 2	-0.097	0.41	-0.076	0.14	0.047	0.54	0.059	0.41	-0.003	0.96
Region 3	0.054	0.61	-0.007	0.90	-0.015	0.83	0.119	0.09	-0.055	0.36
Region 4	-0.101	0.32	-0.008	0.87	-0.072	0.32	0.120	0.11	-0.091	0.14
Region 5	-0.120	0.38	-0.047	0.43	0.013	0.86	0.081	0.30	0.002	0.98
Region 6	-0.053	0.67	-0.033	0.62	0.022	0.75	0.036	0.66	-0.046	0.54
Region 7	0.081	0.49	-0.070	0.31	0.018	0.82	0.019	0.82	-0.149	0.03
Region 8	0.001	0.99	-0.021	0.74	-0.025	0.74	-0.036	0.62	-0.096	0.26
No owner-operator use	-0.012	0.86	-0.053	0.20	-0.070	0.01	-0.046	0.24	-0.107	0.00
Number of Observations	27		72		59		48		281	
F = Value	19.67		196.53		44.44		23.43		73.99	
P_F	0.0001		0.0001		0.0001		0.0001		0.0001	
R^2	0.96		0.98		0.94		0.92		0.81	

Table A-2
Regression of Log of Traffic and Sales Cost per Ton Various Carrier Groups, 1977 Data

	Heavy Machinery		Petroleum Products		Refrigerated Products		Building Materials		Other Specialized	
	β	P_t	β	P_t	β	P_t	β	P_t	β	P_t
Intercept	-5.206	0.31	-2.894	0.44	-2.087	0.59	-3.557	0.54	-6.024	0.00
Log (miles)	0.040	0.92	0.098	0.65	-0.117	0.58	0.179	0.65	0.005	0.58
Log (average revenue)	1.547	0.12	0.721	0.07	0.437	0.55	0.531	0.77	1.786	0.00
Log (average haul)	0.947	0.24	0.354	0.40	0.767	0.13	0.968	0.17	1.226	0.00
Log (average load)	0.699	0.55	-0.285	0.71	-0.149	0.85	-1.092	0.57	0.687	0.00
Radial	-0.009	0.99	0.948	0.05	-0.727	0.16	-0.980	0.26	0.295	0.00
Contract	-1.266	0.46	-1.016	0.16	-0.436	0.40	-0.810	0.40	-1.185	0.20
Region 1	0.267	0.89	0.520	0.76	-0.107	0.95	-0.715	0.71	-0.612	0.29
Region 2	1.311	0.31	-0.359	0.63	0.222	0.87	-2.507	0.08	-0.279	0.46
Region 3	1.214	0.28	-1.579	0.05	0.023	0.99	-1.676	0.21	-0.170	0.65
Region 4	0.922	0.40	-2.069	0.01	0.111	0.93	-2.955	0.05	-0.732	0.07
Region 5	1.261	0.40	-1.073	0.22	-0.527	0.72	-2.031	0.18	0.048	0.92
Region 6	0.343	0.79	-1.005	0.30	-0.631	0.65	-1.070	0.50	-1.015	0.04
Region 7	-0.083	0.95	-0.239	0.80	0.321	0.82	-2.461	0.17	0.144	0.74
Region 8	0.807	0.63	-1.079	0.26	-0.792	0.57	-0.605	0.66	0.680	0.22
No owner-operator use	-0.337	0.64	-0.047	0.94	-0.291	0.47	-0.533	0.49	-2.39	0.02
Number of Observations	26		67		57		44		263	
$F = Value$	1.10		1.88		0.77		1.52		13.44	
P_F	0.453		0.048		0.704		0.163		0.001	
R^2	0.62		0.36		0.22		0.45		0.44	

Table A-3
Regression of Log of Insurance and Safety Cost per Mile, Various Carrier Groups, 1977 Data

	Heavy Machinery		Petroleum Products		Refrigerated Products		Building Materials		Other Specialized	
	β	P_t	β	P_t	β	P_t	β	P_t	β	P_t
Intercept	-11.404	0.19	-16.13	0.00	-14.57	0.00	-14.45	0.02	-7.86	0.00
Log (miles)	0.021	0.97	0.435	0.06	0.459	0.01	0.455	0.17	0.149	0.160
Log (average revenue)	-0.892	0.57	1.202	0.00	2.574	0.00	0.524	0.77	1.641	0.00
Log (average haul)	1.029	0.45	0.940	0.03	0.312	0.46	0.033	0.95	0.094	0.50
Log (average load)	-1.447	0.45	1.144	0.15	2.521	0.00	1.109	0.54	1.412	0.00
Radial	0.039	0.98	1.209	0.01	0.065	0.89	-0.681	0.33	0.186	0.45
Contract	0.763	0.78	-0.072	0.92	0.561	0.24	1.075	0.13	-0.215	0.35
Region 1	1.120	0.74	3.498	0.05	0.848	0.56	-0.049	0.98	-0.404	0.54
Region 2	0.382	0.85	0.879	0.24	-0.185	0.88	1.143	0.34	0.204	0.64
Region 3	-1.247	0.49	-0.691	0.38	-0.916	0.43	0.146	0.90	0.274	0.53
Region 4	1.257	0.48	-0.243	0.74	0.45	0.70	1.658	0.21	0.844	0.07
Region 5	-0.411	0.87	-0.160	0.09	-1.182	0.34	0.096	0.94	0.387	0.48
Region 6	-0.779	0.72	-0.889	0.36	0.492	0.68	1.567	0.23	0.450	0.40
Region 7	-3.597	0.21	0.280	0.77	0.366	0.76	0.530	0.72	0.386	0.46
Region 8	1.343	0.63	1.538	0.09	0.289	0.81	0.176	0.89	0.979	0.13
No owner-operator use	1.505	0.24	-0.605	0.33	-0.542	0.12	-0.788	0.28	-0.440	0.08
Number of Observations	25		66		55		40		246	
F = Value	0.59		2.51		2.45		1.16		5.20	
P_F	0.82		0.008		0.013		0.365		0.0001	
R^2	0.50		0.43		0.48		0.42		0.25	

Table A-4
Regression of Log of Administrative Cost per Ton, Various Carrier Groups, 1977 Data

	Heavy Machinery		Petroleum Products		Refrigerated Products		Building Materials		Other Specialized	
	β	P_t	β	P_t	β	P_t	β	P_t	β	P_t
Intercept	-4.713	0.07	-3.51	0.02	-0.528	0.72	-2.573	0.20	-0.570	0.40
Log (miles)	-0.097	0.59	-0.004	0.67	-0.253	0.01	0.020	0.87	-0.130	0.00
Log (average revenue)	1.917	0.00	0.811	0.00	1.403	0.00	1.682	0.00	1.130	0.00
Log (average haul)	1.419	0.00	1.084	0.00	1.241	0.00	1.314	0.00	1.048	0.00
Log (average load)	1.224	0.03	-0.017	0.95	0.164	0.60	0.013	0.98	-0.082	0.43
Radial	-0.003	0.99	-0.288	0.09	-0.331	0.13	-0.285	0.29	0.143	0.16
Contract	-1.114	0.17	0.287	0.27	0.163	0.42	-0.295	0.32	-0.289	0.00
Region 1	0.655	0.47	0.155	0.81	0.575	0.29	0.113	0.86	0.200	0.43
Region 2	0.085	0.89	0.300	0.28	0.722	0.12	-0.145	0.76	-0.075	0.65
Region 3	-0.353	0.51	0.137	0.63	0.719	0.10	-0.943	0.04	0.062	0.71
Region 4	0.094	0.85	0.007	0.98	0.835	0.05	-0.963	0.04	-0.027	0.88
Region 5	0.178	0.80	-0.088	0.79	0.604	0.20	-0.565	0.27	-0.117	0.59
Region 6	0.156	0.81	-0.043	0.91	0.573	0.18	-0.419	0.43	-0.280	0.19
Region 7	-0.846	0.17	-0.049	0.89	0.963	0.05	-0.680	0.23	0.199	0.31
Region 8	0.137	0.87	-0.065	0.85	0.707	0.11	-0.071	0.88	-0.377	0.13
No owner-operator use	0.133	0.71	0.324	0.15	-0.127	0.42	0.243	0.31	0.024	0.80
Number of Observations	27		72		62		48		285	
F = Value	2.97		8.80		4.99		5.88		48.82	
P_F	0.037		0.001		0.001		0.001		0.001	

Table A-5
Regression of Log of Operating Ratio, Various Carrier Groups, 1977 Data

	Heavy Machinery		Petroleum Products		Refrigerated Products		Building Materials		Other Specialized	
	β	P_t	β	P_t	β	P_t	β	P_t	β	P_t
Intercept	-0.069	0.72	-0.014	0.91	-0.108	0.55	0.257	0.05	0.055	0.44
Log (miles)	-0.040	0.01	0.008	0.26	-0.002	0.89	-0.020	0.02	-0.006	0.22
Log (average revenue)	-0.054	0.16	0.005	0.72	-0.008	0.82	-0.020	0.54	-0.008	0.40
Log (average haul)	0.102	0.00	0.000	0.97	0.015	0.51	-0.000	0.97	-0.000	0.97
Log (average load)	-0.040	0.35	-0.036	0.15	-0.024	0.52	-0.002	0.94	-0.009	0.39
Radial	0.077	0.03	-0.004	0.79	0.010	0.69	0.019	0.25	0.010	0.35
Contract	-0.016	0.80	0.000	0.99	0.018	0.47	-0.025	0.17	-0.005	0.61
Region 1	0.088	0.23	0.069	0.23	0.048	0.47	-0.022	0.61	0.010	0.71
Region 2	-0.022	0.64	-0.033	0.18	0.074	0.19	-0.024	0.42	0.009	0.61
Region 3	0.015	0.73	-0.029	0.24	0.059	0.26	-0.012	0.66	0.007	0.71
Region 4	-0.036	0.37	-0.037	0.11	0.020	0.69	0.005	0.88	-0.008	0.67
Region 5	-0.054	0.33	-0.020	0.48	0.015	0.79	-0.011	0.74	0.007	0.77
Region 6	-0.038	0.45	-0.058	0.07	0.073	0.17	-0.067	0.06	-0.022	0.34
Region 7	-0.007	0.87	-0.049	0.13	0.054	0.35	-0.002	0.96	-0.029	0.17
Region 8	0.065	0.33	-0.017	0.56	0.022	0.68	-0.052	0.10	-0.021	0.43
No owner-operator use	0.016	0.56	-0.019	0.32	-0.012	0.53	0.024	0.12	-0.015	0.14
Number of Observations	27		72		62		50		293	
F = Value	2.83		0.88		0.62		1.55		1.03	
P_F	0.044		0.589		0.843		0.14		0.42	
R^2	0.79		0.13		0.17		0.41		0.05	

Table A-6
Regression of Log of Return on Equity, Various Carrier Groups, 1977 Data

	Heavy Machinery		Petroleum Products		Refrigerated Products		Building Materials		Other Specialized	
	β	P_t	β	P_t	β	P_t	β	P_t	β	P_t
Intercept	4.595	0.00	4.476	0.00	4.573	0.00	4.679	0.00	4.602	0.00
Log (miles)	0.003	0.07	0.006	0.42	0.001	0.55	-0.005	0.13	0.001	0.71
Log (average revenue)	0.002	0.67	0.007	0.64	0.005	0.29	-0.009	0.49	0.001	0.79
Log (average haul)	-0.006	0.05	0.000	0.98	0.004	0.10	-0.000	0.93	0.002	0.14
Log (average load)	0.005	0.24	0.002	0.93	0.002	0.65	-0.007	0.55	-0.002	0.44
Radial	-0.004	0.16	0.009	0.57	0.000	0.88	0.010	0.11	-0.000	0.96
Contract	0.022	0.00	0.013	0.61	0.003	0.37	-0.002	0.79	-0.002	0.26
Region 1	0.003	0.63	-0.086	0.17	0.007	0.38	-0.001	0.95	-0.003	0.62
Region 2	0.011	0.03	0.015	0.57	0.010	0.15	0.000	0.99	-0.005	0.20
Region 3	0.001	0.75	0.002	0.94	0.002	0.70	0.004	0.74	0.002	0.62
Region 4	0.006	0.17	0.019	0.45	0.002	0.74	-0.004	0.72	-0.002	0.57
Region 5	0.005	0.38	-0.007	0.83	0.003	0.63	0.009	0.68	-0.004	0.41
Region 6	0.004	0.43	-0.096	0.01	-0.002	0.74	-0.025	0.06	-0.000	0.92
Region 7	0.003	0.46	0.004	0.91	0.001	0.88	0.008	0.54	0.002	0.71
Region 8	0.005	0.41	0.000	0.99	0.004	0.54	0.003	0.81	0.003	0.58
No owner-operator use	-0.003	0.33	0.048	0.03	-0.003	0.16	-0.011	0.06	-0.001	0.71
Number of Observations	27		72		62		50		293	
F = Value	2.18		1.69		0.97		1.10		0.97	
P_F	0.10		0.08		0.97		0.39		0.49	
R^2	0.75		0.31		0.24		0.33		0.05	

markets. In the case of petroleum products and building materials, the percent increase in line-haul costs more closely matches the full percent increase in average revenue per ton-mile (or vice versa), since these coefficients are closer to 1.

We have already noted a close relationship between average revenue per ton-mile and the degree of owner-operator use. The inclusion of both these variables in the equations shown in table A-1 allows us to detect whether carriers that use owner-operators predominantly have lower line-haul costs per mile than those carriers that do not, apart from any differences in traffic "quality." It may be seen in table A-1 that such differences *do* exist for the refrigerated-products group and the "other specialized" group of carriers (though not for carriers of heavy machinery, petroleum products, or building materials). In the case of refrigerated products, coefficient of -0.070 for the "no-OO use" variable indicates that carriers that do not use owner-operators have line-haul costs per miles that are $e^{-0.070}$, or 93.2 percent of those for owner-operator carriers. In the case of "other specialized" carriers, the relevant factor is $e^{-1.07}$, or 90 percent.

These results are somewhat surprising in that *if* owner-operators are being used because of their greater productivity and/or lower labor cost, we would expect to see higher per-mile line-haul costs for non-owner-operator carriers. Two possible explanations may be given. First, these results might indicate that lower labor cost is *not* an important rationale for using owner-operators in these two sections. Second, we might attribute this result to accounting procedures. Owner-operators may not only for line-haul activities but also some insurance, maintenance, and so on, and their compensation reflects this. If all payments to owner-operators are appearing as line-haul costs, then these will appear high for owner-operator carriers.

As would have been predicted, the coefficient for log (miles), a measure of carrier size, is not significant for any of the carrier groups, with the exception of "other specialized carriers." This indicates that there are no economies of scale in line-haul costs. For the "other specialized" group, line-haul costs per mile seem to increase with size of carrier.

The attempt to explain variations in traffic and sales expenses per ton (table A-2) was not successful, except for petroleum and other specialized carriers. For petroleum haulers the coefficient for owner-operator use was not significant, while for other specialized carriers the effect of not using owner-operators appears to be to lower traffic and sales cost by 91 percent ($e^{-2.39}$ equals .09)! This dramatic result could not be explained and should be treated with extreme caution. In no case does there appear to be any economies of scale (that is, a significant coefficient for the log of total miles).

The regressions of line-haul and safety cost per mile (table A-3) appear successful for petroleum, refrigerated and "other" haulers. Only for "other" haulers does the "no-OO" coefficient have significance at the 10 percent level: the effect is to raise costs by 36 percent for those carriers that use owner-operators. Significant economies of scale appear for petroleum and refrigerated-products haulers: the respective elasticities are 0.435 and 0.479.

The regressions of general and administrative costs (table A-4) appear successful, but there does not appear to be a signficant owner-operator effect. Very substantial economies of scale appear in the refrigerated and "other" product categories.

Regressions of the log of operating ratio (table A-5) were not successful: only for heavy machinery was the F-statistic significant below the 20 percent level. Owner-operator use does not appear to be a major determinant of operating ratio. The regressions of the log of return on equity have significant F values only for the heavy-machinery and petroleum-products groups. Of these two, only the petroleum haulers exhibit an owner-operator effect: carriers that do *not* use owner-operators have an average return on equity that is 105 percent of that of owner-operator carriers! Although the overall regression is not significant, the building-materials carriers also possess a signficant coefficient relating to owner-operators; carriers that do not use owner-operators have a return on equity that is 99 percent of those that do. These results are counterintuitive: we would have expected owner-operator carriers to require less capitalization that non-owner-operator carriers, and hence to receive higher returns. This does not, however, appear to be the case.

The statistically-minded reader should note that the results presented here are but a few of the analyses performed. Experiments with the data base were also conducted using all the applicable data (that is, not only negligible and predominant users of owner-operators), and with linear functional form. While specific results varied, the general conclusions of this appendix were supported by these other analyses. However, there can be no doubt that there is the opportunity for further research in this area.

Notes

Chapter 1
The Owner-Operator System

1. See, for example, U.S. Department of Justice, Antitrust Division, *The Effects of ICC Regulation on Independent Owner-Operators in the Trucking Industry*, Report of the Attorney General Pursuant to Section 10(c) of the Small Business Act, as amended (Washington, D.C.: no date, mimeograph).

2. Gary B. Kogon, "A Study of Regular Route Motor Common Carrier Special Commodity Division" (Master's thesis, The Pennsylvania State University, November 1979).

3. For a good discussion of the history of ICC leasing regulations, see R.J. Corber, *Motor Carrier Leasing and Interchange Under the Interstate Commerce Act* (Washington, D.C.: Common Carrier Conference—Irregular Route, 1977). It should be noted that Corber's book was published before the revisions to the leasing regulations described in chapter 5 of this book.

4. See P. Cavanaugh, "Private Carriers Urged to Make More Use of Owner Operators," *Transport Topics*, June 19, 1978, and D.N. Nisserberg, "Leasing to Private Carriers," *Open Road Magazine*, February 1977, p. 22.

5. For the assertion, see the testimony of William Hill in *Regulatory Problems of the Independent Owner-Operator in the Nation's Trucking Industry (Part I)* (Washington, D.C.: U.S. Government Printing Office, 1976). For rebuttal, see *Allegations and Answers about Independent Truck Owners* (Washington, D.C.: Common Carrier Conference—Irregular Route, July 1977).

6. *The Independent Trucker, A Preliminary Report on the Owner Operator*, Bureau of Economics, Interstate Commerce Commission, Washington, D.C., November 1977, p. 5.

7. Ibid.

8. D.D. Wyckoff and D.H. Maister, *The Owner-Operator: Independent Trucker* (Lexington, Mass.: Lexington Books, D.C. Heath, 1975), chapter 1.

9. See *Regulatory Problems of the Independent Owner-Operator in the Nation's Trucking Industry*, Report No. 95-1812 (Washington, D.C.: U.S. Government Printing Office, 1978), p. 5.

Chapter 2
Understanding the Owner-Operator System

1. D.D. Wyckoff and D.H. Maister, *The Owner-Operator: Independent Trucker* (Lexington, Mass.: Lexington Books, D.C. Heath, 1975), chapter 2

2. Interstate Commerce Commission, *Lease and Interchange of Vehicles*, Ex Parte No. MC-43 (Sub-No. 7), 131 MCC 141 (16 January 1979).

3. L.G. Harter, Jr., "Are They Employees or Independent Contractors?" *Labor Law Journal*, December 1978, pp. 779-785.

4. Comptroller General of the United States, *Tax Treatment of Employees and Self-Employed Persons by the Internal Revenue Service: Problems and Solutions*, GGD-77-88, November 21, 1977.

5. See, for example, A.R. Oxenfeldt and M.W. Watkins, *Make or Buy: Factors Affecting Executive Decisions* (New York: McGraw-Hill, Consultant Reports on Current Business Problems, 1956); J.W. Culliton, *Make or Buy* (Boston: Division of Research, Harvard Business School, 1942); C.C. Higgins, "Make or Buy Re-Examined," *Harvard Business Review* 33 (1955):109-119.

6. See, for example, N.E. Harlan, *Management Control in Airframe Subcontracting* (Boston: Division of Research, Graduate School of Business Administration, Harvard University, 1956); A.S. Borstein et al., *A Special Report on Contract Maintenance* (Salt Lake City: Contract Maintenance Associates, 1964); M.K. Chandler and L.R. Sayles, *Contracting-Out: A Study of Management Decision Making* (New York: Graduate School of Business, Columbia University, 1959); U.S. Bureau of Labor Statistics, *Subcontracting Clauses in Major Collective Bargaining Agreements*, Bulletin No. 1304 (August 1961); U.S. Bureau of Labor Statistics, *Subcontracting*, Bulletin No. 1425-8 (April 1969).

7. D. Izraeli, *Franchising and the Total Distribution System* (London: Longman Group Limited, 1972), pp. 22-23.

8. D.N. Thompson, *Franchise Operations and Antitrust* (Lexington, Mass.: Lexington Books, D.C. Heath, 1971), pp. 7-8.

9. R. Metz, *Franchising: How to Select a Business of Your Own* (New York: Hawthorn Books, 1969), pp. 250-258.

10. *Regulatory Problems of the Independent Owner-Operator in the Nation's Trucking Industry*, Hearings Before the Subcommittee on Special Small Business Problems of the Committee of Small Business, House of Representatives, 95th Congress, First Session, 1976 (Part 1), 1977 (Part 2), 1978 (Part 3).

11. Taken from H. Kursh, *The Franchise Boom*, New Revised Edition (Englewood Cliffs, N.J.: Prentice-Hall, 1968), p. 42.

12. Adapted from "The Franchise Business," Small Business Advisory Service, *Small Business Reporter* 6, as quoted in H. Kursh, *The Franchise Boom*.

13. See D.N. Thompson, *Franchise Operations and Antitrust*, pp. 33-34.

14. See, for example, "Franchising, No End to Its Growth," *Printers Ink*, August 13, 1965, p. 3.

15. Interstate Commerce Commission, *Lease and Interchange of Vehicles; Regulatory Problems. . . .*

16. R.J. Emmons, *The American Franchise Revolution* (Newport Beach, Calif.: Burton House, 1970), pp. 6-7.

17. H. Brown, *Franchising: Trap for the Trusting* (Boston: Little, Brown, 1969).

18. H. Brown, *Franchising: Realities and Remedies* (New York: Law Journal Press, 1973), p. 6.

19. Louis P. Bucklin, "The Economic Base of Franchising," in D.N. Thompson, *Contractual Marketing Systems* (Lexington, Mass.: Lexington Books, D.C. Heath, 1971, pp. 33-62 at p. 37.

20. S.D. Hunt and J.R. Nevin, "Full Disclosure Laws in Franchising: An Empirical Investigation," *Journal of Marketing* 40 (April 1976): 53-62.

21. S.D. Hunt, "Franchising: Promises, Problems, Prospects," *Journal of Retailing* 53 (Fall 1977):71-84.

22. Charles L. Vaughn, *Franchising: Its Nature, Scope, Advantages and Development* (Lexington, Mass. Lexington Books, D.C. Heath, 1974), pp. 20-22.

23. *Distribution Problems Affecting Small Business*, Hearings before the Subcommitte on Antitrust and Monopoly of the Committee of the Judiciary, U.S. Senate, 80th Congress, First Session: Part 1, Franchising Agreements (March 2, 3, 4, 1965).

24. T.G. Moore, *Trucking Regulation: Lessons from Europe* (Washington, D.C.: American Enterprise Institute for Public Policy Research, 1976), pp. 111-117.

25. Price Commission, *The Road Haulage Industry* (London: Her Majesty's Stationery Office, 1978), pp. 32-33.

26. Ibid., p. 33.

27. P.J. Rimmer, *Freight Forwarding in Australia* (Canberra: Department of Human Geography Publication H G/4, Research School of Pacific Studies, Australian National University, 1970).

28. Ibid., p. 144.

29. Western Australia, *Inquiry into the Road Transport Industry* (1974), p. 21.

30. Ibid., p. 23.

31. For a discussion of Canada's regulatory environment, see Maister, "Regulation and the Level of Trucking Rates in Canada," in *Workshop on Economic Regulation of the Motor Carrier Industry* (Washington, D.C.: National Academy of Sciences, 1978).

32. Statistics on Canada are taken from Statistics Canada, *Motor Carriers: Freight* (Ottawa: Queen's Printer, 1976).

33. D.H. Maister and W. Behrenbruch, *The Owner Operator Study: Phase One, A Review of Current Laws*, An Interim Report Prepared for the *Canadian Conference of Motor Transport Administrators*, November 1978 (mimeograph).

34. Ibid.

35. *Report of the Select Committee of the Legislative Assembly Reviewing Intraprovincial Trucking Regulations* (Edmonton, Alberta, March 1977).

36. Quoted in J. Strickland, "Where Have All the Owner-Operators Gone?" *Commercial Car Journal*, February 1977, pp. 99-104.

37. *Susser* v. *Carvel Corp.*, 206 F. Supp. 636 (SDNY 1962), at 640.

38. E. Patrick McGuire, *Franchised Distribution* (New York: The Conference Board, 1971), p. 4.

39. Bucklin, "The Economic Base," p. 37.

40. Hunt, "Franchising," p. 73.

Chapter 3
An Overview of Owner-Operator Management

1. C.L. Vaughn and Slater, D.B., eds., *Franchising Today 1966-67* (Chicago: Matthew Bender, 1967), p. 252.

2. Ibid., p. 256.

3. P.R. Stephenson and R.G. House, "A Perspective on Franchising: The Design of an Effective Relationship," *Business Horizons* 14 (August 1971):36.

4. Ibid.

5. R.J. Emmons, *The American Franchise Revolution* (Newport Beach, Calif.: Burton House, 1970), p. 45.

6. For a general overview of channel theory see B. Mallen, *Principles of Marketing Channel Management* (Lexington, Mass.: Lexington Books, D.C. Heath, 1977).

7. Ibid., p. 223.

8. L.P. Bucklin, "A Theory of Channel Control," *Journal of Marketing* 37 (January 1973):39-47.

9. Mallen, *Principles*, p. 267.

10. D. Dixon, "Intra-Channel Conflict Resolution," *Houston Business Review*, Spring 1967, pp. 36-48.

11. Mallen, *Principles*, pp. 232-233.

12. D.L. Price, "Key Elements in a Sound Distributor System," *Building a Sound Distributor Organization* (New York: National Industrial Conference Board, 1964), pp. 13-14.

13. D.N. Thompson, *Franchise Operations and Antitrust* (Lexington, Mass.: Lexington Books, D.C. Heath, 1971), p. 53.

14. A.R. Oxenfeldt and A.O. Kelly, "Will Successful Franchise Systems Ultimately Become Wholly-Owned Chains?" *Journal of Retailing* 44 (Winter 1968-69):75. Reprinted with permission.

15. D. Daryl Wyckoff, *Organizational Formality and Performance in the Motor Carrier Industry* (Lexington, Mass.: Lexington Books, D.C. Heath, 1974).

16. S.W. Gellerman, *Motivation and Productivity* (New York: American Management Association, 1963).

17. A.H. Maslow, *Motivation and Personality*, 2nd ed. (New York: Harper and Row, 1970).

18. D.D. Wyckoff and D.H. Maister, *The Owner-Operator: Independent Trucker* (Lexington, Mass.: Lexington Books, D.C. Heath, 1975), chapter 4.

19. D. McGregor, *The Professional Manager* (New York: McGraw-Hill, 1967), pp. 3-5. See also the same author's *The Human Side of Enterprise* (New York: McGraw-Hill, 1960).

20. F. Hertzberg, "One More Time: How Do You Motivate Employees?" *Harvard Business Review* 46 (January-February 1968):53-62.

Chapter 4
Recruiting

1. E.H. Lewis and R.S. Hancock, *The Franchise System of Distribution* (Minneapolis: University of Minnesota, 1963), p. 80.

2. A.R. Oxenfeldt and D.N. Thompson, "Franchising in Perspective," *Journal of Retailing* 44 (Winter 1968-69):9.

3. See any standard marketing text. For example, P. Kotler, *Marketing Management*, 2nd ed. (Englewood Clifs, N.J.: Prentice-Hall, 1967), chapter 18.

4. "Carrier-Contractor Pacts: Communication's the Key," *Heavy Duty Trucking*, August 1976, p. 37

5. H. Wattel, "Are Franchisors Realistic and Successful in Their Selection of Franchisees?" *Journal of Retailing* 44 (Winter 1968-69):58.

6. R. Jasmon, "Ten Rules for a Successful Trucker," *Open Road Magazine*, March 1978, p. 47.

7. K.H. Thomas, "You Hire Your Own Problem," *Terminal Operator*, September 1977, p. 7.

8. "Red Ball Motor Owner-Operators Strong on Business Skills," *Transport Topics*, May 8, 1978.

9. R.M. Rosenberg and M. Bedell, *Profits from Franchising* (New York: McGraw-Hill, 1969), p. 49.

10. *Motor Fleet Safety Manual* (Chicago: National Safety Council, 1966), p. 108.

11. *Regulatory Problems of the Independent Owner-Operator in the Nation's Trucking Industry (Part I)*, Hearings before the Subcommittee

on Activities of Regulatory Agencies of the Committee on Small Business, House of Representatives, 94th Congress, 2nd Session, 1976, pp. 91-92.

12. *The Independent Trucker: A Preliminary Report on the Owner-Operator*, Interstate Commerce Commission, Bureau of Economics, Washington, D.C., November 1977, p. 13.

13. C.L. Vaughn, *Franchising* (Lexington, Mass.: Lexington Books, D.C. Heath, 1974), p. 46.

Chapter 5
Contracts and Payment Systems

1. E.P. McGuire, *Franchised Distribution* (New York: The Conference Board, 1971), p. 54.

2. D.D. Wyckoff and D.H. Maister, *The Owner-Operator: Independent Trucker* (Lexington, Mass.: Lexington Books, D.C. Heath, 1975), chapter 6.

3. McGuire, *Franchised Distribution*, p. 54.

4. *Lease and Interchange of Vehicles*, 49 CFR 1057.

5. *Lease and Interchange of Vehicles*, Ex Parte No. MC-43 (Sub-No. 7), January 9, 1979, 131 M.C.C. 142.

6. 48 CFR 1057.12 (d).

7. Administrative Ruling No. 126, Revised March 1, 1979, Question and Answer 20.

8. Ibid., Question and Answer 24.

9. 49 CFR 1057.12 (e).

10. 49 CFR 1057.12 (f).

11. 49 CFR 1057.12 (i).

12. 49 U.S.C. 10927.

13. *Transamerican* v. *Brada Miller*, 96 S. Ct. 229 (1975).

14. ICC Bureau of Operations, *Truck Leasing: Staff Report on Motor Common Carrier Leasing Practices and the Owner Operator*) mimeo, August 1977). ICC Bureau of Economics, *The Independent Trucker: A Preliminary Report on the Owner-Operator*, Washington, D.C., November 1977. ICC Bureau of Economics, *The Independent Trucker: Nationwide Survey of Owner-Operators*, Washington, D.C., May 1978.

15. *The Independent Trucker: A Preliminary Report*.

16. See *Transamerican* (footnote 13); *Tanksby*, 110 MCC 674 (1969); and *Diamond*, 117 MCC 706 (1973).

17. McGuire, *Franchised Distribution*, p. 55.

18. J.G. Van Cise, "A Franchise Contract," in *Franchising Today* (1970), C.L. Vaughn, ed. (Lynbrook, N.Y.: Farnsworth Publishing Co., 1970), pp. 296-317.

Chapter 6
Operations

1. D.D. Wyckoff, *Organizational Formality and Performance in the Motor-Carrier Industry* (Lexington, Mass.: Lexington Books, D.C. Heath, 1974).
2. R. Eads, "Managing Specialized Carriers," *Motor Freight Controller*, February 1978, pp. 4-8.
3. "Salespatchers Find New Business For Craig," *Refrigerated Transporter*, April 1975, pp. 20-21.
4. Ibid.
5. Smiley, "What Turns Drivers . . . On . . . Off," *Heavy Duty Trucking*, January 1978, pp. 36-38.
6. Ibid.
7. D. McRae, Jr., "Computer Assisted Dispatching," *Proceedings: American Trucking Associations—Management Systems Council Conference—1974* (Washington, D.C.: American Trucking Association, 1974), pp. 129-136. Reprinted with permission.
8. Ibid.
9. "On Line Computer Helps C & H Solve Dispatch Problems," *Transport Topics*, December 5, 1977.
10. *Owner-Operator Divisions, Irregular Route Structure and Carrier Agencies*, Department of Transportation (no date), cited in *Regulatory Problems of the Independent Owner Operator in the Nation's Trucking Industry (Part 1)*, Washington, D.C.: Government Printing Office, 1976, p. 71.
11. See, for example, "Carrier Agent Is Indicted for Fraud in Trip Leasing Deal," *Transport Topics*, July 18, 1977.
12. "ICC Adopts Final Rules Establishing Simplified Property Broker Licensing," *Traffic World*, September 24, 1979, p. 121.
13. D.D. Wyckoff, *The Truck Driver in America* (Lexington, Mass.: Lexington Books, D.C. Heath, 1979), p. 87.
14. See, for example, T.A. Patten, Jr., *The Foreman: Forgotten Man of Management*, American Management Association, 1968; S.W. Gellerman, "Supervision: Substance and Style," *Harvard Business Review*, March-April 1976, pp. 89-99; A.Q. Sartain and A.W. Baker, *The Supervisor and His Job* (New York: McGraw-Hill, 1972).

Chapter 7
Information and Control Systems

1. R.J. Emmons, *The American Franchise Revolution* (Newport Beach, Calif.: Burton House, 1970), pp. 55-56.

2. *Motor Carrier Rates—Owner Operators*, 341 I.C.C. 28 (1972).

3. *Iron and Steel Scrap from Conn., Mass., and R.I. to Pa.*, 318 I.C.C. 567 (1962).

4. *Eastern Central Motor Carriers Ass'n* v. *United States*, 239 F. Supp. 600 (1965). See also 251 F. Supp. 483 (1966).

5. Ex Parte No. MC-71 (Sub-No. 1), *Owner-Operator Cost and Impact on the Rate Structure*, Comments of American Trucking Associations, Inc., March 31, 1978, p. 2.

6. D.D. Wyckoff and D.H. Maister, *The Owner-Operator: Independent Trucker* (Lexington, Mass.: Lexington Books, D.C. Heath, 1975), chapter 2.

7. Ibid.

8. E.E. Hamel, Letter to I.C.C. Re Docket No. Ex Parte No. 71 (Sub-No. 1), February 27, 1978. Reprinted with permission.

9. See, for example, D.F. Silver, "Bekins Van Lines Manager Sees Big Revenue Gains, Views Mover Problems," *Traffic World*, July 17, 1978, pp. 29-30.

10. Emmons, *The American Franchise Revolution*.

11. R.J. Mockler and H.E. Easop, "The Art of Managing a Franchise," *Business Horizons*, August 1968, p. 31.

12. R.M. Rosenberg and M. Bedell, *Profits From Franchising* (New York: McGraw-Hill, 1969), p. 114.

Chapter 8
Independent Contractors, Employees, and Unions

1. D.D. Wyckoff and D.H. Maister, *The Owner-Operator: Independent Trucker* (Lexington, Mass.: Lexington Books, D.C. Heath, 1975).

2. *Restatement of the Law of Agency* 220, p. 373.

3. 450 F. 2d at 1328, fr. 4, as cited by R.J. Corber, *Motor Carrier Leasing and Interchange under the Interstate Commerce Act* (Washington, D.C.: Common Carrier Conference—Irregular Route, 1977), pp. 72-73.

4. *Wall Street Journal*, August 30, 1978, p. 1.

5. *NLRB* v. *Hearst Publications, Inc.*, 322 US 111 (1944), 8 LC 51, 179.

6. Ibid., p. 130.

7. *NLRB* v. *United Insurance Company of America*, 390 US 254, 88 S. Ct 988, 1968.

8. *Allied Chemical and Alkali Workers* v. *Pittsburgh Plate Glass Co.*, 404 US 157, 92 S. Ct. 383, 1971.

9. See, for example, *Conley Motor Express, Inc.* 197 NLRB no. 56, 1972 CCH NLRB 24.320.; *Ace Doran Hauling and Rigging Co.* v. *NLRB*,

462 F. 2d 190 (6 Cir. 1972); *NLRB* v. *Cement Transportation*, 490 F. 2d 1924 (6 Cir. 1974).

10. H.H. Aitken, Jr., "Breakdown of NLRB Position on Owner-Operators," *Trucking Labor Relations Information Special* 28 (October 15, 1973).

11. *Deaton*, 76 LRRM 1132, 1971.

12. *George Transfer and Rigging Company, Inc.*, 208 NLRB no. 25 1974, CCH NLRB.

13. L.G. Harter, Jr., "Are They Employees or Independent Contractors?" *Labor Law Journal*, December 1978, pp. 779-784.

14. Ibid., pp. 783-778.

15. *Local 814, Int. Bro. of Teamsters, Inc. etc.* v. *NLRB*, 546 F. 2d 989, 991 (1976).

16. *Molloy Brothers Moving and Storage, Inc.*, 208 NLRB 276 (1974).

17. *Santini Brothers, Inc.*, 208 NLRB 184 (1975).

18. *Local 814, Int. Bro. of Teamsters, Inc., etc.* v. *NLRB,*, 512 F. 2d 564 (1975).

19. *Local 814* (1976).

20. *Harrison* v. *Grayvans, Inc.*, US 704, 718-719.

21. *Rutherford Food Corp.* v. *McComb*, 331 US 722 (1947).

22. *Clarkson Construction Co.* v. *Occupational Safety and Health Review Commission*, 531 F. 2d 451 (10 Ar. 1976).

23. See *Heavy Specialized Carriers Conference Newsletter*, July 6, 1973.

24. See *Trucking Labor Relations Information Special* 31 (September 15, 1976).

25. *Tax Treatment of Employees and Self-Employed Persons by the Internal Revenue Service: Problems and Solutions*, A Report to the Joint Committee on Taxation, Congress of the United States by the Comptroller General of the United States, GGD-77-88, November 21, 1977.

26. Ibid., p. iii.

27. "Treasury Urges Tax Withholding Plan for 'Independent Contractor' Workers," *Wall Street Journal*, June 21, 1979, p. 18.

28. "Withholding Tax Proposals," *Transport Topics*, July 23, 1979, p. 1.

29. Ibid.

30. D.C. Nevins, *Owner Operators: Employees or Independent Contractors?* (Washington, D.C.: Industrial Relations Department, American Trucking Associations, Inc., 1965), p. 26.

31. A. Larson, *The Law of Workmen's Compensation* (Chicago: Matthew Bender and Company, 1952), volume 1, p. 632.

32. Corber, *Motor Carrier Leasing*, pp. 75-76.

33. J. Seidenberg, "Evolution of the Current Pay Practices and Fringe Benefits in the Over-the-Road Motor Freight Industry," in *Report of the Presidential Railroad Commission*, Washington, D.C., February 1962.

34. *In the Matter of Manor Carling Co., and Private Sanitation Union, Local 813, Affiliated with IBT*, N.Y. Labor Board. See *Trucking Labor Relations Information* 16 (January 1, 1961).

35. D. Garnel, *The Rise of Teamster Power in the West* (Berkeley: University of California Press, 1972), p. 114.

36. "Justice Department Owner-Operator Position Raises Ire of Teamster's Union Leader," *Traffic World*, May 15, 1978, p. 23.

37. F. Dobbs, *Teamster Politics* (New York: Monad Press, 1975), p. 243.

38. D. Muldea, *The Hoffa Years* (New York: Paddington Press, 1978), p. 30.

39. Ibid., p. 31.

40. Ibid.

41. Ibid., p. 45.

42. *Local 24, I.B.T.* v. *Revel Oliver, A.C.E. Transportation Company, Inc. and Interstate Truck Service, Inc.*

43. *The . . . Independent Trucker*, p. 14.

44. Ibid., chapter 5.

45. "Federal Judge Orders End to FASH Strike," *Traffic World*, January 15, 1979, p. 11.

46. *Interim Agreement, Iron, Steel, and Special Commodities Rider to Central and Eastern Conference Areas Supplemental Agreements* (mimeo).

47. *Agreement between FASH and Tajon, Inc.* (mimeo).

48. B. Anthony, *Owner-Operators Leased to Regulated Carriers: Industry Overview; Compensation Systems; Operating Costs*, Transportation Systems Center, U.S. Department of Transportation, December 15, 1975.

49. *Traffic World*, May 15, 1978.

50. Ibid.

51. Ibid.

Chapter 9
The Economics of Owner-Operator Use

1. *Allegations and Answers about Independent Truck Owners*, Washington, D.C.: Common Carrier Conference—Irregular Route, 1979.

2. L.S. Case, "Examination of Competition in the Truckload Intercity Motor Carrier Freight Industry," *Proceedings of 1979 Annual Meeting of the Transportation Research Forum*, Oxford, Ind.: Richard B. Cross, 1979, pp. 116-125.

Chapter 10
The Future of the Owner-Operator System

1. "ICC Small Business Office," *Transport Topics*, November 14, 1977.

2. "ICC Asks Carriers Name Liaison for Owner Operators," *Transport Topics*, March 19, 1979, p. 5.

3. L. Dash, "Truckers Violate Law in Use of Lumpers," *Washington Post*, April 13, 1978, p. A-7.

4. "ICC Proposes Law to Curb Lumpers Fees," *Transport Topics*, June 19, 1978.

5. L. Witconis, "Will Lumpers Get Their Lumps?" *Owner Operator*, July-August 1978, pp. 79-82.

6. "ICC Asked to Take Another Look at Detention Rules," *Transport Topics*, July 23, 1977, p. 25.

7. D.D. Wyckoff and D.H. Maister, *The Owner-Operator: Independent Trucker* (Lexington, Mass.: Lexington Books, D.C. Heath, 1975), chapter 4.

8. "Surcharge Rate on Fuel Stays at Same Level," *Transport Topics*, September 17, 1979, p. 1.

9. "Federal Working Group Marks Progress in Relief for Independent Truckers," *Traffic World*, September 17, 1979, p. 31.

10. *Traffic World*, March 5, 1979, p. 38.

11. K.C. Hoffman, "Training Program Seen Stabilizing Owner-Operator Field," *Transport Topics*, September 10, 1979, p. 9.

12. "ATA, CCC-IR Ask ICC Review of 0/0 Survey," *Transport Topics*, September 3, 1979, p. 3.

13. See *Traffic World*, September 10, 1979, p. 25.

14. D.D. Wyckoff, *The Truck Driver in America* (Lexington, Mass.: Lexington Books, D.C. Heath, 1979), p. 12.

15. C.M. Lillis, C.L. Narayana, and J.L. Gilman, "Competitive Advantage Variation over the Life Cycle of a Franchise," *Journal of Marketing*, October 1976, pp. 77-80.

16. "A Moderate Teamsters' Past?" *Business Week*, August 21, 1978, pp. 86-87.

17. Ibid.

18. Ibid.

Bibliography

Trucking

Books and Monographs

Allegations and Answers about Independent Truck Owners. Washington, D.C.: Common Carrier Conference—Irregular Route, July 1977.

Anthony, B. *Owner-Operators Leased to Regulated Carriers: Industry Overview; Compensation Systems; Operating Costs.* Transportation Systems Center, U.S. Department of Transportation, December 15, 1975.

Baker, F. *Owner-Operator Divisions: Irregular Route Structure and Carrier Agencies.* Salt Lake City: University of Utah, 1975.

Charles River Associates. *Impacts of Proposals for Reform of Economic Regulation on Small Motor Carriers and Small Shippers, Final Report,* Contract No. DOT-OS-60527, Office of the Secretary, U.S. Department of Transportation, July 1977.

Corber, R.J. *Motor Carrier Leasing and Interchange under the Interstate Commerce Act.* Washington, D.C.: Common Carrier Conference—Irregular Route, 1977.

Dobbs, F. *Teamster Politics.* New York: Monad Press, 1975, p. 243.

Garnel, D. *The Rise of Teamster Power in the West.* Berkeley: University of California Press, 1972.

Hudson, W.J., Constantin, J.A. *Motor Transportation: Principles and Practices.* New York: Ronald Press, 1958.

Interstate Commerce Commission, *Initial Report of the Motor Carrier Task Force.* Washington, D.C., May 1979.

Interstate Commerce Commission, Bureau of Economics. *The Independent Trucker: Nationwide Survey of Owner-Operators.* Washington, D.C., May 1978.

———. *The Independent Trucker: A Preliminary Report on the Owner-Operator.* Washington, D.C., November 1977.

Interstate Commerce Commission, Bureau of Operations. *Truck Leasing: Staff Report on Motor Common Carrier Leasing Practices and the Owner-Operator.* Washington, D.C., August 1977.

James, R., and James, E. *Hoffa and the Teamsters: A Study of Union Power.* Princeton, N.J.: D. Van Nostrand, 1965.

Kogon, G.B. "A Study of Regular Route Motor Common Carrier Special Commodity Divisions" (Master's thesis, The Pennsylvania State University, November 1979).

Levinson, H.M., et al. *Collective Bargaining and Technological Change in American Transportation.* Evanston, Ill.: The Transportation Center at Northwestern University, 1971.

213

Maister, D.H., and Behrenbruch, W. *The Owner Operator Study: Phase One, a Review of Current Laws*, An Interim Report Prepared for the *Canadian Conference of Motor Transport Administrators*, November 1978 (mimeograph).

Moore, T.G. *Trucking Regulation: Lessons from Europe*. Washington, D.C.: American Enterprise Institue for Public Policy Research, 1976.

Motor Fleet Safety Manual. Chicago: National Safety Council, 1966.

Muldea, D. *The Hoffa Wars*. New York: Paddington Press, 1978.

Price Commission. *The Road Haulage Industry*. London: Her Majesty's Stationery Office, 1978, pp. 32-33.

Regulatory Problems of the Independent Owner-Operator in the Nation's Trucking Industry, Hearings before the Subcommittee on Special Small Business Problems of the Committee of Small Business, House of Representatives, 95th Congress, First Session, 1976 (Part 1), 1977 (Part 2), 1978 (Part 3).

Report of the Select Committee of the Legislative Assembly Reviewing Intraprovincial Trucking Regulations. Edmonton, Alberta, March 1977.

Regulatory Problems of the Independent Owner-Operator in the Nation's Trucking Industry, Report No. 95-1812. Washington, D.C.: U.S. Government Printing Office, 1978.

Rimmer, P.J. *Freight Forwarding in Australia*. Canberra: Department of Human Geography Publication H G/4, Research School of Pacific Studies, Australian National University, 1970.

Seidenberg, J. "Evolution of the Current Pay Practices and Fringe Benefits in the Over-the-Road Motor Freight Industry," in *Report of the Presidential Railroad Commission*. Washington, D.C.: Government Printing Office, February 1962.

Taff, C. *Commercial Motor Transportation*. Cambridge, Md.: Cornell Maritime Press, 1975.

United States Department of Justice, Antitrust Division. *The Effects of ICC Regulation on Independent Owner-Operators in the Trucking Industry*, Report of the Attorney General Pursuant to Section 10(c) of the Small Business Act, as amended (no date).

Western Australia. *Inquiry into the Road Transport Industry*, 1974, p. 21.

Wyckoff, D. Daryl. *Organizational Formality and Performance in the Motor Carrier Industry*. Lexington, Mass.: Lexington Books, D.C. Heath, 1974.

_____. *The Owner-Operator: Independent Trucker*. Lexington, Mass.: Lexington Books, D.C. Heath, 1975.

_____. *The Truck Driver in America*. Lexington, Mass.: Lexington Books, D.C. Heath, 1979.

Wyckoff, D. Daryl and Maister, D.H. *The Motor Carrier Industry*. Lexington, Mass.: Lexington Books, D.C. Heath, 1977.

Articles

Begley, C.R. "Computer Applications for Irregular Route Carriers," *Proceedings: American Trucking Associations—Management Systems Council Conference*, 1973.

"Bekins' Recruitment Program Opens Up New Opportunities," *Transport Topics*, November 7, 1977.

Brown, C.D. "ICC Small Business Office to Aid Independents and Minorities," *Transport Topics*, November 14, 1977.

"Carrier Agent Is Indicted for Fraud in Trip Leasing Deal," *Transport Topics*, July 18, 1977.

"Carrier-Contractor Pacts: Communication's the Key," *Heavy Duty Trucking* 55 (August 1976).

Case, L.S. "Examination of Competition in the Truckload Intercity Motor Carrier Freight Industry," *Proceedings of 1979 Annual Meeting of the Transportation Research Forum*.

Cavanaugh, P. "Private Carriers Urged to Make More Use of Owner-Operators," *Transport Topics*, June 19, 1978.

Clark, B. "Private Fleets: A Potential Goldmine for Owner Operators," *Owner Operator*, July-August 1977, pp. 79-80.

_____ . "The Private Fleet Dilemma," *Owner Operator*, January-February 1978, pp. 63-65.

Classification of Motor Carriers of Property, Ex-Parte No. MC-10, 2 M.C.C. 703, 1937.

Cochran, F.E. "Keeping Owner-Operators in Business," *Refrigerated Transporter*, February 1977, p. 90.

"Coping with Costs," *Heavy Duty Trucking*, April 1977, pp. 36-41.

Eads, R.D. "Managing Specialized Carriers," *Motor Freight Controller*, February 1978, pp. 4-8.

"Ellsworth Sets Up Retirement Plan for Its Independent Contractors," *Refrigerated Transporter*, September 1977, p. 19.

"Fueling Terminals Help Control Widespread Produce Carrier Fleet," *Refrigerated Transporter*, May 1977, pp. 32-37

Harter, L.G., Jr. "Are They Employees or Independent Contractors?" *Labor Law Journal*, December 1978, pp. 779-785.

"Helping Owner-Operators Find Income Security," *Refrigerated Transporter*, April 1975, pp. 20-21.

"How Do Your Linehaul Costs Measure Up?" *Fleet Owner*, February 1978, pp. 71-72.

"ICC Detention Time Rule Stirs Major Controversy," *Open Road Magazine*, September 1977, pp. 16ff.

"ICC Proposes Law to Curb 'Lumper' Fees," *Transport Topics*, June 19, 1978.

Interstate Commerce Commission, *Lease and Interchange of Vehicles*, Ex Parte No. Mc-43 (Sub-No. 7), 131 MCC 141 (16 January 1979).

Jasmon, R. "Ten Rules for a Successful Trucker," *Open Road Magazine*, March 1978, p. 47.

"Justice Dep't Owner-Operator Position Raises Ire of Teamsters' Union Leader," *Traffic World*, May 15, 1978, pp. 23-26.

"Kentucky Sues HHG Carrier; Charges Abuse of Owner Drivers," *Heavy Duty Trucking* 57 (August 1978):15.

Maister, D.H. "Regulation and the Level of Trucking Rates in Canada," in *Workshop on Economic Regulation of the Motor Carrier Industry*. Washington, D.C.: National Academy of Sciences, 1978.

"Making It without the Teamster's Union," *Heavy Duty Trucking* 57 (June 1978):96-98.

"Managing Driver Performance," *Refrigerated Transporter*, May 1978, pp. 32-37.

"Massive MEMA Survey Probes Truckers Buying Habits," *Transport Topics*, October 31, 1977.

McRae, D., Jr. "Computer Assisted Dispatching," *Proceedings: American Trucking Associations—Management Systems Council*. Washington, D.C.: American Trucking Associations, 1974, pp. 129-136.

Menaker, L.J. "Yardsticks to Measure Linehaul Efficiency," *Terminal Operator*, August 1977, pp. 6-7ff.

"Midwestern Distribution Chief Sees On-Line Computer in 1977," *Transport Topics*, January 10, 1977.

Moore, L. "Heavy Specialized Hauling the C & H Way," *Owner Operator*, March-April 1976, pp. 15-20.

Nissenberg, D.N. "Fair Compensation Needed to Offset Downtime Losses," *Open Road Magazine*, March 1978, p. 12ff.

_____ . "Leasing to Private Carriers," *Open Road Magazine*, February 1977, p. 22.

"On-Line Computer Helps C & H Solve Dispatch Problems," *Transport Topics*, December 5, 1977.

Pfaff, Michael A. "Computer Applications for Irregular Route Carriers," *Proceedings: American Trucking Associations—Management Systems Council Conference*, 1973, pp. 173-179.

"Recruiting and Motivating Owner-Operators," *Refrigerated Transporter*, August 1976, pp. 32-35.

"Red Ball Motor Owner-Operators Strong on Business Skills," *Transport Topics*, May 8, 1978.

" 'Salespatchers' Find New Business for Craig," *Refrigerated Transporter*, May 1975, pp. 44-45.

Sanders, Bill L. "Computer Applications for Irregular Route Carriers,"

Proceedings: American Trucking Associations—Management Systems Council Conference, 1973, pp. 157-171.

Silver, D.F. "Bekins Van Lines Manager Sees Big Revenue Gain, Views Mover Problems," *Traffic World*, July 17, 1978, pp. 29-30.

Smiley, C. "What Turns Drivers . . . On . . . Off," *Heavy Duty Trucking*, January 1978, pp. 36-38.

"Special Driver Recruitment Section," *Open Road Magazine*, March 1978, pp. 37-53.

Strickland, J. "Where Have All the Owner-Operators Gone?" *Commercial Car*, February 1977, pp. 99-104.

Swart, B. "Where Do You Stand on the Payroll Line?" *Fleet Owner*, May 1978, pp. 68-72.

"Teamsters and FASH Head for Bitter Confrontation," *Open Road Magazine*, October 1977, pp. 22-23.

Tebb, A. "Why Workers' Compensation Is Costing You More," *Terminal Operator*, September 1977, pp. 4-6.

Thomas, K.H. "You Hire Your Own Problem," *Terminal Operator*, September 1977, p. 7ff.

Winsor, J., and Warner, R. "Driver Professionalism = Productivity, Profits, Performance," *Terminal Operator*, November 1977, pp. 4-7ff.

Witconis, L. "Bernard Gaillard: The Man Who Cuts through Red Tape at the ICC," *Owner Operator*, January-February 1978, pp. 24-28.

_____ . "How Many Bad Apples in the Trucking Industry?" *Owner Operator*, January-February 1978, pp. 31-34.

_____ . "I Now Pronounce You Man and Wife . . . And Truckers," *Owner Operator*, May-June 1978, pp. 22-28.

_____ . "Will Lumpers Get Their Lumps?" *Owner Operator*, July-August 1978, pp. 79-82.

Franchising

Books and Monographs

Atkinson, L.F. *Franchising: The Odds-On Favorite*. Chicago: International Franchise Association, 1968.

Brown, H. *Franchising-Realities and Remedies*. New York: Law Journal Press, 1973.

_____ . *Franchising: Trap for the Trusting*. Boston: Little, Brown, 1969.

Curry, J.A.H., et al. *Partners for Profit*. New York: American Management Association, 1966.

Diaz, R.M., and Gurnick, S. *Franchising: The Investor's Complete Handbook*. New York: Hastings House, 1969.

Distribution Problems Affecting Small Business, Hearings before the Subcommittee on Antitrust and Monopoly of the Committee of the Judiciary, U.S. Senate, 89th Congress, First Session, Part I: Franchising
Agreements. Held on March 2, 3, and 4, 1965.

Emmons, R.J. *The American Franchise Revolution*. Newport Beach,
Calif.: Burton House, 1970.

Franchising in the Economy, 1974-76. Washington, D.C.: U.S. Government Printing Office, 1976.

Gillespie, S.M. *An Analysis of Control in Franchise Distribution Systems*.
Unpublished Master's thesis, Graduate College, University of Illinois,
Urbana, Illinois, 1966.

Heivitt, C.M. *Automobile Franchise Agreement*, Bureau of Business Research Study No. 39, Indiana University, School of Business. Home-
wood, Ill.: Irwin, 1956.

Ingraham, S.M. *Management Control Potentials and Practices of Franchise Systems*. Ann Arbor, Mich.: University Microfilms, 1963.

Izraeli, D. *Franchising and the Total Distribution System*, London: Longman Group Limited, 1972.

Kursh, H. *The Franchise Boom*, New Revised Edition. Englewood Cliffs,
N.J.: Prentice-Hall, 1968.

Lewis, E.H., and Hancock, R.S. *The Franchise System of Distribution*.
Minneapolis: University of Minnesota, 1963, p. 80.

McGuire, E.P. *Franchised Distribution*. New York: The Conference Board,
1971.

Metz, R. *Franchising: How to Select a Business of Your Own*. New York:
Hawthorn Books, 1969.

Mockler, R.J., and Easop, H.E. *Guidelines for More Effective Planning
and Management of Franchise Systems*, Research Paper 42. Atlanta:
Georgia State College, Bureau of Business and Economic Research,
May 1968.

Ozanne, U.B., and Hunt, S.D. *The Economic Effects of Franchising*.
Washington, D.C.: U.S. Government Printing Office, 1971.

Rosenberg, R.M., and Bedell, M. *Profits from Franchising*. New York:
McGraw Hill, 1969.

Thompson, D.N., ed. *Contractual Marketing Systems*. Lexington, Mass.:
Lexington Books, D.C. Heath, 1971.

————. *Franchise Operations and Anti-Trust*. Lexington, Mass.: Lexington Books, D.C. Heath, 1971.

U.S. Senate Committee on Commerce. *Fairness in Franchising Act: Hearings*, April 7-8, 1976, 94th Congress, 2nd Session.

U.S. Senate Select Committee on Small Business. *Impact of Franchising
on Small Business*. Washington, D.C.: U.S. Government Printing Office, 1970.

Vaughn, C.L. *Franchising*. Lexington, Mass.: Lexington Books, D.C. Heath, 1974.

_____ , ed. *Franchising Today 1969*, Lynbrook, N.Y.: Farnsworth Publishing Company, 1969.

Vaughn, C.L., and Slater, D.B., eds. *Franchising Today 1966-67*. Chicago: Matthew Bender, 1967, p. 252.

Walker, B.J. *An Investigation of Relative Overall Position Satisfaction and Need Gratification among Franchised Businessmen*. Unpublished Ph.D. Dissertation, Graduate School of Business Administration, University of Colorado, 1971.

Articles

Bucklin, Louis P. "The Economic Base of Franchising," in D.N. Thompson, *Contractual Marketing Ssytems*. Lexington, Mass.: Lexington Books, D.C. Heath, 1971.

Cady, J.F. "Structural Trends in Retailing: The Decline of Small Business?" *Journal of Contemporary Business* 5 (Spring 1976):67-90.

Candilis, W.O. "The Growth of Franchising," *Business Economics* 13 (March 1978):15-19.

Clutterbuck, D. "Lending a Helping Hand to Suppliers," *International Management* 31 (September 1976):48-51.

Douds, H.J. "The (Non) Franchising Relationship of the Life Insurance Agent," *Journal of Risk and Insurance* 43 (September 1976):513-520.

Etgar, M. "The Economic Rationale for Becoming a Franchisee in a Service Industry," *Journal of Business Research* 4 (August 1976):239-254.

Hair, J.F., Jr.; Cattanach, R.L.; and Bowing, A.L. "Profit-Cost Relationship of Franchise Operations," *Managerial Planning* 24 (November-December 1975):17-24.

Hall, W.P. "Franchising—New Scope for an Old Technique," *Harvard Business Review* 42 (January-February 1964):60-72.

Hunt, S.D. "Franchising: Promises, Problems, and Prospects," *Journal of Retailing* 53 (Fall 1977):71-84.

_____ . "Full Disclosure and the Franchise System of Distribution," in *Dynamic Marketing in a Changing World*, Boris W. Becker and H. Becker, eds. Chicago: American Marketing Association, 1973, pp. 301-304.

_____ . "The Socioeconomic Consequences of the Franchise System of Distribution," *Journal of Marketing* 36 (July 1972):38.

Hunt, S.D., and Nevin, J.R. "Full Disclosure Laws in Franchising: An Empirical Investigation," *Journal of Marketing* 40 (April 1976):53-62.

Lewis, E.H., and Hancock, R.S. *The Franchise System of Distribution*.

Washington, D.C.: Prepared by the University of Minnesota for the Small Business Administration, 1963.

Lillis, C.M.; Narayana, C.L.; and Gilman, J.L. "Competitive Advantage Variation over the Life Cycle of a Franchise," *Journal of Marketing* 40 (October 1976):77-80.

Lusch, R.F. "Franchise Satisfaction: Causes and Consequences," *International Journal of Physical Distribution* 7 (1977):128-139.

Markland, R.E., and Furst, R.W. "A Conceptual Model for Analyzing Discrete Alternative Franchising Portfolios: Design and Validation," *Operational Research Quarterly* 25 (1974):267-281.

Mockler, R.J., and Easop, H.E. "The Art of Managing a Franchise," *Business Horizons*, August 1968, pp. 27-36.

———. "Guidelines for Establishing Franchisor Services and Controls," *Business Review* 27 (Summer 1968):12-23.

Oxenfeldt, A.R., and Kelly, A.O. "Will Successful Franchise Systems Ultimately Become Wholly-Owned Chains?" *Journal of Retailing* 44 (Winter 1968-69):75.

Oxenfeldt, A.R., and Thompson, D.N. "Franchising in Perspective," *Journal of Retailing* 44 (Winter 1968-69).

Price, D.L. "Key Elements in a Sound Distributor System" *Building a Sound Distributor Organization*. New York: National Industrial Conference Board, 1964, pp. 13-14.

Sklar, F. "Franchises and Independence: Interorganizational Power Relations in a Contractural Context," *Urban Life* 6 (1977):33-52.

Stephenson, P.R., and House, R.G. "A Perspective on Franchising: The Design of an Effective Relationship," *Business Horizons* 14 (August 1971):35-42.

Tatham, R.L.; Bush, R.F.; and Douglass, R. "An Analysis of Decision Criteria in Franchisor/Franchisee Selection Processes," *Journal of Retailing* 48 (Spring 1972):16-21ff.

Van Cise, J.G. "A Franchise Contract," *Antitrust Bulletin* 14 (April 1969): 325-346.

Wattel, H. "Are Franchisors Realistic and Successful in Their Selection of Franchisees?" *Journal of Retailing* 44 (Winter 1968-69):54-68.

Other Topics

Books and Monographs

Borstein, A.S., et al. *A Special Report on Contract Maintenance*. Salt Lake City: Contract Maintenance Associates, 1964.

Chandler, M.K., and Sayles, L.R. *Contracting-Out: A Study of Management Decision-Making*. New York: Graduate School of Business, Columbia University, 1959.

Comptroller General of the United States. *Tax Treatment of Employees and Self-Employed Persons by the Internal Revenue Service: Problems and Solutions*, GGD-77-88, November 21, 1977.

Culliton, J.W. *Make or Buy*. Boston: Division of Research, Harvard Business School, 1942.

Gellerman, S.W. *Motivation and Productivity*. New York: American Management Association, 1963.

Harlan, N.E. *Management Control in Airframe Subcontracting*. Boston: Division of Research, Graduate School of Business Administration, Harvard University, 1956.

Kotler, P. *Marketing Management*, 2nd ed., Englewood Cliffs, N.J.: Prentice-Hall, 1967.

Larson, A. *The Law of Workmen's Compensation*. Chicago: Matthew Bender, 1952, volume 1.

McGregor, D. *The Human Side of Enterprise*. New York: McGraw-Hill, 1960.

_____ . *The Professional Manager*. New York: McGraw-Hill, 1967.

Mallen, B. *Principles of Marketing Management*. Lexington, Mass.: Lexington Books, D.C. Heath, 1977.

Maslow, A.H. *Motivation and Personality*, 2nd ed. New York: Harper and Row, 1970.

Oxenfeldt, A.R., and Watkins, M.W. *Make or Buy: Factors Affecting Executive Decisions*. New York: McGraw-Hill, Consultant Reports on Current Business Problems, 1956.

Patten, T.A., Jr. *The Foreman: Forgotten Man of Management*. Chicago: Ill.: American Management Association, 1968.

Sartain, A.W., and Baker, A.W. *The Supervisor and His Job*. New York: McGraw-Hill, 1972.

United States Bureau of Labor Statistics. *Subcontracting*, Bulletin No. 1425-8 (April 1969).

_____ . *Subcontracting Clauses in Major Collective Bargaining Agreements*, Bulletin No. 1304 (August 1961).

Articles

Bucklin, L.P. "A Theory of Channel Control," *Journal of Marketing* 37 (January 1973):39-47.

Dixon, D. "Intra-Channel Conflict Resolution," *Houston Business Review*, Spring 1967, pp. 36-48.

Gellerman, S.W. "Supervision: Substance and Style," *Harvard Business Review*, March-April 1976, pp. 89-99.

Hertzberg, F. "One More Time: How Do You Motivate Employees?" *Harvard Business Review*, January-February 1968, pp. 53-62.

Higgins, C.C. "Make or Buy Re-Examined," *Harvard Business Review* March-April 1955, pp. 109-119.

Index

Index

About the Author

David H. Maister is an assistant professor at the Harvard University Graduate School of Business Administration. He received the B.Soc.Sci. in mathematics, economics, and statistics from the University of Birmingham, the M.Sc. in operations research from the London School of Economics, and the D.B.A. from the Harvard Business School. After working as a statistician for Bell Canada in Montreal, he lectured for four years in economics and statistics at the Polytechnic of the South Bank, London. He was an assistant professor at the University of British Columbia for three years before joining the Harvard faculty. He has been a consultant in management, transportation, and logistics to governments, transportation and distribution companies, and manufacturing concerns in the United States and Canada.

Dr. Maister is coauthor of *The Owner-Operator: Independent Trucker* (Lexington Books, 1975), *The Motor-Carrier Industry* (Lexington Books, 1977), and *The Domestic Airline Industry* (Lexington Books, 1977). His articles on transportation and logistics have appeared in *International Journal of Physical Distribution and Materials Management, Logistics and Transportation Review, Transportation Journal,* and *Motor Truck*. In 1979 Dr. Maister was awarded the Regular Common Carrier Conference/Transportation Research Forum prize for the best research paper on trucking operations.